D0296593

000000759035

Backstabbers and Bullies

Backstabbers and Bullies

How to Cope with the Dark Side of
People at Work

Adrian Furnham

Bloomsbury Information
An imprint of Bloomsbury Publishing Plc

B L O O M S B U R Y
LONDON · NEW DELHI · NEW YORK · SYDNEY

Bloomsbury Information
An imprint of Bloomsbury Publishing Plc

50 Bedford Square	1385 Broadway
London	New York
WC1B 3DP	NY 10018
UK	USA

www.bloomsbury.com

BLOOMSBURY and the Diana logo are trademarks
of Bloomsbury Publishing Plc

First published 2015

© Adrian Furnham, 2015

Adrian Furnham has asserted his right under the Copyright, Designs
and Patents Act, 1988, to be identified as Author of this work.

All rights reserved. No part of this publication may be reproduced or
transmitted in any form or by any means, electronic or mechanical,
including photocopying, recording, or any information storage or retrieval
system, without prior permission in writing from the publishers.

No responsibility for loss caused to any individual or organization
acting on or refraining from action as a result of the material in this
publication can be accepted by Bloomsbury or the author.

British Library Cataloguing-in-Publication Data
A catalogue record for this book is available from the British Library.

ISBN: HB: 978-1-4729-1550-4
ePDF : 978-1-4729-1552-8
ePub: 978-1-4729-1551-1

Library of Congress Cataloging-in-Publication Data
Furnham, Adrian.
Bac~~kstabbers and bullies : how to cope with the dark side of~~
~~people at work / Adrian Furnham. – First edition.~~
~~pages cm~~
ISBN 978~~-1-4729-1550-4 (hardback) – ISBN 978-1-4729-1552-8 (ePDF e~~ook) –
ISBN 978-1-47~~29-1551-1 (ePub ebook) 1. Psychology, Industrial.~~ 2. Negativism.
3. Harassme~~nt. 4. Bullying in the workplace. 5. Interpersonal relations~~. I. Title.
~~HF5548.8.F815 2015~~
~~158.7–dc23~~
~~2015003~~

DUDLEY LIBRARIES	
000000759035	
Askews & Holts	11-May-2015
	£25.00
DU	

For Alison and Benedict as always...

Contents

Preface

I got interested in this topic for both personal and academic reasons. Like most of us, I have worked with, and for, people who could be variously described as bad, mad or sad. They can cause not only misery for many but also mayhem, distress and disaster for whole organizations. Further, we read about them more and more in the press. Indeed, it has been suggested that more fail and derail at leadership than thrive and excel.

The question that always intrigued me most was how these people climb the greasy pole in the first place and get to such exalted positions without being found out. How do deeply dishonest, egocentric and flaky persons rise to positions of power and responsibility? How do they possibly get elected and then promoted? Has it not been apparent what difficult, devious, devils they were early on in their careers? Surely, all or many of the signs were there.

Most of us have encountered nasty, negative, narcissists at work. The problem for those who believe in a Just World were we get what we deserve is that often these traits are rewarded rather than punished. The meek do not inherit the earth: the Machiavellians do. Worse, some never seem to get their 'come-uppance' in this life: though it remains uncertain about the next.

Many have encountered a nasty, selfish, bullying manager. Some people seem to have only ever had bad bosses. Sometimes it is just luck on who you get as your boss or leader. But it does depend on the sector in which you work and the country where the organization is located.

I hope that in this book I will not be accused of pathologizing all management problems. Indeed, very early on I make a distinction between Bad, Mad and Sad managers. And, I am clear that just as for fire to occur you need heat *and* fuel *and* oxygen, so for derailment you need not only personal pathology but also situations that allow it to play out.

Equally, I feel it as my duty to alert people to the fact they could well be working with or for a Corporate Psychopath, a Business Narcissist or a Histrionic Show-Off. It is all very well to diagnose or label people, and it is equally important to understand how they operate in the world of work.

As I say to various groups: if you are articulate, educated, good-looking…and a narcissistic psychopath, the world is your oyster. We read daily about powerful business people, politicians and celebrities whose cold-blooded, manipulative deception is revealed only years after their crimes were committed. The question is how, when and why these bastards, bullies and backstabbers achieved so much for themselves before they were unmasked.

I recall going to a school reunion 25 years after matriculating and finding how well the class psychopath had done. He had three wives by the age of 40, which must have entailed some costs. He was a callous, fearless bully – feared and hated by most of the more 'academic boys', whom he sought to torture in a variety of ways. At University I encountered a couple of more, one of whom was in effect a petty criminal. If they were privileged and charming, they could get away with anything…and often did.

Also, as an academic and consultant, it became clear that people with a lot of 'dark-side issues' could exploit their predictions and do rather well in the world of work. I have dealt with many very charming 'movers and shakers', who had the reputation for being tough change agents. Many left behind a trail of destruction at every level.

My other experience was academic. I have been very fortunate to have known Robert and (the late) Joyce Hogan for nearly 20 years. They not only pioneered work on the 'dark side' of personality but they have been also very generous with their ideas. Bob and I discuss and debate lots of issues in emails, conferences, fine hotels and airport lounges. Hogan's work inspired me a dozen years ago and still does. He remains a man of great curiosity and generosity whose impact on psychology will endure for many decades.

Others working on this topic, like Delroy Paulhus and Tim Judge, have been an inspiration. The 'dark-side' area is at the intersection of various different specialist areas in psychology: differential, clinical and work psychology as well as psychiatry. Few academics have the breadth to cover such a range to see the connections. Currently, I have a number of PhD students (Mary-Clare Race, Kat Palaiou and Simmy Grewal) working in this area, and I am sure that I learn as much from them as they do from me. It is surely a great privilege to have bright, fit, forward-looking people to work with.

I have written a number of previous books on this topic but the literature in this erstwhile backwater is moving ahead fast. It has been pointed out that there are around 60,000 to 80,000 books on leadership in the English language and most are on the brighter side. The idea of leadership failure and derailment has been brushed under the carpet for far too long and only now are the statistics on the sheer numbers who fail coming out.

Boddy, C. (2011). *Corporate Psychopaths*. Basingstoke: Palgrave.

Dotlich, D., & Cairo, P. (2003). *Why CEOs Fail*. New York: Jossey Bass.

Finkelstein, S. (2003). *Why Smart Executives Fail*. New York: Portfolio.

Furnham, A. (2010). *The Elephant in the Boardroom: The Psychology of Leadership Derailment*. Bracknell: Palgrave MacMillan.

Ghaemi, N. (2011) *A First-Rate Madness*. Harmondsworth: Penguin.

Hogan, R. (2007). *Personality and the Fate of Organizations*. Mahwah, NJ: Lawrence Erlbaum.

Kets de Vries, M. (2006). *The Leader on the Couch*. Basingstoke: Palgave.

Kets de Vries, M. (2006). *Coach and Couch*. Basingstoke: Palgrave.

Miller, L. (2008). *From Difficult to Disturbed*. New York: Amacon.

Oldham, J., & Morris, L. (1991). *Personality Self-Portrait*. New York: Bantam.

Owen, D. (2009). *In Sickness and in Power*. London: Methuen.

Owen, D. (2012). *The Hubris Syndrome*. London: Methuen.

Ronson, J. (2011) *The Psychopath Test*. London: Picadore.

I have tried to write an up-to-date, referenced and topical book in this area. I hope that it is both informative and useful, approachable but sound, critical (in the best sense) comprehensive yet sufficiently succinct. I have drawn at times heavily upon previous work in papers, books and chapters and tried to be strictly up to date.

I have been fortunate in having had a number of people help me. Luke Treglown has helped in many ways as my 'top' Research Assistant. Luke has done a lot of leg work on many of these chapters, and I am ever grateful for his positive work ethic and fine mind. I have relied in sections for his detailed and careful work and I am most grateful. He will, I am sure, have a 'stellar career' as an academic if he is unwise enough to choose to become one.

I have also had many 'dark-side' chats with John Taylor, David Pendleton and others. They have dealt with some of the chaos that these people leave in their wake. Moreover, I have had, over the past few years, some very direct contacts with people I have to consider as members of the 'forces of darkness'. This book has been an attempt to shed light on the causes and consequences of that darkness.

And, as always, I need to thank my long-suffering wife and son for being absent so often in the office. I hope one day to find a cure for my workaholism.

Islington, London

November 2014

Chapter 1

The incidence and cost of management failure

1.1 Introduction

This book is about leadership failure and derailment. It is about the surprisingly high number (estimated between 20 and 50 per cent) of executives who cause chaos and mayhem. The cause is usually associated with unethical or fraudulent behaviour; aggression, bullying and adversarial styles; poor deal-making and conflict resolution skills; consistent and serious errors in decision making, forecasting and judgement as well as deceptive, incoherent or unreliable communication.

The book is about executives who undermine and destroy the effectiveness of the 'top team' and the board, as well as senior and middle managers who adversely affect the well-being of those around them.

Leadership is *a contact sport*. It is done with others: it is always distributed. There are enormous pressures and opportunities for the leader of today. Every generation believes that it lives in particularly challenging and difficult times, but any analysis of the past shows this not to be true. It is tough at the top and often very difficult to get there. Unfortunately, the evolutionary selection method for finding those who can make it often favours the selfish, unethical, showman rather than the wise leader.

So how can you measure whether an appointed leader is, or has been, a success and failure? How do you define failure? Though this is a simple question, it has a complicated set of answers. There are a number of standard metrics that one might use:

1. *Financial metrics*: There are lots of these to choose from and include revenue, profit and share-price. The problem with using these most desirable of metrics is that many factors contribute to the bottom line, not only managerial incompetence.
2. *Client satisfaction and repeat purchasers*: This idea from the Service Profit Chain concept suggests that once a company loses the loyalty of their customers they are doomed. Staff and clients desert bad managers.
3. *Employee engagement, recognition and retention*: The opposite of this can be measured by the usual triad of gloomy metrics: absenteeism, accidents and turnover. It is well established that people resign from organizations most often because of poor management.
4. *Company and personal awards and prizes* which are non-existent under poor leadership.
5. *Sustainability indexes* which are essential.

In short, there are many ways to measure company performance though, of course, this cannot be attributable solely to the leader or the board.

Many failed and derailed leaders have been very successful and as a result have climbed the 'greasy pole' to positions of power and influence where they have pretty much unrestrained control of an organization's resources. An increasingly inflated opinion of their ability to control and predict outcomes may lead them to loot those resources and indeed remain undetected in doing so. Hence a great deal of white-collar crime. Hubris precedes Nemesis as we shall see in this book.

Most, but alas not all, derailed leaders have their careers 'involuntarily terminated'. Some 'leap before they are pushed' and a large number previously judged as 'high potential' executives derail at some stage. It seems as if they 'come off the track' for a specific number of reason: they fail to meet agreed objectives and targets; they have many problems with many of their work (and personal) relationships; they find adaptation and change increasingly difficult; they are beset by problems of building and leading teams; and many have had too limited business and leadership experience (Zhang et al., 2013). Whilst there clearly are country, sector and level effects and differences, these derailers seem surprisingly consistent.

Derailed leaders, through their incompetence, pathology or criminality, cause mayhem in the workplace. They can cause whole companies to collapse. Whilst they might bring about short-term success for the organization, this is nearly always short-lived and in the long term lead to the inability of people to work together productively in the organization. They often pay no attention to the needs and expectations of followers (and all stakeholders), leading to a collapse of morale and productivity. They do it mainly because they are totally self-centred and only interested in their own agenda and in essence are unable or unwilling to consider how their actions might affect others. Some are insecure, others arrogant, but the result is much the same.

Derailment can happen suddenly. Whilst there may be a noticeable pattern and even long history of a leader's failings, the actual process is usually triggered by misjudgements in a variety of critical situations. Suddenly *trap doors* open when a leader has no game plan and is unable to deal with a complex situation. Trap doors are usually about four issues: setting directions, executing a plan, building a team and influencing stakeholders (Dailey, 2013). The bewildered and inadequate leader oscillates between *freeze, flight and flight*, all responses of which are, at times, inappropriate.

There are themes to this growing literature. Most derailed leaders have been successful in the past, but their early strengths that led to their rise later became their weaknesses. Their early success often caused hubris which exacerbated the demise. Long-standing flaws (poor people skills and inability to adapt) become particularly salient when some sudden and dramatic change occurs. Some, of course, are just unlucky being at the wrong place at the wrong time.

Organizations are as much to blame as individuals in their selection, mentoring and support. So, the following points are notable:

1. Strengths, particularly when identified early, can become weaknesses. Success can lead to perseveration and repetitious behaviour without evidence of learning.
2. Personal problems and issues eventually matter especially as people climb up organizations.
3. Acute and chronic problems and challenges test people and show up their flaws.
4. People can too easily become victims of their own success.
5. Derailment is much more common in some situations than others.

Equally, as we shall see, it is important not always to 'rush to the dispositional' as Zimbardo (2004) insists when studying evil. He points that trying to explain (leadership) success and failure exclusively in individual terms is naïve and simplistic. This lets groups and organizations 'off the hook' as blameworthy. It is clear that for derailment to occur you need more than a leader who is bad, mad or sad. For derailment to occur, we need an environment that allows or encourages it, as well as people happy to go along with all the acts associated with derailment. There are sick organizations that encourage and legitimize acts of abuse and corruption.

Three areas of research have come together over the past twenty years that have encouraged a serious examination of leadership failure. *First*, the rapprochement between personality psychologists and psychiatrists interested in the personality disorders. This has provided a way to both describe and explain some of the paradoxes of leadership derailment. *Second*, some psychoanalysts have used their well-known conceptual scheme to try to understand why some very high-profile leaders 'fall from grace'. As is often the case, many people are intrigued and enchanted by the neo-Freudian explanations for pathology. *Third*, the neuro-scientists have come to the party with their attempts to investigate the biological basis of those leaders who fail and derail and get caught as opposed to those who succeed.

1.2 Business leadership

Over the past decade, there have been some spectacular corporate failures that have encouraged researchers to try to understand the relationship between charismatic leadership and corporate failure. For example, the dramatic cases of Enron in the United States (Tourish & Vatcha, 2005) and the Royal Bank of Scotland in Great Britain make leadership sound heroic and relatively simple. The reality suggests otherwise.

To many, it is a great shock when an eminent leader stumbles, fails and derails. Most have had a 'stellar' career; they have been carefully selected and very well rewarded for their efforts.

Factors that contribute to the challenges of leadership include:

- **Transparency, scrutiny, accountability**: The rise of the web and social media means that leaders are under the spotlight as they never have been before. Their all activities and conversations are watched, judged and often recorded. It is almost impossible to get away from the job and have a 'down' time. This can put considerable stress on even the most robust and resilient executive.
- **Democratization, cynicism, disrespect**: These are all challenges to power and control. The exercise of authority is much easier in hierarchical, stable, authoritarian organizations. Leaders feel more and more that they have to consult and negotiate with people inside and outside the organization who constantly challenge their decisions. Furthermore, they are often met by derision and scorn by those who seem to have little respect for those in leadership roles.
- **International competition and threats**: Nearly all medium-sized businesses are affected strongly by international events. Changes in technology mean that whole products can be made redundant overnight. An economic slowdown in a major economy (American, Chinese) can affect the whole world. Cheap labour and technology means that many traditional industries in the west are challenged as they never have been before.

- **Mixed messages**: The leaders of big businesses get many contradictory pieces of advice. They are told to be tough and focussed. They are told to be fearless with battle-hardened confidence. But they are also told they need emotional intelligence and empathy. They must show confidence but also humility. They must be, at different times, both very masculine and feminine.
- **Intrapersonal**: Being self-aware and self-controlled; having emotional maturity and adaptability. Early signs of problems include frequent emotional outbursts, overreacting and loosing composure; doubtful integrity, loyalty or sincerity; acute and chronic stress; inability or unwillingness to take responsibility for problems; proneness to gossiping and rumour mongering; and inappropriate communications.
- **Interpersonal**: Having social skills and empathy and being able to establish relationships. Having little 'interpersonal savvy' and inability to deal with conflict. Early warning signs include reports of abrasive, abusive and insensitive behaviour with colleagues and reports; a tendency for others to prefer not to work with that individual; a tendency to blame others for all problems; a (deserved) reputation for being untrustworthy; and a history of office-politics misjudgements.
- **Leadership**: The inability to build a functional team, influence others and model the behaviour that they want. This may be seen in over- or under-managing. Early signs include poor team morale; high turnover; demotivated and angry supports; a reputation for being autocratic and authoritarian; and a history of poor staffing decisions.
- **Business**: The ability to plan, monitor and organize; to generally administer and to have a strategic vision. Early signs include obvious issues like poor returns, customer complaints, missed objectives as well as being overwhelmed by complexity, inability to prioritize and being too reliant on technical skills.

Hogan et al. (2011), the pioneers of research in this area, have argued that derailment occurs in one or more of four reasons.

Others have taken a less psychological perspective. Consider the book *Why Smart Executives Fail* by Finkelstein (2003). It is written by a management academic rather than a psychologist, but, as well shall see, many of the issues and concepts are similar.

He argues that failure in multiple, otherwise irrelevant, companies from different areas suggests general patterns, which are mostly due to seven 'faulty habits' of CEOs:

1. **Assuming dominance**: Being overconfident about their own and the company's predominance in the market reduces proactivity and care which potentially leads to failure. Underestimating the role of chance and overestimating their abilities and skills leads to delusions of excessive control and to viewing other people as tools to execute their goals. Moreover, those CEOs often consider their company's products as best in the market and therefore assume that their clients should consider themselves lucky to have access to them. Ultimately, customer and company roles are reversed and competitors take advantage of that. They treat customers better leading them to leave their current preferred supplier.

2. **Identifying with the company**: Two of the major problems that companies might face are the principal–agent and the principal–principal problems.
The former occurs when CEOs act on behalf of their own self-interest rather than on that of the shareholders. The latter occurs when one person is both the CEO and the owner of a company. In this way, this person obtains absolute power and overidentifies with the company to such degree that they can no longer distinguish between the company's and their own interests. In these cases, CEOs become less careful with the company's assets and more likely to use corporate funds for personal reasons. They also lose the ability necessary to be able to make critical evaluation in order for the company to benefit. Moreover, having total control and power removes any authority from the board of directors. Therefore, they cannot offer effective feedback or criticism to the actions of the CEO, and they may even be afraid to confront them. This leads to a toxic work environment and consequently harms the organization as the board members are not able to prevent or report mistakes before it is too late.

3. **Thinking they have all the answers**: It is impossible to know the answers to every issue in general and especially in a business environment where change is a constant phenomenon. CEOs who feel they have all the answers assume total control, as discussed earlier. Therefore, they believe that there is no need for them to learn new things, refuse any suggestions and advance or reject criticism and opposition and consequently trust no one. Once again, this leaves the board of executives powerless and intoxicates the organization's culture.

4. **Eliminating anyone who does not follow by 100 per cent**: Another problem of a 'faulty' CEO is that in the rare case of showing opposition to their actions, the CEO eliminates the opposing party. The CEO feels that employees and board members who do not blindly follow their aspirations, undermine their vision. However, these kinds of actions affect organizational culture but their most negative consequence is that they leave the CEO without any chance of being corrected. By firing people who oppose to some of their actions, CEOs are let loose to keep doing what they consider to be correct which in such cases is actually harmful for the organization.

5. **Obsessing over the company's image**: CEOs who have this habit tend to focus excessively on the image of the company. Although this may prove beneficial in the long run, this habit often leads the CEO to overlook everyday operations that are essential for the normal functioning of the organization and consequently their management efforts become shallow and ineffective. When shifting their focus from the running to the image of the company, they tend to settle for what appears to be an accomplished thing and not the actual accomplishment. Clearly, this habit once again leads to catastrophic consequences for the organization since problems are not really dealt with.

6. **Underestimating major obstacles**: Similar to the previous one, this habit focuses too much on the ultimate strategy, the vision of the corporation, and this leads to overlooking other major obstacles. Although more subtle at the beginning, minor issues can grow and have a significant negative impact if left unsupervised. CEOs who ignore these signs tend to not admit that their past choices are

wrong and commit to them even more in order to prove their effectiveness. Using these ineffective strategies can cause damage to the organization.

7. **Stubbornly relying on what worked for them in the past**: This habit derives from the aforementioned one and causes CEOs to lack flexibility as far as the solutions they use are concerned. They use patents that have worked for them in the past because they consider them the characteristics of their success. This mentality, however, can only prove destructive for the corporation since flexibility and openness are essential.

1.3 Upper Echelon Theory

Over thirty years ago, an Upper Echelon Theory was proposed and has been discussed a great deal since then (David et al., 2012). It is neither complicated nor counterintuitive. The idea is that the senior executives who make crucially important strategic decisions for their company do so not only based on cold logic but also on their background, personality and values. That is, all important strategic decisions which can make or break a company are as much a function of the psychology of those in the upper echelon as the objective or economic conditions. They can in effect even encourage illegal activity (Daboub et al., 1995).

Upper Echelon Theory is a very psychological theory as it locates company success and failure in the psychological processes of those CEOs and top team leaders who make business decisions. The sorts of factors that have been highlighted by those working in the area are as follows:

1. The Age of the Top Executives which relates to risk-taking, information processing and skills.
2. Functional Expertise or Track which is concerned with their initial sources of expertise: are they training in marketing, engineering and finance?
3. Career Experience including their work in different jobs in different companies.

4. Education, both formal and informal, in different areas like finance, law and psychology.
5. Socio-economic background, which it is alleged, has an impact on a CEO appetite for diversification, growth and acquisitions.
6. Homogeneity of top teams which relates to creativity and morale in groups as well as the generation of alternative ideas.
7. Ethnicity and minority status.
8. Military Service: where and whether a person had served in the military.

As the theory has developed, various other factors have been identified. Thus, it has been argued that job demands are important and as these increase there is an even stronger relationship between executive characteristics and strategic choices. Furthermore, the way power is distributed in top teams is important: the less the team/board engages as a group in information processing and decision making, the more important the characteristics of CEO on the decision making.

Some of the studies within the Upper Echelon Theory tradition have identified other factors and processes. Thus, Zona et al. (2013) showed that CEO traits influenced an imbalanced corporate strategy which placed the organization at risk for managerial fraud. Clearly, the pathology of boards is an important issue in organizational derailment.

1.4 Some evidence

The US-based Institute for Policy Studies recently published a study called *Executive Excess 2013: Bailed Out, Booted and Busted*.

They noted that many CEOs had 'delivered' for the shareholders by dubious means: manipulating marketplace monopolies, freezing worker's pay cheques or cutting corners on environmental protection. They described in some detail who, when and how these CEOs had derailed and caused their company significant problems. On the first page they note:

Our data set draws from the top-paid CEO lists for the years from 1993 through 2012. CEOs who performed poorly – by the most basic of definitions – occupied 38 per cent of the 500 slots in these 20 annual lists. These poorly performing chief executives either wound up getting fired, had to pay massive settlements or fines related to fraud charges, or led firms that crashed or had to be bailed out during the 2008 financial crisis.

- **The Bailed Out**: CEOs whose firms either ceased to exist or received taxpayer bailouts after the 2008 financial crash held 22 per cent of the slots in our sample. Richard Fuld of Lehman Brothers enjoyed one of Corporate America's largest 25 paychecks for eight consecutive years – until his firm went belly up in 2008.
- **The Booted**: Not counting those on the bailed out list, another 8 per cent of our sample was made up of CEOs who wound up losing their jobs involuntarily. Despite their poor performance, the 'booted' CEOs jumped out the escape hatch with golden parachutes valued at $48 million on average.
- **The Busted**: CEOs who led corporations that ended up paying significant fraud-related fines or settlements comprised an additional 8 per cent of the sample. One CEO, Jerald Fishman of Analog Devices, had to pay a penalty out of his own pocket for back-dating his stock option grant for personal gain. The other companies shelled out payments that totalled over $100 million per firm.

They provided a number of examples listed in Table 1.1:

Table 1.1 Some recent examples of derailed leaders

Name	Year of Derailment	Company	Reason
Alan Fisherman	2008	Washington Mutual	For recording a quarterly loss of $3.3 billion in his 17 days at the job
Andy Mason	February 2013	GroupOn	Mason was expected to be fired, but finally done after business lost net $81 million for the previous quarter

(Continued)

Name	Year of Derailment	Company	Reason
Bernard Ebbers	2002	MCI Inc.	Used fraudulent accounting methods to inflate stock in order to keep stock prices high. Currently in prison
Bernard Madoff	2008	NASDAQ	Running the largest Ponzi scheme ever, and is currently in prison for life
Bob Diamond	2012	Barclays PLC	For having a lack of humility and modesty, poor levels of pay, and money market rate manipulation
Brian Dunn	April 2012	Best Buy	Inappropriate relations with a female employee
Chris Kubasik	2012	Lockheed Martin	Fired before he started having a personal relationship with a subordinate and going against company policy
David Petraeus	2012	C.I.A	Admitting to an extramarital affair with his biographer
Denis Abrams	June 2012	Berkshire Hathaway	Fired by Warren Buffet for taking a boat vacation on company money
Dennis Kozlowski	2002	Tyco	Using company money as his personal fund
Ernst Lieb	2011	US Mercedes-Benz	For using company money to pay for personal expenses
Jacob Alexander	2006	Comverse	Backdating, fraud, money laundering, etc., all related to stock options. Currently in prison
Joseph Nacchio(?)	2002	Qwest	Sharp decline in stocks; imprisoned for fraud and insider trading
Mark Hurd	August 2010	Hewlett-Packard	Ousted by board for violating standards of business conduct, and rumours of sexual harassment

(Continued)

Name	Year of Derailment	Company	Reason
Robert O'Connel	2005	MassMutual	Fired for ethical breaches including personal gain, misuse of company assets, and obstructing internal investigation
Ron Johnson	April 2013	JC Penny	'Bold new pricing strategies clearly failed' (according to Forbes article 'Did J.C. Penney Pick The Exact Wrong Time To Fire Ron Johnson?')
Scott Thompson	May 2012	Yahoo	Lying on his resume that he had another degree
Walter Forbes	2007	Cendant	Inflating reported incomes of the company by $500 million over three years. Currently in prison

The study documented the capricious, callous and cocky style of chief executives whose greed appeared to know no bounds. It is more a business report than one that tries to uncover the motives or psychological processes associated with the executives.

It is more concerned with legal reforms (CEO–worker pay ratio disclosure; pay restrictions on certain executives; limiting the deductibility of executive function) as well as establishing principles for better systems that prevent this happening. However, it remains shocking reading not only for investors but also for taxpayers as a whole, and it is very easy to explain the growing cynicism around executive greed.

1.5 Definitions

There are a very large number of books and papers that use the image of light to think about derailment. Words and concepts like bright side and dark side are used as well as concepts like gloom, glare, shadow and spot-light. Much of the work and these ideas should be attributed to

Robert Hogan who has pioneered the measurement of dark-side traits (of which, we discuss much more later).

In Jungian psychology, the *shadow* or *'shadow aspect'* may refer to (1) an unconscious aspect of the personality which the conscious ego does not identify in itself. Because one tends to reject or remain ignorant of the least desirable aspects of one's personality, the shadow is largely negative, or (2) the entirety of the unconscious, that is, everything of which a person is not fully conscious. There are, however, positive aspects that may also remain hidden in one's shadow (especially in people with low self-esteem).

Many writers have noticed the plethora of words/concepts used to describe the harmful behaviour associated with bad leaders (McCartney & Campbell, 2006). Thus, Pelletier (2010) tried to distinguish between six concepts: *abusive, tyrannical, destructive, bullying, toxic* and *laissez-faire*. Excluding the latter concept, he noted that some behaviours (demeaning, marginalizing, degrading, ridiculing, mocking) are true for all the different concepts, whilst some are exclusive like emotional volatility and pitting in-group members against out-group members. In his examination of toxic leaders, he identified eight different dimensions: attacking followers' self-esteem, lack of integrity, abusiveness, social exclusion, divisiveness, promoting inequality, threats to follower's security and laissez-faire attitudes.

Aasland et al. (2009) proposed a simple model of destructive leadership with two dimensions: *pro versus anti subordinate and pro versus anti-organization*. Thus, the derailing leader is anti-subordinate, whilst the tyrannical leader is anti-subordinate but pro-organization. In their study, they noted two findings often quoted: *first* the surprising high prevalence of destructive leadership and *secondly* that most leaders display both constructive and destructive leadership.

In the literature, some researchers seem to prefer different concepts. Thus, Goldman (2008, 2011) refers to *toxic leadership*, whilst Wille et al. (2013) talk of *aberrant personality* tendencies which are made of key features of six personality disorders: antisocial, narcissistic, borderline, schizotypal, obsessive compulsive and avoidant.

1. **Aberrant (leaders)**: This emphasizes abnormality, atypicality and deviance for the right or normal type. It has two themes: both unusualness but also a departure from acceptable standards. That is, it has statistical and moral side to it.

2. **Antisocial (leaders)**: This echoes the immoral nature of leaders who can be antisocial in the way selfish people may be, but more likely in the way delinquents are antisocial. It echoes the new term for psychopath: antisocial personality disorder.

3. **Dark Side (Triad) (leaders)**: This is to contrast the bright and the dark; the outside, the obvious and the straightforward with the inside, the obscure and the devious. Dark implies evil, dismal and menacing. The triad suggests three separable constituents of evil.

4. **Derailed (leaders)**: This emphasizes the idea of being thrown off course. Trains on tracks derail. Leaders set fair in a particular direction deviate from the path unable to move forward. It is sometimes hyphenated with the next word in the dictionary, namely deranged which implies not only a breakdown in performance but also insanity.

5. **Despotic (leaders)**: This is taken from the historical literature emphasizing the misuse and abuse of power by oppressive absolutist leaders. It emphasizes the autocratic type or style of leadership.

6. **Destructive (leaders)**: Used by historians in this context to look at a particular style, it speaks to the ruining, spoiling or neutralizing of a group or force led by a particular person.

7. **Incompetent (leaders)**: This is used to suggest inadequate, ineffective, unqualified. It implies the absence of something required rather than the presence of something not required. Incompetent leaders are ineffective because they are lacking in particular qualities.

8. **Malignant (leaders)**: Those are leaders who spread malevolence, the antonym of benevolence. Malevolence is misconduct, doing harm such as maliciously causing pain or damage. Malignant leaders grow fast like cancer and are deadly.

9. **Toxic (leaders)**: This refers to the poisonous effect leaders have on all they touch. Toxic substances kill rather than repel. Again this refers to the consequences of a particular leadership style.

10. **Tyrannical (leaders)**: Tyrants show arbitrary, oppressive and unjust behaviour. Tyrants tend to usurp power and then brutally oppress those they command.

Similarly, there are various descriptions of 'bad behaviour' at work. So there is:

- **Deviant behaviour** which violates work norms and threatens the well-being of organizations and the workers in them.
- **Aggressive behaviour** where individuals attempt to deliberately harm others.
- **Antisocial behaviour** which are work behaviours that have the potential to cause economic, emotional, physical and psychological harm.
- **Violent behaviour** which is an extreme form of aggression involving direct assaults.
- **Dysfunctional behaviour** which is employee behaviour intended to have negative consequences for other work individuals, teams or the organization as a whole.
- **Incivility** which is the 'exchange of seemingly inconsequential inconsiderate words and deeds that violate conventional norms of workplace conduct' (Porath & Pearson, 2010).

In this book, many of the terms will be used interchangeably; however, three distinctions will be made: between derailment and incompetence (see Chapter 3), between serious mental illness and a devious behaviour pattern (see Chapter 2), and between individually and organizationally driven problems (see Chapter 4).

1.6 Causal chains

There are consequences to good and bad management. There is no shortage of descriptions of good management: setting goals, monitoring performance, aligning incentives with performance. There are established principles of good management which are linked to individual and organizational success. Equally bad management leads to misery and failure for many. Some do not work hard enough; others make bad decisions or put in place rigid and inappropriate processes.

Still others exploit all aspects of the company for their own ends which has been called 'self-dealing' (see Figure 1.1).

Figure 1.1   The causal chain that leads to bad management

There are many studies and reports which demonstrate how bad leadership affects corporate culture and significant work outcomes. Many of them talked of a cascading or trickle-down effect of the abusive leader (Liu et al., 2012). Abusive supervision can have significant consequences though much depends on context and the personality of the worker (Sulea et al., 2013).

There is also the possibility of negative spirals occurring. Thus, if someone at work whistle-blows on their boss or organization because of malpractice this might lead to even further bullying (Bjorkelo, 2013).

Many have tried to document the cost of a negative style. Thus, Porath & Pearson (2010) suggests that 88 per cent of workers who are treated uncivilly get even with their organization: 48 per cent decrease work effort; 47 per cent time at work and 38 per cent work quality.

Hence the idea of a causal chain where a leader's personality, ability and values determine their leadership style which impacts on the corporate culture which may actively encourage deviant behaviour of many kinds.

1.7 Conditions that allow for the emergence of dark-side leaders

There are clearly many factors that account for why potentially derailing leaders make it to the top. Many have pointed out that just as you need three components for fire, namely heat, oxygen and fuel, so you are unlikely to get leadership derailment if you do not have leaders with a derailment profile, people who are prepared to follow derailing leaders and environments which 'allow it' (see Figure 1.2).

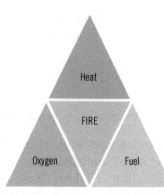

Figure 1.2 The essential components of fire

Many people have tried to moderate the simple-minded and individualistic trait approach to leadership derailment by stressing the nature of leader-follower dynamics. Ouimet (2010) noted three factors:

1. **Cultural Factors**: There are national and corporate cultural factors that favour the dark-side manager making it to the top. First, individualistic cultures (mainly in the West) more than collectivistic cultures (mainly in the East) value personal achievement over group success. Thus, in these cultures it is more natural to look for, and select, people who draw attention to themselves and have significant self-belief.

Furthermore, if the organization promotes and trumpets values like immediate results, audacity, ambition, individual initiative, financial success, professional prestige and social celebrity they become a breeding ground for dark-side leaders (Duchon & Burns, 2008). Thus, inevitably dark-side types are drawn to organizations in which they can thrive. This is particularly the case for organizations in sectors which are fast moving and poorly regulated.

2. **Environmental Factors**: There is considerable historical evidence that dark-side leaders emerge in times of political and economic crisis. Where people perceive an imagined or real and significant

threat to their well-being and livelihood they are often drawn to the 'superman, heroic' leader who promises them he or she can save them. People are drawn to the rhetoric, the self-confidence and the bravado of leaders who can mobilize people and give them confidence.

Crises occur for all sorts of reasons. Political crises can trigger economic crises and vice versa. Sudden changes in technology or international law can have an immediate and massive impact on organizations of all sizes who look for immediate solutions. If at this point, the bold, mischievous, Machiavellian steps forward, the emergence of a dark-side leader is usually guaranteed.

3. **Organizational Structural Factors**: All organizations for not only historical but also legal reasons have processes and procedures which can, in effect, facilitate or frustrate the emergence of a dark-side leader. Some place serious restrictions on an individual's power and freedom to make decisions. Some organizations have strict rules and procedures about group decision making and record keeping. Others are more relaxed.

Furthermore, most organizations have rules about corporate governance. There may be non-executive directors whose explicit task it is to 'keep an eye on' maverick leaders and their decisions. There also may be rules about reports and statements and shareholders' meetings which make all sort of procedures public. In short, the better the corporate governance, the less chance the dark-side leader has to emerge.

There is a great deal of literature which supports the idea that some environments inhibit and others almost encourage illegal behaviour. Thus, Baucus and Near (1991) showed that large firms operating in a dynamic, munificent environment, with a history of prior violations and certain industry sectors, were more likely to take part in illegal acts.

1.8 The bully and the backstabber

This book was to be titled Bullies, Bastards and Backstabbers, but the second descriptor was dropped so as not to offend people. There are many books about difficult bosses. Many of these are self-help books not always informed by research evidence.

1.8.1 The bullying boss and the toxic manager

The idea of the manager as a bully is a much more common lay explanation for why workers may react badly at work. Very occasionally, sabotage or stealing, or some other dark-side behaviour, is the direct result of the bullying by one or more supervisors or boss. The dark-side behaviour is usually the attempt of a deeply frustrated individual or group to have their revenge for the humiliation, hurt and powerlessness that they have felt at the hands of a bullying boss.

There are various models of the bullying boss. One is that he or she bullies because he or she does not have the social and political skill to charm and persuade others and thus resort to bullying. However, some researchers have identified the skilful bully as one who is particularly good at navigating and influencing the organizational environment to achieve his or her own ends (Treadway et al., 2013). Inevitably skilful bullies are harder to identify and are much more successful at pursuing their own agendas.

Indeed, some organizations or parts of them may approve, even require, a bullying culture. That is, it is normative to bully. So what is workplace bullying? There are no agreed definitions, but they all share certain themes: first, it is an inappropriate, repeated and unreasonable behaviour, which is experienced as demeaning, humiliating, insulting, intimidating, offensive and even physically painful.

It is possible to distinguish between *personal* bullying and a *corporate* bullying culture, which can range from teasing, practical jokes, rumour-mongering to persistent targeted criticism. There is also *procedural, corporate culture* bullying, which may involve excessive workloads, unreasonable and unacceptable demands and paranoid monitoring of work.

The bullied suffer reduced self-esteem. Their concentration goes down and their absenteeism up. This inevitably affects productivity. But, it is common for morale in the whole section to go down, particularly of the silent group that knows about the bullying, disapproves of it, but is too scared to say anything.

It is important for managers to realize that bullies rarely work alone. They need actual or tacit support. Often investigators find that many in the work group often collude with bullies. They assist, instigate and praise bullies. Or they turn a blind eye to the whole thing. It really is a lot like the classroom of one's youth.

Bullying works at three levels. *First*, there are the characteristics of the bullies, who may be relatively easy to spot. They have very low emotional intelligence; they can't charm, persuade or influence. They often are a short-fuse and have poor coping skills. They want their own way but don't know how to get it in the adult world. Occasionally they are callous, smarmy individuals with superficial charm. But most are characterized by charmlessness.

Second, there is the work group, often characterized by win-lose, unsupportive, competitiveness. Work group attitudes or norms often start or stop bullying. The way people help or hinder each other at work is a function of their tasks, their environment and also how they are managed. It is possible to change group norms to both deter and increase bullying. The divide-and-conquer autocratic manager may easily be unwittingly the source of the bullying behaviour.

The *third* factor is the corporate culture. The work-hard, tough-guy macho corporate culture may well support bullying. It is the high-risk, quick-return world that fosters immaturity and distrust. The process-oriented, bureaucratic culture is more cautious and ritualistic and probably not as prone to physical bullying. The latter may be more exclusionary.

The list of bullying behaviours specified by the literature in the area is indeed long. It includes:

- Verbal abuse: name-calling, rudeness, screaming, profanities.
- Ridicule via insults, slander, belittling or patronizing comments.
- Malicious teasing, pranks and practical jokes.
- Unwanted and inappropriate physical contact.

- Consistent criticism, accusations and blame.
- Isolation, ignoring or giving the person the 'silent treatment'.
- Unreasonable/impossible targets, deadlines, tasks, pressure.
- Assigned meaningless, pointless, dirty-work tasks.
- Devaluing work efforts, giving no credit for effort/outcome.
- Withholding and distorting work-related information.
- Refusing reasonable requests for training, equipment.
- Unexplained, unnecessary, erratic changes introduced.
- Constant threats of job loss.
- Tampering with a worker's individual property or work equipment.

Bullying is a difficult problem because it can be so subjective. One man's firm and directive supervision is another's bullying. To this extent it is in the eye of the beholder. Jokes can be seen as insults; promotion refusal could be attributed to bullying rather than poor progress.

The law tends to side with the person who is complaining and if the employer fails to deal adequately with the complaint, a worker may intend to resign and claim constructive unfair dismissal. If the bullying is serious, the worker may also bring in a civil or criminal claim (Kibling & Lewis, 2000, p. 241).

What is clear is that perceived or real (if distinguishable) bullying has powerful consequences on the bully, the bullied and the work group. Usually the most manifold consequences of bullying are on the health and well-being of the bullied. But there are usually noticeable increases in absenteeism and staff turnover and a decrease in productivity.

Some researchers have attempted to count the costs and benefits of taking no action such as the introduction of prevention and redressal measures. Much of this is about creating awareness and providing employee support systems as well as managing incidents well.

A central question is why some managers bully. Is it a result of the personality, leadership style or lack of skill? Is it because of different expectations or even an awareness of their behaviour on others? Are bullies simply people with low social/emotional intelligence with an inability to influence and persuade? And as a result should they be punished or helped or both?

This book is not about the cause of bullying but possible reactions to it. Some people who feel bullied simply resign; others retreat; some others complain; and yet others take revenge. It seems logical that dark-side behavioural revenge against individuals and organizations can be significantly reduced by developing both a healthy workplace culture and sensitive and sensible set of procedures to deal with bullies.

Corporate cultures that condone bullying, explicitly or inexplicitly, invite revenge. Certainly all organizations can experience problems particularly at times of change and restructuring. Handled well, the incidences of reported bullying should decrease as well as some of the negative consequences of those who felt bullied.

Walton (2007) in a piece based on *'personal consulting and coaching assignments'* described toxic leaders and how they are *'silent killers who inhibit openness, creativity and healthy workplaces'* (p. 19). They are abrasive and abusive, insensitive, arrogant and aloof, self-serving, manipulative micro-managers. Like all others he stresses that for toxic leadership to flourish one needs also vulnerable and demeaned followers as well as conducive context which allow the toxic leader to emerge and flourish.

Reading the list of typical characteristics of the dysfunctional parent in the toxic family, it is not difficult to see why children from these families end up as they do. Moody, egocentric, uneducated, immoral 'care-givers' give little care. Instead of providing the loving, stable environment, they do the opposite, which can have a disastrous long-term effect on the child.

Dysfunctional managers create toxic offices. They manage, often in a brief period of time, to create mayhem, distrust and disaffection. And even in stable adults this can have long-term consequences. That perfidious issue of 'stress at work' and its more serious cousin, the nervous breakdown, are often caused by the dysfunctional manager.

To many, especially young people, a manager is *in loco parentis*. They can have considerable influence over one's health, happiness and future. They can create an environment that allows employees to give their best. They can stretch their staff by setting reachable but challenging goals and they can give them support in doing so. They can be helpful and encouraging and consistent – or not.

But there are some seriously poor managers who create a working environment at the precise opposite end of the spectrum. What are the symptoms of the dysfunctional manager? Check the list.

The dysfunctional boss, like the delinquent child, may have come from a dysfunctional home or socialized in a dysfunctional organization. Management consultants often talk about management practices they have come across that are little short of startling. They cause unhappiness and reduce productivity and morale, which, over time, can lead to the breakdown of the staff.

The workplace can become psychologically as well as physically toxic. The dysfunctional manager is a sort of Typhus Mary of stress and incompetence, taking the disease around with them wherever they go. Worse, they model dysfunctionality to young staff, who may consider their behaviour normal. The cure, alas, is often not worth the candle. Dysfunctional managers need more than counselling: they really need cancelling.

1.9 Conclusion

We have discovered, only relatively recently, the high cost of management failure and leadership derailment. The question this book addresses is how and why this occurs and what we can do about it. Whilst the book will take a strongly individual difference perspective, it is recognized that organizational factors play an important part in causing leadership derailment.

Chapter 2

Management derailment

2.1 Introduction

Over the past twenty years the academic psychological literature on management derailment has really 'taken off'. Some of the early researchers like Lombardo et al. (1988), McCall (1998) and Hogan and Hogan (1997) began to sketch out the issues and develop theories.

Thus, McCall (1998) noted that most derailing leaders had early success. He suggested five usual reasons as shown in Table 2.1.

Table 2.1 Sources of initial success (based on McCall, 1998)

Track record	Most executives have a strong track record, consistently achieving bottom-line results or making an impressive impact in a functional or technical area. This reputation and work history have often been exemplary and they get rated as highly talented.
Brilliance	Being seen as very bright was a common reason for success. Brilliance might be manifest in technical or functional speciality, in analytical and problem-solving skills, or in a singular burst of genius. Some have their brilliance in fluid and others in crystalized intelligence. It is difficult to make it to the top without being both clever and educated.
Commitment	Many list their loyalty to the organization as a strength, which is often expressed as a willingness to work long hours and accept whatever assignments they are asked to take on. The question is who or what they are committed to: their boss, career, team or company?

(Continued)

Charm	Many are capable of exuding considerable charm, charisma or personal warmth when dealing with others. They are known for their social and emotional intelligence. This quality is used effectively and is often expressed upward and outward to those who hold power.
Ambition	Although some are 'drafted' into the management ranks, many others actively seek it, doing whatever is required to achieve success. They always seem to be driven to achieve fame, money and power.

Likewise the early work suggested a few more common pathways to failure (Table 2.2).

Table 2.2   The dynamics of derailment (based on McCall, 1998)

Strengths become weaknesses	The particular strengths that made the person successful become liabilities in situations where other strengths are more important. Equally the strengths are overused and other skills and approaches are not learnt or used.
Blind spots matter	Weaknesses and flaws that did not matter previously or were forgiven in the light of strengths or results become central in a new situation. Early allowable weakness or overlooked problems that were not really dealt with become manifest.
Success leads to arrogance	Success goes to a person's head, leading to the mistaken belief that he or she is infallible and needs no one's help. This is the classic route from high self-esteem to clinical narcissism. Moreover, this often occurs at precisely the time when these assumptions are least viable.
Bad luck	Sometimes derailment results from a run-in with 'fate' that is not a reflection of the person's talent. Sometimes, however, bad luck is exacerbated by one of the other dynamics. To some extent you make your luck.

As Denton and van Lill (2006) in their review noted, the early literature seemed to indicate that more effective leaders will possess most of the following characteristics:

- Handling the demands of the management job, through resourcefulness, doing whatever it takes and decisiveness
- Dealing with subordinates by leading subordinates, setting developmental climate, confronting problem subordinates, work-team orientation and hiring talented staff
- Respect for self and others through building and mending relationships, compassion and sensitivity, candour and composure, balance between personal life and work, self-awareness, putting people at ease, and acting with flexibility. (pp. 236–237)

It was Lombardo, who could be considered to be the 'founding father' of research in this area, who provided the first description of the derailment process. It is set out in a useful summary in Table 2.3.

Table 2.3   The derailment process (Lombardo & Eichinger, 1999)

Early Strengths	Latent Problems/ Untested Areas	Changing Demands	Reasons for Discord
a) Brilliant	a) Overambitious	a) Interpersonal effectiveness	Poor treatment of others
b) Driver	b) Needs no one else	b) Building and mending relationships	
c) Ambitious	c) Abrasive		
d) Tough on laggards	d) Lacks composure	c) Stability required for trust development	
	e) Handles others' mistakes poorly		
	f) Does not know how to get the most out of people		

(*Continued*)

Early Strengths	Latent Problems/ Untested Areas	Changing Demands	Reasons for Discord
a) Independent b) Likes to do it alone c) Dislikes doing it alone d) Overmanages e) Suppresses subordinates f) Extremely loyal to organization	a) Does not develop subordinates b) Does not resolve conflict c) Poor delegator d) Selects according to own image e) Has never chosen or built staff	a) Team-building b) Staffing c) Developing others d) Increase in importance	Cannot mould staff
a) Controlling b) Results-orientated c) Single-minded d) Technical detail e) Extremely personable f) Relies on relationships	a) Has trouble with new jobs, situations, people b) Easily irritated c) Has not developed a strategic perspective d) Does not adapt well to new culture or changes e) Has not made transition to an unknown area	Giving up old way of doing things, which is essential to success at more complex assignments	Cannot make transition to more strategic, complex roles
a) Creative b) Conceptually strong c) Ball of fire d) Finger in	a) Lack of attention to essential detail b) Disorganized c) 'Speedboats' along; leaves people dangling d) Has not really completed an assignment in detail	Depth as well as awareness of how one is perceived if one does not follow through on commitments/ detail	Lacks follow-through

(Continued)

Early Strengths	Latent Problems/ Untested Areas	Changing Demands	Reasons for Discord
Has a single notable characteristic, such as tons of energy, raw talent, or being a long- term mentor	a) Too many eggs in one basket b) Staying with the same person too long c) Has not stood alone	Increasing complexity requires broader skills; standing on one's own without a shield	Overdependence on single strength
a) Contentious b) Loves to argue c) Takes strong stands d) Usually right	a) Does not known how to sell position, cajole b) Has to win c) Trouble adapting to those with different styles	Cajoling, persuasion, understanding of group processes required	Strategic differences with upper management

In a qualitative study done in South Africa, Denton (2000) found a range of factors related to derailment. In all, 193 people took part and their scores on completely agreeing about a range of causes of derailment are given in Table 2.4.

Table 2.4 Beliefs about the causes of derailment

Question	% Completely Agreeing
1. Overambitious	5.2
2. Does not need anyone else	15. 5
3. Abrasive	9. 3
4. Lack of composure	9. 8
5. Handles mistakes poorly	17. 1
6. Does not know how to get the most out of people	27. 5
7. Does not develop subordinates	27. 5
8. Does not resolve conflict	26. 4

(*Continued*)

Question	% Completely Agreeing
9. Poor delegation	23. 8
10. Selects persons in own image	15. 0
11. Has never chosen or built staff team	11. 4
12. Trouble with new jobs, people	13. 0
13. Easily irritated	15. 5
14. Does not adapt to new cultures or changes well	20. 7
15. New at making transitions into the unknown	10. 4
16. Lacks the attention to essential detail	7. 3
17. Disorganized	19.2
18. 'Speedboats' along and leaves people dangling	13. 0
19. Has not really completed an assignment in detail	7. 8
20. Too many eggs in one basket	18. 1
21. Stayed with the same person too long	5. 2
22. Never stood alone	5. 2
23. Does not know how to sell a position	6. 7
24. Has to win at all costs	27. 5
25. Has difficulty adapting to those with different styles	20. 7
26. Poor treatment of others	18. 1
27. Cannot mould staff	13. 0
28. Cannot make the transition to more strategic, complex roles	20. 7
29. Lacks follow-through	16. 1
30. Overdependence on single strength	14. 5
31. Strategic differences with upper management	19. 7

Many of the writers have pointed out that derailment happens in all sectors to all groups of people though there are some interesting differences. Thus, Furnham et al. (2014b) showed how dark-side trait patterns were very different when comparing those in the private and public section. Equally, and more controversially perhaps, Morrison et al. (1992) suggested sex differences in derailment, though this issue has not be fully explored or explained (Table 2.5).

Table 2.5 Derailment factors of women versus men (from Morrison et al., 1992)

	Derailed Women Said to Have This Flaw (%)	Derailed Men Said to Have This Flaw (%)
Unable to adapt	50	35
Performance problem	50	65
Too ambitious/wants too much	50	20
Unable to lead subordinates	44	35
Not strategic	38	25
Presented a poor image	38	5
Poor relationships	38	100
Skill deficits	31	20
Not driven to success	25	2
Too narrow	19	–

2.2 Three crucial indicators

The modern literature based on both psychological and psychiatric theory suggests that underlying all the leader derailment (and all personality disorders) there are three very fundamental markers. Whilst there are a large number of factors that might indicate the possibility that a leader could derail, there are three which are always most important. They concern issues like empathy, intimacy, identity and adaptation.

2.2.1 Relationships: Can the person establish and maintain healthy, happy, long-term relationships with various sorts of people?

Leadership is done with and through people. It is almost impossible to conceive of a leadership position which does not involve groups and teams. Leaders have to get the trust and loyalty of their team to succeed. They need to build team spirit and understand team dynamics. They must help teams cope with both triumph and disaster and learn new skills and ways of working together.

The ability to form and maintain relationships starts early. People make friends at a very young age for various reasons and some keep them for very long periods. There is vast literature in psychology on the psychological importance of friendship formation and social support. It is essential to establish relationships to be able to maintain mental health.

What is clear from the work on the personality disorders and dark-side traits is that for different reasons those with these disorders have difficulty with relationships. It is possible to consider the number of relationship problems that an individual has had including parent-child, sibling, partner, colleague, neighbour etc., over the years.

The psychiatrists have listed some of the issues:

1. Recurring arguments, conflict, even physical violence between two individuals which cause preoccupation and/or distract from the normal activities of daily living.
2. Acute and chronic lack of communication and/or withdrawal from others which results in frustration and/or anger.
3. Inappropriate communication and expectations from others which can include unrealistic expectations, withdrawal or criticism.
4. Avoidance of the people who are felt to be causing the stress.
5. Stress related to threat of separation either by ending the relationship.
6. Increased irritability, sleeplessness, depression and/or social withdrawal.
7. A pattern of angry responses towards others.
8. Tearfulness, low energy, withdrawal related to concerns about the relationship.
9. Arguments which never resolve due to insufficient conflict resolution strategies.
10. Overprotection or overinvolvement in another individual's life activities.
11. Arguments with spouse that cause preoccupation and detract from work performance.

Whilst nearly all researchers have demonstrated that problems with interpersonal relationships are at the heart of the problem for derail managers, it has been suggested that these are often complemented by a whole number of self-defeating behaviours. These include being rigid, hostile, defensive, overcommitted, suspicious and defensive (Williams et al., 2013). However, it seems these self-defeating behaviours themselves play a big part in derailment because they are related to the inability to establish good relationships.

From the 1960s to the mid-1990s, it was common to talk of *communications, interpersonal or social skills*. These were loosely defined as a set of learned, specific but related skills which allow us to understand and communicate relating to others: initiating and maintaining social relationships. People who worked in the area maintained that there were various specific assumptions made by social skills researchers. Most would have agreed that social skills are essential.

Those who focused on communication focused on verbal, vocal and non-verbal behaviour. They noted that people could be taught to communicate what they felt and thought more accurately and effectively. Hence the emphasis on presentation skills and public speaking.

Others were more interested in the ability of people to initiate and sustain relationships. These skills concerned being assertive and relationship building. Social skills deficit was thought of as the cause of many problems.

Some adults often tend to be rigid, with poor self-control and poor social skills, and are weak at building bonds. Understanding and using emotions/feelings are at the heart of business and indeed being human.

Often business people prefer to talk about *emotional competencies* (rather than traits or abilities) which are essentially learned capabilities. Emotional competencies include emotional self-awareness, emotional self-regulation, social-emotional awareness, regulating emotions in others – understanding emotions, etc. If one is to include older-related concepts like social skills or interpersonal competencies, then it is possible to find a literature dating back thirty years showing these skills predict occupational effectiveness and success. Furthermore, there is convincing empirical literature which suggests that these skills can be improved and learnt.

One recognized reason for management failure is lack of emotional intelligence. This is most often found in leaders in highly technical areas (finance, engineering), who my have chosen those subjects because of their poor social skills in the first place.

A more straightforward conceptualization of emotional intelligence is listed in Table 2.6.

Table 2.6   The four components of emotional intelligence

	Self	Others
Emotional Awareness	A	B
Emotional Management	C	D

A. This refers to an insight into where and when and why one experiences (or does not experience in contrast with everybody else) particular emotions. Why do I feel low or jittery on particular occasions? Why do others seem to react to certain events differently from me? This is classic self-awareness but applies specifically to the emotions.

B. This refers to being perceptive, aware and sensitive to how others are really feeling whatever they may be saying. Some people are easier than others 'to read': what are they really thinking, feeling, experiencing. The ability to notice, understand and decide the emotional state of others nearly always involves sensitivity to emotional displays.

C. This refers to the ability of a person not so much to understand as to change and manage their emotions. This may involve controlling anxiety during public speaking or else their anger when dealing with particular customers. It is about the regulation of moods and the presentation of appropriate emotional cues.

D. This involves the management of others emotions. It involves what to do and when to raise spirits in demoralized groups and to change the mood of clients, customers or staff when they are inappropriate.

The bottom line is this. All the evidence suggests that derailed managers are unable or unwilling to initiate and maintain healthy, long-term relationships in the workplace. Either because of their lack of social skill or else their egotism and selfishness they tend to have problems with their clients, team and reports.

2.2.2 Self-awareness: Does the person have insight into themselves?

This is defined as the accurate appraisal and understanding of your abilities and preferences and their implications for your behaviour and their impact on others. It is essentially reality-testing, a calibration against the facts of life.

Self-awareness is partly knowledge about the self: strengths and weaknesses, vulnerabilities and passions, idiosyncrasies and normalness. It can be derived in many ways. Sometimes self-insight comes from a sudden epiphany in the classroom or on the couch. It can even occur at an appraisal. It comes out of success and failure. What others say and yes, even by receiving feedback from a personality test.

There is a pathological form of self-awareness. This is manifest in the hyper-vigilant, counselling-addicted, self-obsessed individuals who are interested in nothing but themselves. It is a phase most adolescents pass through. But some become stuck. It's deeply unattractive and quite counterproductive.

It can take years to find out who you are, where you belong (in the family, organization, community), knowing what you can best contribute to others. Some people are lucky: they are given opportunities to test their skills and see their impact. They become more aware of their potential and how they naturally behave in specific situations.

Are you good in a crisis, or do you provoke them? Do you have a good ear for languages? Are you (really) emotionally intelligent? Why do certain types of people clearly not like you? Are you a natural at negotiation and sales? Are you aware of what stresses you and what your fundamental values are?

Are you self-conscious in the sense that you really have self-understanding? Because with this comes both better self-regulation of emotions and self-management.

Surely, one of the greatest of all faults is to be conscious of having none. So how to improve your self-awareness? Three things help: first, *self-testing*, exploration and try-outs. Try new tasks and situations. Adolescents are famous for saying they do not like something that they have never tried. People make discoveries late in life – often through chance discoveries.

The second feature is *self-acceptance*. This is neither the over- nor under-estimation of your talents. We are not all intelligent, creative, insightful. It is as sad to see people ignoring or underplaying their strengths as their weaknesses.

Third, seeking out *feedback* from others. A good friend, boss or teacher tells it like it is. They help to clarify crucial questions: *What is really important to me? Who is the authentic me?*

The famous Johari window argued that self-awareness comes about as a function of two processes:

Disclosure: We all have skeletons in the cupboard and private hopes and yearnings. We might tell these to our favoured confessor and no one else. But those disclose very little, often through fear of being used or hurt, and are difficult to get to know. Disclosure is usually reciprocated. It is good for building relationships.

Feedback: How do you know whether you are clever, productive, charming, etc.? The answer lies in obtaining and acting upon objective and subjective feedback of one's behaviour. This is the job of all teachers and coaches and fundamental to the whole business of learning.

The Johari window has four boxes: The *Open Self* which is common knowledge, things I know and you know about me. Then there is the *Hidden Self* which is the little box of secrets, things I know about me that others do not. The third box is labelled *Blind Self* which is about things other people know about, see in, are sure of, me but which they have not told me. The fourth box is the *Unknown Self* – things neither I nor others know about me. These include buried, repressed or long forgotten thoughts. Perhaps they can be mined by therapists interested in, and supposedly able to, drag things from the murky unconscious into the bright light of day.

The bottom line is that most derailed leaders are poorly informed about their strengths and weaknesses. They do not understand how they come across and their effect on others. This is potentially a serious issue.

2.2.3 Adaptability, learning and transitioning

It has frequently been observed that derailed leader's early career success was often responsible for their later failure because they failed to learn. At various times in a work career people have to learn to let go of old, odd, dysfunctional assumptions and beliefs. Furthermore, they need to acquire new skills and ideas. This often means exposing oneself to learning situations that can be threatening and which may involve failure.

Some organizations do a good job in preparing people for senior positions. Through a series of planned experiences and courses they hope to transition them to take on the responsibilities of higher management. All potential leaders need to upgrade and extend their social and technical skills and move from tactical to strategic thinking. Both incompetent and derailed leaders often have too narrow a range of experience and an overemphasis and reliance on either technical or social skills.

Senior leadership is often about dealing calmly and rationally with ambiguous, threatening and uncertain situations. The inflexible and unadaptable executive seems often to change their mindset and grow to meet changing situations.

There are a range of transitions that most people go through. These include promotion to senior and then general management, losing a supportive boss or coherent team, going through a difficult merger or simply experiencing disruptive organizational change. Some are offered coaching, mentoring and other ways to help over this period. They might be given a mature and functional team. Most importantly they are given feedback on their strengths, limitations and blind spots.

But change happens all the time. Technology and the law change. Internationalization means new competitors. Companies can appear and disappear overnight. People therefore need to be adaptable and able to cope with change. Some are clearly better at this than others. The more inflexible, unadaptable and rigid a manager is, the more likely that he or she will derail.

2.3 Five fundamental issues

Over the years it appears that there are five issues that lead to potentially derailing people being appointed, promoted and managed. It seems failure to take heed of these fundamental issues is a major cause of management failure and derailment.

2.3.1 Selecting in, as well as, screening out

Now, more than ever, we are getting used to the idea of screening out people who volunteer or are required to work with children, highly sensitive information or under conditions where safety is paramount. People have to be properly 'checked out' partly for legal reasons.

Traditionally, the areas of concern (red flags) include alcohol and drug abuse, a criminal record, conflicts with authority, misconduct, chronic financial problems, and poor and inconsistent performance. A particular interest for psychologists has been how people handle anger and frustration.

However, it is rare for chief executives, military or political leaders to experience any select out process.

Table 2.7 A Simple Selection Model

	Good	Bad
Select	A. Excellent candidate: the right person for the job	B. Decision Error: chosen for the wrong reason
Reject	C. Decision Error: not recognizing particular characteristics; personal biases; little insight	D. Good Decision: For various reasons the wrong person for the job

The simple box in Table 2.7 illustrates the issue. The aim of selection is to accept and select good candidates (A) while rejecting the bad, less able or less suitable (D). However, selectors make mistakes. Nearly everyone has made a bad selection decision and lived to regret their error (B). Few know about the other common mistake which is when they reject a candidate who later turns out to be the ideal candidate (C).

But what of select out? Most people are not selected because they do not have enough of some skills or competency. It is comparatively rare for selectors to have a set of specific select-out factors. These may be things like impulsivity or obsessionality. Some people may argue that not having enough of a quality like integrity or honesty implies the presence of a select out factor. However, if you are not a brilliant scholar it does not mean that you are unintelligent. If you are not strongly creative, it does not mean that you are totally lacking in creativity.

It is centrally important to look for evidence of things you do not want. Few organizations think like this and fewer actually have select out processes. The consequences are often that leaders with potential derailers sail through. Indeed, as will be noted, paradoxically some of their derailers may actually assist them in the selection process.

2.3.2 Too much of a good thing

With very few exceptions, *all human characteristics are normally distributed*. Handedness is one exception, gender another. Roughly one in ten people are left-handed and half the population male, the other half female.

The issue is now called 'the spectrum hypothesis'. It means that extreme normality is non-normality. By definition, people at extremes are rare/few and therefore not average or normal. Nearly all human characteristics are normally distributed from creativity to conscientiousness. Consider height. People who are unusually tall or short often experience socio-emotional as well as physical problems.

Even factors thought to be beneficial and healthy can occur at extremes. Healthy high self-esteem becomes narcissism; out-of-the-box creative thinking becomes schizotypal; sociable, optimistic extraversion becomes impulsive hedonism.

Many people believe there is a linear relationship between a 'virtue' and success. The more the merrier. However, it is clearly apparent that leaders can be too vigilant, too tough, too hardworking. Selection errors occur because of linear, rather than cut-off thinking. Too much of a good thing becomes a bad thing.

This idea has also been conceived as strengths overused. Hogan and Kaiser (2008) note that strengths become weaknesses because one type of response is used too much and too often and other different behaviours are not learnt.

2.3.3 Ignoring the past

It might be a truism, but it is true that the best predictor of the future is the past. People are products of their past, not necessarily victims of it. They have a history which gives strong clues to their current lives.

For instance, there is a fascinating literature on the misfortunes of youth and how they have long-term effects on individuals. In studies of famous individuals from a wide range of backgrounds (arts, business, literature, science), five 'setbacks' seemed to be particularly important, which helped people become more resilient and helpful. They are as follows:

Bereavement: Parental death or divorce can make or break people as can long tern illness. The death of a sibling or a child can have much the same effect.

Parental cruelty: By physical or psychological means, neglect or humiliation.

Isolation: Being brought up in physical or social isolation from others of one's own age group.

Lack of fixed abode: Being highly peripatetic moving from one place to another.

Dependence: The unwelcomed feeling of dependence on others for everything that is important.

The psychobiographical research has suggested the importance of early insecurity, feelings of inferiority and identity confusion. Much has been made of acute and chronic relationship problems as well as emotional problems leading to unusual manifestations of anxiety, jealousy, resentment and depression. Health problems and their consequences are also thought to be important as are early social problems, particularly when a person was discriminated against on the basis of his colour, religion or class.

Those interested in biography suggest that it gives great clues to whether and why a person is resilient and hardy and at what point they might crack. They also suggest that it is possible to get a great insight into a person's attitudes to authority.

Many writers have mentioned the compensation hypothesis which suggests that some people are driven to compensate for some early, even imagined weakness, handicap or shortcoming. It is also suggested that early life points to an individual's social skills and their social adaptability. Equally early peer group contacts are often established in youth.

The issue is this. Because of nature and nurture, we are products of not only our genetics but also our environment. Nearly all in-depth studies of derailment suggest that the clues to a person's derailment could have been spotted much sooner had people spend the effort in looking a potential leader's past history.

2.3.4 Halos and horns

There is a very long list of systematic biases and errors that people commit when rating others at interviews. The most famous are described here.

- **Halo/Horns effect**: The tendency to make inappropriate generalizations about an individual which can be either positive or negative. Thus, there are either all good/excellent/competent/talented or all hopeless. It is essentially a result of an inability or unwillingness to discriminate and differentiate between good and bad features of the individual.
- **Leniency**: The tendency to evaluate all people as outstanding and to give inflated ratings. These people or 'softies' are unwilling to rate anything as poor.

- **Central tendency**: The tendency to evaluate every person as average regardless of differences in performance.
- **Harshness**: The tendency to rate all people at the low end of the scale seeing everyone and everything about them as weak, inferior and inadequate.
- **Contrast effect**: The tendency for a rater to evaluate a person relative to other individuals. That is there are contrast effects with no base rate.
- **First impression error**: The tendency for a manger to make an initial favourable or unfavourable judgement about someone, and then ignore subsequent information.
- **Similar-to-me effect**: The tendency to more favourably judge those people perceived as similar to the leader.

2.3.5 The power(less)fullness of training

There is, for some people, the belief that everything is changeable and trainable. Thus, there are cases where the serious shortcomings of a potential leader are noted – which subsequently lead to their demise – but it is argued that they can be dealt with by training. It is suggested that a comparatively short but very expensive training course, plus a mentor or coach, can bring about dramatic positive consequences.

The problem here is not differentiating enough when judging people. They are seen to be all good or all bad. One 'bad mark' against a person's name can have great consequences. The issue here is differentiating attitudes and skills within and between people.

2.3.6 Helping people change (if they want to)

Some argue that all human behaviour is (relatively easily) *changeable*: your own and others', if you swallow a magic pill. The major problem for all managers is that it is very difficult to change people's attitudes and/or their work-related behaviours. Perhaps this explains why there are so many books on change management.

There are a very large number of self-help books that promise to provide the answer of how to change behaviour, from the 'curing' of addictions to general health and happiness. Many offer simple solutions to complex psychological phenomena and processes and often make claims that are not supported by disinterested, peer-reviewed, empirical research (Lilienfeld et al., 2010).

In an attempt to 'review with unflinching candour the effectiveness of most different kinds of treatment for the major psychological disorders', Seligman (2007, p. xi) provided some facts about psychological change. In his book he reviewed the changeability of sixteen disorders including sexual preferences, identity orientations and dysfunction. He provides ten facts about change.

There are debates in various areas of psychology about how to change individuals as well as groups and organizations as a whole. In personality theory there are debates between those who argue that people do change (considerably and significantly over time) and those who suggest they do not (Ardelt, 2000). Equally there are studies in clinical psychology that examine theories of change as a function of therapy (Furnham et al., 2013).

There is also a debate about whether intelligence can change; that is, whether people can become more intelligent. Individuals holding an *entity* theory of intelligence believe that intelligence levels remain constant over a person's lifetime regardless of their education, effort and experience gained. This is the result of what Dweck (2012), who pioneered research in this area, calls a *Fixed Mindset*. Entity theorists believe that they can learn new things (skills, knowledge), but their underlying intelligence level essentially never changes. By contrast, *incremental* theorists believe that intelligence can be increased and cultivated over a lifetime through hard work and continued learning. Fixed mindset theorists tend not to increase their level of effort in educational and work environments because they do not believe they can improve their performance. Incremental theorists, however, tend to acknowledge the importance of effort when approaching a learning task (Dweck, 2012).

Entity theorists are essentialists with regard to their beliefs about intelligence. Indeed, the whole issue of malleability and immutability of abilities and temperament is at the heart of many psychological debates including the 'talent myth' and 10,000-hour rule which suggests all expert/elite performance can be trained if people put in sufficient effort.

This is a topic of considerable academic debate with some arguing that people can, and others that they cannot, increase their intelligence. Kuszewski (2011) concluded thus: 'Fluid intelligence is trainable. The training and subsequent gains are dose-dependent – meaning, the more your train the more you gain. Anyone can increase their cognitive ability, no matter what your starting point is. The effect can be gained by training on tasks that don't resemble the test questions' (p. 2). Some studies have supported this assumption (Jausovec & Jausovec, 2012).

Furnham (2014) looked at the extent to which people believed they could increase their multiple intelligences. He found whilst verbal, naturalistic and intra-personal intelligence was seen to be relatively easy to change, creative and musical intelligence was seen as much less so. He also found that core self-evaluation and growth mindset were both significant positive correlates on beliefs about growing/changing intelligence.

We know that change is difficult and that learning new behaviour patterns is far from easy. A serious and recurrent error with respect to derailed managers is the assumption that all skills and attitudes can be trained. That is, people can be trained to avoid certain behaviour patterns and acquire other.

2.4 The avoidable behaviours

As we shall see in other chapters in this book, one of the most useful of all the ways to understand the causes, manifestations and consequences of leadership derailment is through the personality disorders. This approach was pioneered by the Hogans but enthusiastically taken up by others.

In their short but very clear book *Why CEOs Fail: The 11 Behaviours That Can Derail Your Climb to the Top – and How to Manage Them*, Dotlich and

Cairo (2003) provided a very useful and clear summary of the whole issue in common sense language.

They identified 11 behaviours that corresponded to the DSM III Personality Disorders but gave them labels different from the Psychiatric Manual or the Hogan and Hogan (1997) report. The essential ones (see Chapter 4) are worth considering briefly.

a. *Arrogance*: They talk of the self-blinding brilliance of the arrogant leader with the tell-tail signs of a diminished capacity to learn; an off-putting refusal to be accountable, a resistance to change and an inability to recognize one's limitations (Table 2.8a).

Table 2.8a Have you crossed the line into **Arrogance** (based on Dotlich & Cairo, 2003, p. 6)

Arrogance		You're Right and Everybody Else Is Wrong
You're willing to fight for what you believe in	vs.	You're unwilling to give up a fight no matter what
You believe that your perspective is the correct one after evaluating other points of view	vs.	You believe that your perspective is the correct one before evaluating others' ideas
You hold yourself accountable when your strategy or idea doesn't work	vs.	You refuse to take responsibility when your strategy or idea doesn't work
You adapt your strongly held viewpoint to jibe with new information or developments	vs.	You reinterpret events to fit your point of view
You possess a powerful ego that allows you to make an impact on others	vs.	You possess a powerful ego that causes you to dominate others

b. *Melodrama*: They talk sparks flying and everything being a show. They note typical signs as lack of focus, a failure to develop people, having a showboating team and having elevated expectations (Table 2.8b).

Table 2.8b Have you crossed the line into **Melodrama** (based on Dotlich & Cairo, 2003, pp. 18–19)

Melodrama		You Always Grab the Centre of Attention
You command attention when you speak	vs.	You dominate meetings by speaking constantly
You use charisma to involve and motivate people	vs.	You use attention-getting styles to create unquestioning compliance
Your showmanship helps attract outside attention from media, analysts and prospective recruits	vs.	Your highly theatrical style creates the impression that your style of leadership is the issue for discussion
You know exactly when to be charming or deliver an eloquent talk to achieve a key goal	vs.	You are consistently flamboyant rather than strategically dramatic
You can turn off the style and listen and learn from others	vs.	You're always 'on' and rarely reflect on what you're trying to achieve

c. *Volatility*: They talk of mood swings which lead to decision variance. They note that people hold back in their interactions with this type; that there is a lot of mood management going around; that people feel like they become increasingly distant (Table 2.8c).

Table 2.8c Have you crossed the line into **Volatility** (based on Dotlich & Cairo, 2003, pp. 32–33)?

Volatility		Your Mood Swings Drive Business Swings
You lose your temper because of major screw-ups or other significant problems	vs.	You explode over minor mistakes or for reasons you can't articulate
Feedback tells you that your people know what they can expect from you	vs.	Feedback tells you that your people don't know who's going to show up from one day to the next

(Continued)

Volatility		Your Mood Swings Drive Business Swings
You generally act on way most of the time	vs.	You move back and forth between optimistic and pessimistic stances
You consistently generate energy and enthusiasm through your words and deeds	vs.	You create energy and enthusiasm one day and intimidate others the next through your words and actions

d. *Mischievousness*: These are rebels without a cause, should they argue note four things: People question their commitments and the projects they have started; they do not take the time to win people over; everything is a challenge; they often find themselves 'finessing' their mistakes; and they are easily bored (Table 2.8d).

Table 2.8d Have you crossed the line into **Mischievousness** (based on Dotlich & Cairo, 2003, pp. 83–84)?

Mischievousness		Rules Are Made to Be Broken
You test limits and push boundaries	vs.	You break rules because you believe rules are boring and unnecessary
You are impulsively creative	vs.	You are destructively impulsive
You enjoy risk-taking and don't dwell on mistakes	vs.	You make decisions and take risks without considering the consequences
You use your charm and creativity to achieve organizational goals	vs.	You use your charm and creativity as a matter of personal style and not to achieve specific goals
You make provocative statements in order to foster debate and discussion	vs.	You speak your mind for your own amusement or without any real objective

e. *Eccentricity*: They are people who march to their own drum and are unable to prioritize, tend to go it alone and are frequently not taken seriously by others (Table 2.8e).

Table 2.8e   Have you crossed the line into **Eccentricity** (based on Dotlich & Cairo, 2003, pp. 96–97)?

Eccentricity		It's Fun to Be Different Just for the Sake of It
You have a million great ideas	vs.	You have a million great ideas that rarely get executed
You keep people on their toes with your unpredictable and offbeat style	vs.	You confuse and confound people with your style
You've launched many important activities	vs.	You've launched many initiatives but don't follow up on them
You blend your original and sometimes unconventional style with a more conforming approach when necessary	vs.	You refuse to change who you are and be conforming in any way to organizational norms

f.   *Perfectionism*: These are the obsessional nit-pickers who have difficulty delegating and seem obsessed in putting form over function and style over substance. They often short-change people by retreating into processes and can overlook the obvious. Furthermore, they often get caught in a vicious stress cycle (Table 2.8f).

Table 2.8f   Have you crossed the line into **Perfectionism** (based on Dotlich & Cairo, 2003, p. 120)?

Perfectionism		Get the Little Things Right Even If the Big Things Go Wrong
You focus on the details	vs.	Detail focus prevents you from seeing the bigger picture
You find it worthwhile to make sure that presentations look and sound great	vs.	You pay more attention to the form of presentations than to their substance
You feel uncomfortable with uncertainty and ambiguity	vs.	You try to impose structure in every situation to get rid of uncertainty and ambiguity

(Continued)

Perfectionism		Get the Little Things Right Even If the Big Things Go Wrong
You manage processes with skill and determination	vs.	You spend so much time managing processes that people's needs become secondary
You are conscientious about your responsibilities	vs.	You can't let go of any task no matter how small until it's completed exactly as you had wanted

2.5 Conclusion

In many ways the issues discussed in this chapter are the most important in the book. The current psychiatric literature has lighted the three fundamental issues underlying all the personality disorders and other issues: problems with relationships, self-awareness and dealing with change. The chapter also noted five fundamental issues for those selecting and managing senior managers and leaders at work.

Chapter 3

Management incompetence and derailment: Too little and too much of a good thing

3.1 Introduction

Leaders fail for many reasons. Some unanticipated and uncontrollable events overwhelm them: an overseas war that affects the oil price; a radical change of government; the invention of new technologies. Wars, recessions and massive sudden economic changes can, quite quickly, cause chaos in any organization. Some otherwise effective leaders never had a chance: events over which they had no control and probably could not have anticipated overwhelmed them. As British prime minister Harold MacMillan, said when discussing what he feared most, 'Events, dear boy, events'.

However, fate, luck and chance are not the whole story. Some fail because of those they work with and for. Yet, one crucial factor seems to emerge in all the studies in this area and that lies in the ability, personality and values of the leader themselves. They fail because they are '*intellectually underpowered*'; they fail because they *cannot cope with the stress* and make bad decisions; and they fail because of their selfishness, *egoism and lack if integrity*. They fail *for not having sufficient business knowledge or office savvy*. There are many reasons why leaders fail, which is at the heart of this book, but it is most important to make a fundamental distinction.

3.2 Incompetent vs. derailment

It is important to make the distinction between leadership incompetence and derailment.

> A. **Incompetent**: Synonyms include ineptitude, inability, inadequacy, incapacity, ineffectiveness, uselessness, insufficiency, ineptness, incompetency, unfitness, incapability, skill-lessness. In essence incompetence means an inability to perform; lacking some ability, capacity or qualification.

Nearly everyone has worked for an incompetent manager. Some have never worked for anyone else! Essentially the incompetent manager is lacking something: Most are simply overpromoted. Others are there because of favouritism or simply bad selection. They do not have the skills, the energy, the courage or perhaps the insight to do that which is required of a good leader. Nepotism, poor selection techniques and complacency often account for the appointment of an incompetent leader.

Casciaro and Lobo (2005) in an amusing HBR article distinguished four types based on their competence and likability: competent and incompetent jerk and lovable star and fool. They caution, quite rightly, against spending too much time with the lovable fool, who is, in essence, incompetent.

Many have reported that the phenomenon of the incompetent CEO is not new. Toney and Brown (1997) in a paper entitled 'The Incompetent CEO' noted how they often get appointed through flawed promotional practices: ostracizing shining stars; choosing those with a pleasing personality or not examining the nature of their experience. Their advice was: watch out for early warning signs, scrap defective promotional practices, search out and retain really great leaders and train people in the appropriate skills.

> B. **Derailment**: This literally means coming off the tracks and is taken from railroad terminology. It refers to where an otherwise functional train, expectedly 'comes off the rails' and is thus left stranded, unable to move, possibly

blocking the line and potentially irreparable. The derailed leader is not one lacking in ability: indeed often the opposite. Many are highly talented, well-educated and high flyers. But they come unstuck, often because the dark side to their personality does not fully manifest itself until they acquire significant power.

Incompetence and derailment are sometimes difficult to differentiate because the consequences in the business are often similar. They usually include declining customer service, morale and profits, high turnover and negative media coverage as well as simple things like inadequate quality control and stock flow.

In the management literature, derailment has come to mean the demise of an otherwise successful business or political leader who seems to have too much of a good thing like self-confidence, boldness or courage. Indeed, it is for those characteristics that they were often chosen. However, the strengths became weaknesses possibly because of the way they were overused or, in the first place, were compensatory.

3.3 Two perspectives on incompetence

3.3.1 Humorous social psychologist

Nearly forty years ago, the academic psychologist Laurence Peter described the now famous Peter Principle: 'In any hierarchy, individuals tend to rise to their levels of incompetence'. Although his book was rejected by thirteen publishers, when it was finally published, it became an immediate best-seller. Indeed, Peter made the concept of incompetence popular long before competency or incompetency was on the lips of every manager.

In a later book entitled 'Why Things Go Wrong', he spelt out a number of corollaries to the Peter Principle:

- The cream rises until it is sour.
- For every job in the world there is someone, somewhere, who can't do it. Given enough promotions, that someone will get the job.

- All useful work is done by those who have not yet reached their level of incompetence.
- Competence always contains the seeds of incompetence.
- Incompetence plus incompetence equals incompetence.
- Whenever something is worth doing, it is worth finding someone competent to do it.
- The Peter Principle, like evolution, shows no mercy.
- Once an employee achieves a level of incompetence, inertia sets in and the employer settles for incompetence rather than distress the employee and look for a replacement.
- Lust gets us into trouble more than sloth.
- There is a tendency for the person in the most powerful hierarchical position to spend all his or her time performing trivial tasks.
- It's harder to get a job than keep it.
- Equal opportunity means everyone will have a few chances at becoming incompetent.
- The higher up you go, the deeper you get.
- Incompetence knows no barrier of time or place.
- The higher one climbs the hierarchical ladder, the shakier it gets.
- Climb the ladder of success, reach the top and you'll find you're over the hill.
- In a hierarchy, the potential for a competent subordinate to manage an incompetent supervisor is greater than for an incompetent superior to manage a competent subordinate.
- Colleges can't produce competence but they can produce graduates.
- Being frustrated in your work can be disagreeable, but the real disaster may be when you're promoted out of it.
- More competent individuals resign than incompetents get fired.
- The ability of the potentially competent erodes with time, while the potentially incompetent rises to the level where his or her full potential is actualized.

Individuals may be selected on a basis of competence, for their entry-level jobs, but as they move up they tend to become arranged just as distribution theory would predict: the majority in the moderately competent group, with the competent and incompetent comprising the minorities, as illustrated in the graph. (pp. 72–73)

Peter became well known for his wry and funny observations. However, he did not fully discuss the aetiology from a psychological perspective. He seemed to imply organizations get the managers they deserve and that incompetence is more about managerial systems than personal pathology. But organizations do not create incompetence: they may foster it, even reward it. Its origins lie in the individuals: those high and low flyers that end up being managers.

3.3.2 The military historian

Norman Dixon (author of *The Psychology of Military Incompetence*) argued that although military organizations are specialized, they are not unique. Indeed an analysis of management in the military naturally applies to all uniformed services (fire, ambulance, police). In fact, a 'command and control' management style and culture can be found in many organizations that have a uniform code, not of dress, but of behaviour.

Dixon (1981), an ex-military man and experimental psychologist, claimed that military incompetence is tragically expensive, predictable and preventable. Incompetence in the military is fundamentally no different from that in business, politics or state service except that:

- military organizations may attract a minority of people who are particularly prone to failure at high levels of command;
- the nature of militarism serves to accentuate the less adaptive personality traits in leaders;
- military officers are not democratically elected and few are sacked, dismissed or demoted for their incompetence; and
- the consequences of bad military decisions are often incredibly high.

Incompetence involves, first, *a serious waste of human resources and failure to observe one of the first principles of war – economy of force.* This failure derives in part from an inability to make war swiftly. It also derives from certain attitudes of mind. Next, *a fundamental conservatism and clinging to outworn traditions*, as well as an inability to learn from fundamental experience and a refusal to admit past mistakes. It also involves a failure to use or a tendency to misuse available technology. Third, incompetence results from *a tendency to reject or ignore information* that is unpalatable or that conflicts with preconceptions. Another problem is *the tendency to underestimate the enemy and overestimate the capabilities of one's own* side. Fourth, *indecisiveness* and a tendency to abdicate from the role of decision-maker lead to incompetence. Finally, *an obstinate persistence in a given task* despite strong contrary evidence is the hallmark of incompetence.

There are several explanations for military disasters. The first is that military (and indeed managerial) incompetence might be attributed to lack of intellectual ability. Is low intelligence among officers a necessary and sufficient explanation for military disaster? Although there is evidence that some military commanders were not especially bright, and that IQ was never a major criterion for selection or promotion, this does not seem an important, sufficient or parsimonious explanation for military failure. Indeed the opposite is more likely to be true.

What is true, however, is that the military harboured a culture of anti-intellectualism. The tendency to denigrate the intellectual values of inquiry, criticism and innovation, and to promote the values of tradition and conformity is, of course, not unique to the military. If an organization ignores or despises intellect, it will have long-term consequences, most importantly during times of change and the attendant stress. Organizations with incompetent managers are often either deeply anti-intellectual or uncritically in awe of quasi-intellectual (e.g. consultant-based) solutions. Both attitudes towards intellectual inquiry are unhealthy.

Certainly arrogance, pomposity and hubris characterize many captains of industry who later fall from grace. It is the excessive self-esteem that is the clue. In military, like managerial duties, incompetence is really a failure of leadership. Military leaders (i.e. officers) are, however, rather different from managers in most other organizations because of the following reasons:

- They are appointed rather than emerge – the average soldier has no say in the sort of officer (leader) he/she gets.
- Military leaders have considerable power over their subordinates and can literally order them to do their bidding – the force of law rather than persuasion.
- They can be autocratic, and information flows strictly through chain of command.

The concept of authoritarianism may explain military incompetence. The model military leader is a paterfamilias – the all-powerful, all-knowing, father figure in the authoritarian Victorian family. In his discussion of authoritarianism, Dixon relies heavily on the classic psychoanalytic study of prejudice, entitled *The Authoritarian Personality* (Adorno, et al., 1948), published over fifty years ago. The authors of that book were trying to understand the origins of anti-Semitism in Nazi Germany; they traced it to the concept of authoritarianism and identified a number of factors that seemed to cause it.

Authoritarianism contributes to military incompetence in various ways. Research shows that authoritarians are more dishonest, irresponsible, untrustworthy, suspicious and socially conforming than non-authoritarians (authoritarian tendencies can be easily measured). Authoritarians are less insightful and empathic and less likely to understand the opposition's intentions. They seem unable to relinquish cherished traditions and adopt technical innovations. They underestimate the ability of the opposition. They demand obedience and loyalty in juniors at the expense of initiative and innovation. Authoritarians are deeply concerned about their reputations and the criticism of seniors. They are also particularly quick to blame others for their shortcomings. Many authoritarians tend to be obsessive/compulsory types. Authoritarians are more likely to believe in supernatural forces and, therefore, fate. They also have generalized hostility and a lack of humanity.

In short, authoritarians are hostile, dogmatic people with closed minds. Hence, they are attracted to the cult of muscular Christianity and the stoicism and the dominance–submission relationships in military life. Obviously, they may be attracted to other organizations that resemble the uniformed services – for instance, the church and, in many countries, government service. There are, of course, degrees of authoritarianism: it is not an all-or-nothing issue. In addition, many people and organizations try to hide their authoritarianism in an effort to appear 'politically correct'.

Authoritarians are attracted to organizations that fulfil their needs and vice versa. Hence, over time more and more people of the same persuasion populate organizations. The peacetime army, like a large national utility, can soon be a homogeneous mass of crypto- and even proto-authoritarians.

Dixon noted:

> In developing this thesis, emphasis was laid upon those devices whereby fear is stilled, aggression evoked and disorder prevented. Military organisations were depicted as sometimes cumbrous and inflexible machines for the harnessing and direction of intra-species hostility beneath whose often brightly decorated exterior the psychological process of 'bull' authoritarianism, codes of honour, anti-intellectualism, anti-effeminacy, sensitivity to criticism and fear of failure have contributed to incompetence, both directly and indirectly. These processes make for incompetence because, since their primary object is control and constraint, they themselves tend to become inflexible and unmodifiable. They resist change, block progress and hamper thought. Just as once useful but now irrelevant drills rob overt behaviour off any verve or spontaneity, so ancient rules and regulations, precious formulae and prescribed attitudes become an easy substitute for serious cerebration (p. 306).

Dixon argued that the military personality is drawn to, and seems to have, an emotional investment in using force to solve problems and manage others. They are, of course, not unique in this. Incompetent military leaders are (or were) emotionally dependent, socially conforming, religiously orthodox and they distrust the new and strange. They also lack creativity, imagination and aesthetic appreciation; cognitive complexity; independence; and altruism. They are anxious and self-doubting, and the lethal combination of high anxiety and low self-esteem in part makes their behaviour bizarre and unpredictable, with literally awful consequences. The urge to simply give orders, control others and follow rigid codes of conduct epitomizes the failed military manager. They are the classic 'control freak' managers. The opposite traits of tact, flexibility and imagination seem associated with managerial success in the military or elsewhere.

Dixon's analysis was obviously inspired by Freudian ideas and the psychiatric literature. This is not a common approach in the management literature. Certainly, the similarity between military and management incompetence is striking.

3.4 The incompetent manager and leader

Incompetence is not a curious and rare phenomenon in the world of management: it is more often the rule rather than the exception. Ask the average person to rate the people for whom he or she has had to work all his or her life. Typically over half are rated as 'mildly', 'amazingly' or even 'dangerously' incompetent. The same is true if you ask managers to rate their peers. But is this more than just blaming others: an attribution error.

Many lazy, incompetent or unskilled staff blame their performance on their managers as a worker might blame his tools for his poor performance. But competence, unlike beauty, is not just in the eyes of the beholder. It is possible to describe, observe and see the consequences of good management.

Incompetent managers are found in all sectors, in all countries. Some environments are more conducive to incompetent managers than others. Large public utilities, government departments and other 'non-profits' are a sort of club of the incompetent. Incompetent managers select, train, promote and model incompetence. If a potentially competent manager gets hired into a company run by incompetent managers, the only model he/she will ever see is incompetence. Thus, incompetence gets perpetuated.

This process also, in part, accounts for incompetent corporate culture. The entire organization acquires an incompetent style (see below) that influences how the organization does things. Incompetent corporate cultures are not easy to change.

Incompetent managers are often *pessimistic fatalists* who exaggerate failure and spend their energy on finding scapegoats rather than on diagnosing the cause of the failure. Scapegoating often ruins long-term relationships. Good managers understand that exceptions to rules and processes will occur. Few systems can be constructed to take account of all possible situations and, even if they can, they will be extremely cumbersome and complex. When exceptional circumstances occur, they command immediate attention and can be easily dealt with.

Incompetent managers are also often *poor delegators* though they do not know it. They delegate tasks, not objectives; they blur accountability so as to make it impossible for their staff to use their initiative. Hence the person to whom the work is delegated is demotivated and fails... which proves to incompetent managers that delegation doesn't work.

Incompetent managers *forget that their job is to take a longer view*. This does not mean ignoring daily events and recording and analysing them appropriately. Trivia needs to be identified, delegated or ignored. *Incompetent managers believe in luck*; competent ones do not. There is a large psychological literature that shows instrumentalists – people who take charge of their own careers – are likely to succeed, whereas fatalists are likely to fail. Many incompetent managers believe that luck, chance or powerful people, and not themselves, are the key to their success.

Serious adversity often helps weed out managerial incompetence. The possibility of failure helps the competent manager concentrate, assess priorities, make sacrifices, identify key objectives and make tough decisions, while simultaneously ignoring office politics and other distractions. Potential failure may also help management groups pull together into real teams. Crisis is a sort of Darwinian process for revealing incompetence, some of which may be cured, and some not. But it is equally important not to overcompensate when confronted by a problem. Management by crisis rather than reason is the hallmark of an incompetent manager. Failing to plan, monitor and ask difficult questions is yet another sign of incompetence.

Incompetent management encourages crime (e.g. theft, bogus worker compensation claims, sabotage); bad managers don't understand the difference between security and insurance, and the costs of crime can be exorbitant. Insurance is a backstop when security fails. Incompetent managers lead their staff to become whistle-blowers and absentees.

The importance of regular, clear, honest communication cannot be overestimated. Gossip abhors a vacuum: idle speculation and damaging rumours are often the result of employees trying to make sense of what is happening around them. Incompetent managers choose inappropriate media to communicate to the wrong people badly. Often their writing, like annual reports, is boring, costly, incomprehensible, insulting and wrongly aimed. It is a sort of in-house junk mail – volume mailings only expecting a minority response. Bad writers fail to consider how readers will react to their memos; will they be offended, pleased, informed, provoked to respond or apathetic?

3.5 The psychology of managerial incompetence

Furnham (1998, 2000, 2003) has reviewed the topic of management incompetence: although he acknowledged that many incompetent managers may be 'psychologically disturbed', he also notes other reasons for incompetence. One is that managers fall victim to fads perpetrated by consultants. Another reason is that managers often have bizarre beliefs and myths about how to manage. Furnham maintains that many incompetent managers hold and follow management myths for five reasons:

1. They don't get clear, specific feedback on their actual style so they cannot learn from experience.
2. They are superstitious and it takes careful and honest analysis and experimentation to dispose superstition.

3. Most have had a pretty erratic (often poor) formal management education.
4. Many are simply desperate for answers and will follow anyone or any theory that has sufficient self-proclaimed confidence.
5. Many managers hate, and are frightened by, ambiguity and uncertainty and conform to myths simply to avoid these.

Furnham (2000) presented a 'theory' of management incompetence that takes the form of a vicious cycle. It does not explain how managers become incompetent but rather tries to explain why they stay that way.

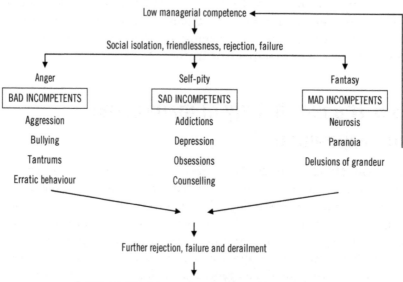

Figure 3.1 The causes and consequences of managerial incompetence (MI)

So the cycle spirals down. The helpless, hapless and hopeless manager simply becomes more so.

Furnham defines the three types as in Table 3.1.

Table 3.1   The sad, bad and mad leader

Sad	The sad, inadequate manager is often one who is prone to depression and self-pity. Many have a fine future behind them and probably will never reach their potential. Colleagues and schoolmates poring over photographs often remark of the sad, incompetent managers that, although they clearly had some promise, it was never fulfilled. They may turn to pharmacological solutions to their sorry state, but with little success.
Bad	Some inadequate and incompetent managers are bad in the moral sense. The bully, the selfish, egotistical bastard and the psychopath are all well known in the managerial dungeons of notoriety. These managers often succeed in the short run. Indeed, it is a sad fact that some also succeed in the long run, threatening the happy myth that good wins out in the end. They can succeed in some companies in particular sectors during specific phrases of the economic cycle. But they rarely last.
Mad	Some incompetent managers simply become deranged over time. They live in a fantasy world where they think they are successful, adaptive, healthy individuals. They start by believing their own press statements and strictly censoring negative feedback. They may develop a whole range of neurotic and psychotic symptoms before anyone seriously thinks of men in white coats. (p. xvii)

3.6 Derailment: Too much of a good thing

Most people think more in linear rather than curvilinear terms. That is, they speak as if when considering two things that both move in unison: the more attractive you are, the happier you are; the richer you are, the more content you are; the healthier your life style, the longer your life.

However, we all know that sometimes the relationship between variables is curvilinear. Consider music: very familiar music *and* very unfamiliar music are rated as moderately appealing, while music that is partly familiar is most appealing. The same is true of most names: John and David and Peter (very familiar) are rated as modestly appealing like rather unfamiliar names like many foreign names. Lower frequency names are most liked, then become more popular, and inevitably then go out of fashion.

The concept of optimality is relatively common in psychological research, but often seems to be ignored in the workplace. Consider the idea of intelligence and success at work.

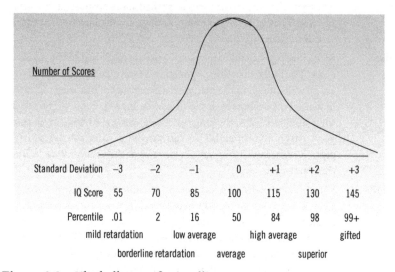

Standard Deviation	−3	−2	−1	0	+1	+2	+3
IQ Score	55	70	85	100	115	130	145
Percentile	.01	2	16	50	84	98	99+
	mild retardation		low average		high average		gifted
		borderline retardation		average		superior	

Figure 3.2   The bell curve for intelligence

Is intelligence related to job success? The answer is indeed yes. In fact, one of the best predictors of job success is intellectual ability. However, what is the relationship? It can be expressed in at least three ways:

- **Linear:** This suggests that the brighter a person is, the more successful they are at work. This may be true in certain jobs – the academic physicist for instance.
- **Cut-off:** This suggests that intelligence is linearly related to work success up to a point, but beyond that point it carries no advantage. The idea is akin to minimum height requirements in certain jobs: As long as you attain the standard cut-off point there is no

advantage to be gained in being taller. Naturally, one could conceive of the cut-off differing for different jobs: the more complex the job, the more intelligent you need to be.

- **Curvilinear**: This graph line suggests that both low and high intelligence leads to poor job success but that average intelligence is best. The idea is of an optimum amount.

Managers are selected and promoted on all sorts of criteria, often called competencies. They are frequently meant to have almost superhuman qualities; some of them are almost contradictions. But can too much competence lead to incompetence? Can a strength become a weakness? Can one simply have too much of a good thing?

McCall (1998) has a clear theory of management incompetence and derailment. Essentially, there are three important themes. The first is that within any business, divided along traditional lines – finance, human resources, marketing, operation – people are *likely to be good at certain things and less likely to be good at others*. Thus, marketing people are action-oriented, entrepreneurial, resourceful and risk-takers *but* they are less likely to be consistent, self-disciplined team-workers who go through the appropriate channels and use company systems. Operations managers, on the other hand, often have considerable strengths in efficiency, teamwork, maintenance and the use of systems. They are, however, less concerned about the big business issues and poor at responding to customers or initiating change. People in finance are good at analytic detail, strategic thinking and cost control but they are often poor at influencing the managers and turning clever ideas into appropriate actions.

There is nothing unusual or surprising about these assertions. Indeed it is the very essence of the stereotypes that people hold. However, the second theme is that of *organizational complicity*. In essence, this means that organizations need to recognize an individual's manifest strengths but they forgive, overlook or suppress evidence of weakness. Thus, the brilliant, technically sophisticated young manager is promoted frequently as reward and soon discovers he/she is attempting to manage others with little or no ability. That is, they get analysis paralysis or bogged down in process unable to inspire others or get things done.

Equally, the marketing manager with a strong track record of getting things done and delivering profit is forgiven the fact that he or she maybe a little egocentric and refuses to use the accounting or performance management systems. The organizational complicity is to reward, rather than punish, rule breaking and promote the person to senior roles where they are overwhelmed with complexity and have no strategic perspective.

Once the golden-child, 'wonder-kind' manager begins to derail, organizational complicity turns into unforgiveableness, leading to total derailment. Be successful and the organization overlooks flaws; fail and they get magnified.

The third theme to this 'theory' is that all competencies have their *'dark-side'*. And this is very much a compensations theory (consider the eight examples suggested by McCall in Table 3.2).

Table 3.2 The dark side, too much of a good thing, theory of derailment (Based on McCall)

Competency	Potential dark side
Team player	Not a risk-taker, indecisive, lacks independent judgement
Customer-focused	Can't create breakthroughs, can't control costs, unrealistic, too conservative
Biased towards action	Reckless, dictatorial
Analytic thinker	Analysis paralysis, afraid to act, inclined to create large staffs
Has integrity	'Holier than thou' attitude, rigid, imposes personal standards on others, zealot
Innovative	Unrealistic, impractical, wastes time and money
Has global vision	Missed local markets, overextended, unfocused
Good with people	Soft, can't make tough decisions, too easy on people

Many organizations have as competencies the eight specified in the left-hand column. However, what McCall is suggesting is that one needs an optimal amount of each. Consider this: integrity and innovativeness. All managers need to have integrity: it refers to honesty, morality, incorruptibility and adherence to a code of ethics and behavioural standards. Indeed, the quality that people *most* want in their boss is honesty. But can one have too much integrity? McCall suggests that it is possible to be overzealous in one's morality, imposing inflexible, possibly unattainable, standards on others. There are many examples from literature of the rigid, moralist, many of whom are portrayed as hypocrites partially because they try to impose on others standards that they personally do not live by.

There are many good reasons why being overzealous is potentially a handicap. Moral and ethical standards have to be adaptable to different times and conditions. Standards of integrity can also be both ego- and ethnocentric in the sense that they can be very particular to an individual and a culture. They are 'imposed' on others. People with very strict standards also tend to be too dismissive and rejecting of those who do not hold their particular views of those with other views. They are prone to absolutist 'black-and-white' thinking. They can be too fundamentalist in their thinking and acting. These characteristics – morality, intolerance, zealotry – can be a source of derailment in any manager. They are often unattractive to customers, shareholders, bosses and subordinates.

Managers need integrity, to follow rules, codes and laws and have ethical standards. But they must know how to apply them sensitively and where appropriate be flexible. A manager without integrity is a serious handicap and their lack of honesty is one of the most important sources of distrust at work.

The message is simple. Integrity, like height and intelligence, can be described on a linear scale. There are degrees of integrity. And there is probably an optimal amount. There are some rules that may rarely be broken, whereas others are much more flexible. The trick is to know which. There is also the distinction between the spirit and the word of the law. Wise leaders know when to turn a blind eye and when to admonish; when to set examples and when to bend the rules.

3.7 Conclusion

Leaders and managers fail for many reasons. Some resign and others are sacked. Some have breakdowns and some remain blissfully unaware of their shortcomings. This chapter suggests their failure is for essentially two reasons: either they do not have what it takes (they are over promoted) and hence incompetent or else they have a surfeit of a quality (mischievousness, self-confidence, emotionality) which becomes their nemesis. In short, their dark side manifests itself and this is a major cause of the problem. This book is primarily about this second factor.

Chapter 4

Corrupt countries and sick corporate cultures: Bad places to be

4.1 Introduction

It was argued in Chapter 1 that for bullies, bastards and backstabbers to survive they need to be supported (accepted, approved and even encouraged) by the work culture and local environment. Corporate cultures condone behaviours both sick and healthy. In a bullying corporate culture, bullies thrive: indeed, if you are not a bully you may soon become a victim. It is easier to be a bad boss in unregulated organizations that do nothing to prevent it.

Whilst there might be differences in various subtle definitions of what is ethical, moral, etc., it is not difficult to get some agreement on the concept of corruption. This chapter is concerned not so much with dark and derailing people as dark environments where it is the norm to be corrupt and immoral: places where bribery and nepotism and illegal practices are normal.

However, it is not always clear as to when a bribe is a bribe, a thank you or a present. What also of jumping up the waiting list because of a personal friendship? Or ensuring nepotistic appointment or promotion? Back-handers, cronyism and favouritism: members of a long list of, what are now called *counterproductive behaviours at work*. Why do they occur and what to do about them? Are they more common in service or manufacturing industries? Why does corruption take different forms?

Three types of factors are usually involved. The *first* is *bad people* – morally bad people: bullies, psychopaths, perverts and the like. They harass, manipulate, cheat, steal, etc. The *second* factor is *poor management*. People have clear expectations of what they expect from their boss. They develop a psychological contract – an emotion laden concept that captures the nature of the exchange between worker and organization. All workers are sensitive to unfairness, to bullying, blame storming bosses. People leave managers, not organizations.

Studies show the following typical organizational causes of corrupt behaviour. People are vengeful because they are passed over for promotion; promises are reneged upon; perks are removed. They feel their appraisals are unjust; their bosses are both demanding and rude, as well as self-serving, political and incompetent. The sense of being unjustly dealt with, being abused or being ignored can soon lead to disillusion, resentment and thence revenge. Bad bosses are probably more common causes of corruption than bad employees.

The *third* factor, which is the topic of this chapter, is *corporate culture*: the well-established patterns of beliefs and behaviours that are in fact corrupt. Some people cheat at work because cheating is the norm (see the last section). In their job they may be able to cheat customers, the taxman and the company. They may receive bribes – called tips, or favours, or 'thank yous'. It is curiously then the organization, or at least part of it, that either turns a blind-eye or even encourages it because it is an alternative source of pay.

Frustrated supervisors, unable to reward materially their hard-working staff, may quite simply put in place a system that provides rewards: stock may be removed and charged to customers; days off are approved; 'fiddles' become the norm. So 'sickies' become a perk of the job, as does finding one in ten bottles of wine 'corked', which are perfectly good and stolen for reselling.

Organizational culture can provoke loyalty or disloyalty. It can perpetuate an atmosphere of surveillance, suspicion and lack of trust. Employers may rely on ineffectual PR and spin to cover up their inefficiency, even illegality. Some corporate cultures are 'squeaky clean' with regard to corruption; others operate in a way which reveals the essence of the definition.

We know stealing and deceit is more common in some jobs compared to others. The following generalizations seem to hold: the more skilled the job holder, the less he/she will be likely to cheat/steal. Flexibility in time keeping will be negatively associated with lying. Higher performance expectations on the part of the boss or company will be associated with more lying, stealing and cheating. People having more than one formal role will be more likely to try to deceive. People with considerable demands (i.e. parental) outside the organizations are likely to be more deceitful. People reporting to more than one boss are more likely to be deceitful.

Workplace theories, on the other hand, emphasize rather different factors. *Organizational climate*: in effect this refers to a moral atmosphere than can even endorse dishonesty (i.e. even encourage theft) or at least turn a blind eye to it. The idea is that the prevailing climate sends clear messages to employers about whether, what, which and when thieving and thefts are acceptable or not.

Deterrence doctrine: This refers to the existence, explicitness and retributive nature of company antitheft policies and the perceived certainty and severity of punishment, as well as the visibility of that punishment. The idea is simple: get tough with deterrence and theft will be reduced.

Perceived organizational fairness: This 'theory' suggests it is exploitation by the employer that causes pilferage. Note that it is the crucial factor. Pay cuts in particular lead to this activity.

A major workplace theory that attempts to explain the origin or maintenance of things like corruption and theft at work is *social exchange theory*. The theory (sometimes called *equity theory*) suggests that all employees are in a social exchange relationship at work: they give and they get. They 'sell' their time, expertise, labour and loyalty and, in return, get a salary, pension, paid holidays, etc. Where the 'equation' is balanced all is well. Where not, people are motivated to establish it. Thus people can ask for a raise, leave, work less hard, go absent or steal.

People who feel frustrated, cheated, humiliated or undervalued often steal as revenge and to right a perceived wrong. This is not to say that *all* dissatisfied people thieve. But there is evidence that thieving is often a restitution and retaliatory response to perceived unfairness. People steal partly because of the way they are treated. People strike back with *reciprocal deviance* if they feel poorly or unfairly treated.

There is an extensive and important social and organizational psychology literature on this topic, much of it pioneering, by Greenberg with his interests in justice in the workplace (Greenberg, 2010). This literature looks at various categories of counterproductive work behaviours like interpersonal (bullying), production (absenteeism), property (theft, vandalism) and political (whistle-blowing, deception) misbehaviours. With ingenious laboratory and field experiments Greenberg has tested equity theory showing how through restitution and retaliation employees 'even the score', as the theory suggests.

Often many large organizations are seen as very rich abusers of power, bullies of their workforce and competitors and hence, just targets of 'Robin Hood' restitution. Companies do not prosecute, however, because of the cost, the nature of the evidence they have, the poor publicity and the effect on the other staff. Thus, employees do not see the activity as necessarily wrong and hence steal happily and without guilt.

Equally supervisors may condone or even encourage theft and other forms of corruption! This may occur because of *parallel deviance* or *passive imitation* which simply means that people follow the lead of their bosses who they notice abusing the system. If the supervisor calls theft 'a perk' so do the staff. There is also the *invisible wage* structure or system of *controlled larceny* which effectively means that supervisors allow, help and even organize employee theft. They often say they do this to enrich jobs and more efficiently motivate staff.

Even more common are work-group norms that support and regulate employee corruption. Becoming part of a group may involve being taught *how to*, *when* and *where* to steal. Indeed work-group thieving may ritualistically and symbolically be linked to becoming a successful employee. Thieving norms involve how people divide the spoils/outcomes of theft. The group helps 'neutralize' their acts with a raft of excuses/explanations like denials of responsibility, injury, the company being a victim, appeals to higher authority and a condemnation of the condemner. Group norms often spell out the parameters of thieving behaviour – that is, what is and is not stolen, and the worth of what has been stolen.

4.2 Terminology and incidence

Table 4.1 When researchers write about the topic they use a wide variety of phrases which include the following

Antisocial behaviour	Usually restricted to the workplace but covering almost everything
Blue-collar crime	Everything from theft, property destruction and record fabrication to fighting and gambling by semi-skilled, often lower class (non-salaried) staff
Counterproductive workplace behaviour	Any behaviour at work that goes counter to the short- and long-term interests and success of all stakeholders in a company
Dysfunctional work behaviour	Intentional, unhealthy behaviour that is injurious to particular individuals who do it to themselves or others
Employee deviance	Unauthorized but intended acts that damage property, production or reputations
Employee misconduct	The misuse of resources from absenteeism to accepting handbacks
Non-performance at work	Both not performing behaviours which are required and performing acts that are not required
Occupational aggressive crime deviance	Negative, illegal, injurious and devious behaviours conducted in the workplace
Organizational misbehaviour	Behaviour that violates societal and organizational norms
Organizational retaliative behaviours	This is deliberate organizational behaviour based on perceptions of unfairness by disgruntled employees

(Continued)

'Political' behaviour	Self-serving, non-sanctioned, often illegitimate behaviour aimed at people both inside and outside the organization
Unconventional work practices	Simply odd and unusual but more like illegal and disruptive behaviours
Workplace aggression, hostility, obstructionism	Personally synonymous behaviours at work
Unethical workplace behaviour	Behaviour that deliberately and obviously infringes some set and accepted ethical/moral code

In certain countries at specific times of great instability there is often considerable evidence of corruption (Table 4.1). People bribe all officials to get things done; fake and fraudulent documents are produced; crimes are committed and ignored. In short the rule of law is replaced by the law of the jungle. In these situations people feel forced or pressurized to behave badly just to survive.

In 2008 PriceWaterhouseCoopers produced a report about corruption in business world-wide. A summary was provided which stated thus:

- There is a strong business case for having an anti-corruption strategy.
- An increasing number of companies recognize their vulnerability to corruption and the benefits of effective anti-corruption programmes and controls.
- Sixty-three per cent indicated that they had experienced some form of actual or attempted corruption.
- Thirty-nine per cent say their company has lost a bid because of corrupt officials.
- Sixty-five per cent of respondents believe a level playing field is crucial to their company's future business activities.
- Reputational (brand) damage from corruption can be crippling.
- Having an anti-corruption programme in place and publicizing it is seen as valuable or very valuable to a company's brand by 86 per cent of respondents.

- Fifty-five per cent say the most severe impact would be to the corporate reputation. Greater than the combined total of those who say legal, financial and regulatory impacts would be the most severe.
- Companies are losing real and significant business opportunities because of corruption risks.
- Almost 45 per cent of respondents have not entered a specific market or pursued a particular opportunity because of corruption risks.
- Forty-two per cent believe their competitors pay bribes.
- More than 70 per cent believe a better understanding of corruption will help them compete more effectively, make better decisions, improve corporate social responsibility and enter new markets.
- Despite being aware of corruption, many companies underlying policies and controls currently do little to identify and mitigate risk due to poor design or implementation.
- Whilst 80 per cent say they have some form of an anti-corruption programme in place, only 22 per cent are confident of their effectiveness.
- Slightly less than half say their programme is clearly communicated and enforced.
- Only 40 per cent of respondents believe their current controls are effective at identifying high-risk business partners or suspect disbursements.

All organizations have a corporate culture, simply defined as 'the way we do things around here'. Further organizations are located in a particular geographic region which is subject to laws pertaining to various issues. Thus in some countries an organization may be subject to various legal processes which discourage corruption and abuse, whilst in others no such laws exist.

The criminal, narcissistic or psychopathic leader is unlikely to emerge and certainly thrive in a healthy, law abiding corporate or national culture. Most people have a dark side which they may or may not be aware of. But there are also dark places where the normative behaviour is dark: corrupt gangs and groups, working in corrupt countries.

4.3 Poor management

A great deal of blame can be laid at the feet of poor managers or poor managerial processes. The hope is that transformational leaders who inspire and model satisfaction (engagement) and productivity encourage trust, loyalty and dedication in their employees. Not all managers are transformational, or even transactional. They may be incompetent, lazy or self-centred, which can have immediate and significant consequences for those that work with them.

That is, bad management just like bad parenting, causes serious long-term problems for all concerned (staff, shareholders, customers, etc.). These bad managers not only alienate staff and lower morale but they can, quite easily, provoke reprisals in the form of counter work behaviours (CWB). In this sense people become backstabbers because they are first stabbed in the back.

Managers have two main roles in issues concerned with disenchantment. First, they are at the front line in *identifying* CWBs and participating in any actions against the individuals. They need to be vigilant about people 'going sour'. Second, they have to generate an atmosphere and environment which actively discourages such behaviours.

They need to generate engagement (commitment, satisfaction), loyalty and a strong work ethic, not distrust and alienation. Studies on 'bad apples' again and again attest to the observation. Too often they are blind to what is happening around them; but worse their actions and own behaviours lead to resentment which in turn leads to staff becoming disillusioned and vulnerable to CWBs.

Good managers are loyal to both the organizational goals and their employees. Tyrannical, autocratic leaders may be only pro-organization (and self) and less concerned with their staff. Poor managers are undisciplined: they flout guidelines and the 'good psychology' of management. They belittle and intimidate, threaten and tease, ignore and exclude their staff. This in turn can lead to employee revenge, then managerial counter-retaliation and then escalating and entrenched conflict. This is the ideal breeding ground of the Insider Threat.

It is important to bear in mind also that people become angry and disappointed when they see *others* treated unfairly such as during redundancies, lay-off, etc. That is, people do not always have to be the 'victim' of injustice themselves. It is enough to see others badly treated to lead them to want to seek revenge.

For managers to be fully involved in the process of developing loyalty in an organization and countering the Insider Threat it is necessary to recognize the nature and potential size of the threat and the motivations of those committing the CWBs.

Finally, although CWBs have always been around, how they are expressed does change with the times. Thus, rapid and widespread developments in technology have led to what is now called *cyberdeviancy, cyberloafing, cyberaggression, workplace blogging* and *cyber whistle-blowing*. As things change so does the opportunity for an incidence of Insider Threats.

Why do insiders leak information, and how can we prevent them? The simple and obvious answer lies in rigorous selection. Don't let these people join your organization and then you won't have any problems. So government departments and the security services take selection very seriously. They screen their applicants very thoroughly. They know the cost of getting it wrong.

It seems there are five reasons why people go from engaged to disenchanted; productive to subversive; a friend to an enemy of the organization.

1. **Organizational lying/hypocrisy**: This is the perception by the employee that what the organization says about itself in public and even to its employees is a pack of lies. The more the organization tries to capture the moral high ground and come out on 'the side of the angels', the more outraged becomes the astounded and angry insider.
2. **Perceived inequity**: The idea that some people in the organization are treated very differently from others. 'One law for the rich, another for the poor'. The hottest word at work is fair: that people

are fairly assessed, promoted and rewarded. Yet, it can seem to some that loyalty, hard work and productivity have less to do with success than some other attributes such as demography, brown-nosing or particular experiences.

3. **Bullying and mistreatment**: This is the belief that some senior people are callous, uncaring, nasty and manipulative and that you are a victim. The workplace attracts all types: the demanding perfectionist, the geeky inadequate, the flamboyant self-publicist. This is to be expected and we all have to adapt to the idiosyncrasies and peculiarities of powerful people at work. Bullies have been shown to have poor emotional intelligence and the ability to charm and persuade. Bullies come from all sorts of backgrounds and can be found in many different organizations.

4. **Distrust**: The feeling that the organization does not even trust its own employees. It may have put in place a number of devious and not-admitted (often electronic monitoring) systems to spy on its own people. Whilst top management may talk about and demand loyalty from the staff, it is clear that they are not trusted by their employees. Trust is a two-way street. If the organization lets it be known that it never really and fully trusts their staff with information, money and materials, why should they trust management?

5. **Broken promises**: This is all about expectations not being met. For some, the selection interview and the induction period are where people set your expectations about working for the organization. They tell you what they stand for, what they expect and how things work. Yet, all too often an employee does not have his or her expectations clarified. Either supervisors do not know how to conduct, or they fudge conversations about what the criteria are for promotion, salary increases or other rewards.

For some time now a research body has tried to measure and compare corruption on an international level. It has come to be known as the *Transparency International Corruption Perception Index*. It tracks and measures perceived levels of public sector corruption in countries and territories around the world. The countries that are at the bottom of the index, those that are perceived to be most corrupt, are fragile, unstable states that are scarred by war and ongoing conflict. The countries at the top of the list, by contrast, are those that have enjoyed longer periods of stability, an established and enforced rule of law, and efficient functioning public institutions. On top are Scandinavian and European countries and countries like New Zealand and Singapore. In the bottom are poor Africa countries and some in central Asia.

The suggestion is that it is very difficult to do business in corrupt countries without either falling victim to, or in some way supporting the corruption. People expect and demand 'back-handers'; they insist that to win a contract large sums of money have to be deposited in European bank accounts; they 'require' lavish 'gifts' and expect their relatives to be 'employed' in certain roles. It remains a considerable challenge to do business with organizations, particularly government and public sector organization in corrupt countries without breaking the law, corporate or personal moral values.

4.4 Corporate cultures

There is no shortage of definitions for corporate culture. Consider:

> *Culture is a system of informal rules that spells out how people are to behave most of the time.* (Deal & Kennedy, 1982)

Some researchers have tried to categorize culture and then delineate those that are thought to be negative and unhelpful. Thus consider the types set out below that may indeed encourage or turn a blind eye towards corruption (Cooke & Lafferty, 1989):

- An **oppositional culture** describes organizations in which confrontation prevails and negativism is rewarded. Members gain status and influence by being critical and, thus, are reinforced to oppose the ideas of others and to make safe (but ineffectual) decisions. (Pointing out flaws; being hard to impress.)
- A **power culture** is descriptive of non-participative organizations structured on the basis of the authority inherent in members' positions. Members believe they will be rewarded for taking charge,

> controlling subordinates and, at the same time, being responsive to the demands of superiors. (Building upon one's power base; motivating others in any way necessary.)
> - A **competitive culture** is one in which winning is valued and members are rewarded for outperforming one another. People in such organizations operate in a 'win/lose' framework and believe they must work against (rather than with) their peers to be noticed. (Turning the job into a contest; never appearing to lose.)
> - A **competence/perfectionistic culture** characterizes organizations in which perfectionism, persistence and hard work are valued. Members feel they must avoid all mistakes, keep track of everything and work long hours to attain narrowly defined objectives. (Doing things perfectly; keeping on top of everything.)

Research by Cooke and Rousseau (1988) indicates that organizations characterized by chief executives as excellent or ideal (i.e. for implementing successful organizational strategies) take the form of satisfaction-orientated cultures. Security-orientated cultures involve uses of organizational sanctions to promote particular behavioural patterns and often are more behaviour-inhibiting (e.g. risk-avoiding), in contrast to satisfaction cultures, which tend to be behaviour-amplifying (e.g. risk-seeking).

Are there identifiable corrupt cultures? In an important paper Campbell and Goritz (2013) showed that organizations with corrupt cultures perceived themselves in a war-like situation where the end justified the means. The summary of their findings was as follows:

> The characteristics of the organizational culture in corrupt organizations...(1) Organizations perceive themselves to fight in a war instead of facing ordinary competition within their market. Due to this war perspective, employees undergo a perception shift that tinges corruption in a positive light. For employees, it is important to receive contracts, relax regulations, or glean other benefits for their organization to face the 'war'. Wartime degrades values such as fairness and sustainability, and

therefore corruption becomes an attractive behavioral alternative. (2) In line with former research and backed up by our own findings, we conclude that the underlying assumption 'the end justifies the means' is the key characteristic of a corrupt organizational culture. This teleological assumption merely considers ends while disregarding means. This assumption directly and indirectly touches most rationalization strategies, values and norms.

(3) Organizations value job and organizational security and connect these values to unethical employee behavior. Under the threat of unemployment, corrupt organizations justify corruption to bring about a win–win situation: If employees show corrupt behavior, then they attain benefits for their organization, which in turn ensures their job security. (4) Because organizational culture does not reward or punish according to ethical values, ethical values do not get reinforced on a daily basis. (5) Employees perceive that they are a community of fate and that every member who fails to support corruption harms this community and needs to be punished. (p. 292)

They also asked the question as to whether managers and employees see the situation quite differently. This was their considered conclusion:

Managers and employees play different roles in the process of normalization of corruption. While managers install an environment supportive of corruption, employees implement work tasks directly in a corrupt manner. According to the model of normalization of corruption, managers rely primarily on institutionalization and employees on rationalization and socialization mechanisms ... managers' norms of goal setting, rewarding and punishing as a manifestation of the institutionalization mechanism, because all of these norms pertain to organizational daily routines and structures that facilitate corruption ... employees' rationalization and the value 'team spirit' and the norms 'coercion' and 'punishment' as manifestations of rationalization and socialization mechanism, because through them, employees reduce cognitive dissonance and increase social support. To sum up, the corrupt organizational culture is a manifestation of the three mechanisms of normalization of corruption 'institutionalization', 'rationalization' and 'socialization' that render employees' behavior supportive of corruption. (p. 295)

Balthazar et al. (2006) in a paper entitled '*Dysfunctional culture, dysfunctional organization*' noted that the dysfunctional organization is characterized much like a disorganized individual; less efficient than its peers, etc. For an individual, whilst external factors play a role it is the inner workings that have the greatest effect, such as the cognitions. For an organization, it is the culture that impacts its function.

They found that constructive norms promote achievement-oriented and cooperative behaviours which should promote individual-level outcomes such as satisfaction, organizational outcomes including quality of service and ultimately knowledge management processes. Conversely, expectations for defensive behaviours should have the opposite impact. Defensive norms create pressures for dependent and avoidant (passive) and/or power-oriented and internally competitive styles (aggressive) and, in turn, are dysfunctional for both the organization and its members.

Corrupt corporate cultures allow, encourage or turn a blind eye towards corruption. Corporate culture is difficult to change but can and does have considerable impact on organizations.

4.5 What is corruption?

Dictionary definitions of corruption stress dishonest and fraudulent conduct characterized by deception, law breaking and such things as bribery, extortion and profiteering. The definitions also refer to the act of making people 'morally depraved' (debauched, decadent) as well as changing the status of something to, in essence, debase it. For some it is easier to have quantitative, rather than qualitative cut-off points. There are personal, legal and national definitions.

It is certainly true that corruption is widespread. It has been estimated that $1 trillion, or 3 per cent of the world GDP are paid annually in bribes. Corruption is contagious: it creates complicity; it acts as a 'demonstration effect'; it provides information about opportunities and the means to exploit them; it creates an atmosphere of impunity. Corrupt actions are usually a symptom of a lack of management quality, conformism and expedience

There are many types of corruption. Argandoña (2001) has provided the following list:

- Extortion and bribery
- Commissions
- Gifts and doubtful favours
- Nepotism
- Favour-currying and favouritism
- Illicit use or sale of insider information
- Misappropriation or embezzlement
- Actions of kleptomaniac or predatory state

Corruption may take place between agents from private sector to private sector: Managers/employees can interact with third parties or other agents in order to gain certain benefits. Companies can misappropriate their assets, funds or financial reports for their own benefit. Argandoña (2001) has argued that corruption occurs when there is an interaction or 'dealing' between one type of agent (individual, company, NGO, etc.) with another agent (civil servant, public sector or another member of the private sector).

Corruption restricts the scope of citizens' rights. It often facilitates opaqueness in actions and eludes political and legal controls. Corruption can undermine the government's and democratic system's legitimacy.

Campbell and Göritz (2013) viewed corruption as 'corrupt behaviour' and not as 'counter-productive behaviour'. This is an important difference because employees regard corruption as useful, not illegal or criminal activity. Counterproductive behaviour are actions that benefit the self, at the harm of the organization. Corrupt organizations seem to expect employees to facilitate criminal behaviour to attain organizational goals.

It is also possible to distinguish between *active corrupt behaviour* and *passive corrupt behaviour*. The former refers to deliberate and active participation in the corruption as the perpetrators/accomplices. Passive refers to employees tolerating the corruption as 'silent observers'. For instance ordinary citizens can take the initiate for corrupt acts for an agent (usually in the public sector) with the following purposes:

- Trying to reduce the amount of taxes they have to pay
- Obtaining goods or services that are not entitled
- Trying to sell goods without being entitled to do so
- Obtaining undeserved rights
- Avoiding certain duties

Equally, administrators/civil servants/the public sector may take the initiative against other agents: denying rights; requiring higher prices for goods that are sold to them; establishing higher taxes; giving citizens a smaller quantity of goods to benefit from the difference/extort payment for the rest; manipulating civil servants by promotion, appointment and remuneration; civil servants offering money or favours in exchange for gained access.

There is also a difference between corrupt organizations and an organization of corrupt individuals (Pinto et al., 2008). Essentially the difference refers to an organization of corrupt individuals which involves the scaling up of personally beneficial corrupt behaviours to organizational level, or a group of employees carrying out corrupt behaviours on behalf of the organization.

According to Finney and Lesieur (1982), distinguishing different types of corruption can be done through understanding if an action is solely beneficial to the individual, or if the benefits extend to the business also. They argue that it is useful to study corruption on the individual and the group level, as well as the links between them in order to understand how individuals acting on personally beneficial corruption without colluding may constitute an organization-level corrupt phenomenon.

- **The benefit of the corruption is solely for the actor**: This could occur through bonuses or stock options where the organization is still the primary and direct financial beneficiary. There are two streams of research looking at how an individual can benefit at the cost of the organization: the principal-agent model and the deviance or unethical behaviour literature. Principal-agent models state the agent will favour some third party at the expense of the principal with the exchange of compensation or gain.
- **Collusion among members**: Sometimes individuals collude to obtain personal benefit at the expense of the organization. Much of what is labelled 'organizational crime' is enacted by a group of individuals. Argue that collusion is necessary for corporate corruption, but not essential to corruption for individual gain.

An organization of corrupt individuals (OCIs) will have individuals acting for personal gain at the expense of the organization, yet a CO (corrupt organization) will have groups collectively acting in order to benefit the organization. OCIs are defined as 'emergent, bottom-up phenomenon in which one or more meso-level processes facilitate the contagion (and sometimes the initiation as well) of personally corrupt behaviours that cross a critical threshold such that the organization can be considered corrupt'. Examples of this include police forces, where individuals act for personal gain, which spreads to such a degree that the whole force can be considered as corrupt. It is considered an organizational-level phenomenon because, whilst the individuals are still the sole benefactors of the actions, the behaviours are sufficiently widespread to characterize the organization as well as the internal meso-level processes that are responsible for, if not facilitating (then at least not inhibiting) the spread of these behaviours.

Campbell and Göritz (2013) argued that engagement in corruption depends on 'department, latitude, and position', as well as other factors. This is important as employees who work in warehouses less likely to act in a corrupt manner than those who work in accounting – 'division of labour forks corruption into different tracts'. Corruption in this sense has 'thresholds' which are not possible to define, but are possible to notice once they have been crossed. *Firstly*, when it is difficult to localize the corrupt portion of an organization because the corruption is so widespread. *Secondly*, if the act of firing a localized group of corrupt individuals is difficult because there are too many of them. *Thirdly*, if the individuals are fired, internal processes are needed to stop a further manifestation among other individuals of the same behaviours.

A corrupt organization (CO) is usually a top-down phenomenon where organization members (typically the organizational elites) undertake collective corrupt actions that benefit the organization, either directly or through their subordinates. This phenomenon is considered as corporate crime. Often when under investigation, senior members of an organization will deny knowledge of the behaviours, and sometimes scapegoat the individual members who have been found to be directly involved in corrupt behaviours. Ashforth and Anand (2003) noted organizational structures and processes are often contrived to insulate senior managers from the blame.

Employees in a corrupt organization see the behaviour as acceptable through three stages: *rationalization, socialization* and *institutionalization*. In the first stage, employees reshape perceptions about their situation, that is, how the action will aid organizational goals. In the second stage, work groups use social influence to normalize corrupt actions, such as gradually introducing corruption to their work life. In the third stage, organizations involve work structure that accommodate for corruption in their daily life. These three work together to form a 'social cocoon': managers and employees share positive attitudes and behaviours towards corruption, making it a norm and thus punishing resistance to act corruptly and rewarding participation.

Corrupt organizational culture needs to address work-related values and norms, including the organization's expectation of the employees' behaviour. It seems that organizations will install and communicate ethical values, yet expect corruption from its employees, giving the sense of 'we follow ethical values, but we don't care'. Ambiguity confuses the employee, and the reinforcement of corrupt behaviour thus solidifies the value places on 'we don't care'.

The 'is-ought' discrepancy can become more tangible when viewing the following:

1. degree of ethical distance impacts corrupt acts;
2. rewards and actual work conditions promote unethical decision making;
3. employees are often unaware they are committing any wrongdoing and behave thoughtlessly. (ethical blindness; Palazzo et al., 2012)

Employees reflect on their managers' expectations in order to make sense of how they should work. Employees learn the necessity and importance of corruption whilst acting upon these values, as well as ensuring their own moral self-image. They may need to assimilate to group norms to overcome the criminal feelings of their actions, depending on rationalization and coping strategies.

4.6 Why does corruption occur?

Psychological processes exist where individuals can selectively disengage internal moral control to permit detrimental conduct. In particular, self-sanctions can be disengaged by reinterpreting one's actions or the negative consequences of one's actions, vilifying the target of one's actions, and, most strongly, by obscuring personal causal agency through diffusion or displacement of responsibility (Mazar et al., 2008). The easier it is for individuals to employ any of these mechanisms and deactivate moral control, the more likely they are to engage in immoral behaviour such as initiating a bribe. The concept of *moral disengagement* is an individual's propensity to evoke cognitions which restructure one's actions to appear less harmful, minimize one's understanding of responsibility for one's actions or attenuate the perception of the distress one causes others.

Moral disengagement is relevant to organizational corruption because it helps initiate corruption by allowing individuals to pre-empt the discomfort of cognitive dissonance. Equally it may facilitate corruption by dampening individuals' moral awareness. It may also help perpetuate corruption by rewarding individuals who have a greater propensity to morally disengage and advance more quickly through the organization. Those individuals who engage in moral disengagement have made habitual use of the cognitive mechanisms which reframe them, actions in ways which downplay their ethical content or import.

Moral disengagement has been found in civic behaviour (Caprara & Capanna, 2006), computer hacking (Rogers, 2001) and reactions to war (Aquino et al., 2007). Moral disengagement mechanisms are involved in mundane and routine decisions by individuals to further their own interests or for profit. Moore (2008) argues that the propensity for individuals to morally disengage may influence not only their awareness of the ethical content of the decisions they make, but also their likelihood of making unethical decisions which advance organizational interests, and ultimately, their ascent up the corporate ladder.

Bandura suggests that moral disengagement comprises of eight different cognitive mechanisms:

- Three facilitate cognitive restructuring of inhumane acts to appear less harmful to the individual occupied in them – moral justification, euphemistic labelling and advantageous comparison
- Two cognitive mechanisms minimize the role of the individual in the harm that is caused by an individual's actions (displacement of responsibility and diffusion of responsibility)
- Three mechanisms reframe the effects of one's actions, either by minimizing the outcomes of those actions or by minimizing the perception of distress those actions have caused (distortion of consequences, dehumanization and attribution of blame). These do not reframe the action in a positive light, but reframe the activity to seem 'victimless' – the victim deserved it.
- Individuals who have a greater propensity to morally disengage might be more likely than others to make those key early decision that are required for corruption to be normalized within organizations.

Being able to more easily make unethical decisions means being able to make unethical decisions without resultant psychological discomfort (Moore, 2008, p.132).

John's (1999) theory of self-serving behaviour suggests that disengaged individuals could be rewarded within organizations because disengagement allows one to rationalize self-serving behaviours, including taking undue credit for success, avoiding taking responsibility for failure and making self-enhancement presentations that assist in resource accrual such as salary gains or organizational advancement.

Essentially there are two research questions here: What are the characteristics of the culture in corrupt organizations? What are managers' and employees' perceptions of corrupt organizational culture?

Campbell and Göritz (2013) argue that corrupt organizations perceive themselves to be fighting in a war. Often corrupt organizations see themselves as a military force, not a normal organization; they see competitors as enemies that need to be defeated to secure continuity of their own company. With this environment, values such as 'success' and 'survival' rise in importance, whilst 'ethical judgement' and 'morality' decline.

Many workers describe corruption as providing a win-win situation; continuous survival of organization is linked to employment of their employees. A cycle emerges of organizations taking advantage of corrupt employees winning contracts whilst the employees assure themselves of their organization's survival. It then becomes necessary to ensure as many contracts as possible. Many researchers claims these are typical conditions of corrupt organizations (Beenen & Pinto, 2009). A perception shift occurs as a result of loose market regulations, need for survival and a war-like working environment, reshaping the employees' perception into one of corruption. The underlying assumption in 'the end justifies the means' emphasizes the importance of results and the non-importance of obtaining them. Rationalization thus occurs in employees who fail to question organizational goals, as well as seeking the most effective and legal ways to obtain these goals.

Essentially it seems there are two *Internal* antecedents of organization-level corruption. The first is *organization structure*. Aspects of the structure that may facilitate corrupt acts include processes and tasks, positional relationships and hierarchical levels/departmental boundaries. At an individual-level some occupations may have built in opportunities for corruption, that is, bookkeeping, and when they are in these autonomous positions it is hard to supervise and prevent corruption. The organizational structure can provide opportunities for corruption-isolating subunits which allow managers to be 'wilfully' blind to important issues.

The second is *results orientation*. This has been called 'performance emphasis', 'incentive systems', 'pressure for performance/output' and 'the call of the share price and share-holder return'; when these systems are in place, low-performing units are likely to engage in corruption. On the other hand, those organizations where compensation is not strongly linked to business results, the high performers may experience injustice and are more likely to act corruptly to redress the experienced inequality (including theft, etc.). The high-performers' perceptions are more likely to cause contagion due to the social networks literature and their high centrality in advice networks (linked to Gladwell's 'law of the few'). If these injustices are ruminated on, then a collective judgement of injustice may form, resulting in the spread of the OCI phenomenon.

Equally the literature suggests two *external* antecedents of organization-level corruption: the first has been called *environmental scarcity*. This and competitive pressures (i.e. strong and sometimes oligopolistic competition) are the most important external pressures for organizational crime. Competition can cause corruption through the need to acquire resources and meet targets. In high-profitability or monopoly industries with weak control/monitoring over expenses, employees could adopt a 'denial of injury' technique of neutralization in which they feel the company has so much money, and stealing will not do any harm.

Second, there is *industry structure and norms*. It is posited that firms in certain industries are more likely to commit corrupt acts (Baucus & Near, 1991), where firms in an industry have similar rates of corruption. In highly regulated industries, regulators may be bribed to 'look the other way' or an agency may decide to protect the organization it is overseeing ('captured' regulator). Industry norms (also known as industry culture) are *'taken-for-granted assumptions which most describe a cohesive industry's character'*. If an industry culture allows for illegal acts, firms are more likely to engage in the wrongdoing; it would be extremely costly to not act illegally in such an environment (Waters, 1978). OCI, however, builds from the accumulation of individual corrupt behaviour and unethical decision making, but it has been found that industry culture has no direct impact on this. This could be that the industry is too far removed from the individual (where behaviours take place).

4.7 Cheats at work

Anthropologists have taken a very different approach to occupational deviance and corruption at work. In a series of books and papers Mars (1982, 2006) showed much cheating at work was a consequence of how jobs were organized. He concentrated, not on individuals but on groups and job families.

His initial focus was on the sorts of rewards people get at work. He divided these into three categories.

- **Formal**: usually linked to official 'compensation' systems usually involving money.
- **Informal**: which includes perks, tips, overtime, time-off
- **Hidden**: taking goods/stock, overcharging customers, etc.

When people cannot easily increase their formal rewards at work, they can increase the other two which may make up a large part of their income. Furthermore, it is the nature of the job that dictates the number and type of informal and hidden rewards (Table 4.2).

Table 4.2   A typology of work and its rewards

	Official	Unofficial	Alternative
	(1)	*(3)*	*(5)*
Legal	*Formal Rewards* Wages, salaries, commissions, overtime	*Informal Rewards* Perks, tips, extra work, consultancy	*Social Economy Rewards* Domestic production, barter, exchange, 'do-it-yourself'
	(2)	*(4)*	*(6)*
Extra-legal or illegal	*Criminal Rewards* Returns from professional crime, prostitution, etc.	*Hidden Economy Rewards* Pilfering, short-changing, overcharged expenses, overloading and underdropping	*Black Economy Rewards* Unregistered production and service organizations, moonlighting

He noted that in the hotel and catering industry, a waiter will receive basic and formal pay from Box 1 in the form of wages and overtime payments. This will be supplemented by informal rewards from Box 3 – the tips he receives and the perks of 'free' meals and 'free' accommodation. From Box 4 he or she may well be allowed to indulge in pilfered food or be afforded a 'winked-at-facility' to 'short-change or short-deal customers'. The contents of Box 4 are usually allocated on an individual basis through an individual contract with a specific contract-maker – usually a first-line supervisor. It is the receipts from Boxes 1, 3 and 4 which, in their entirety, comprise a person's total rewards from work.

Boxes 5 and 6 distinguish the rewards that derive from alternative economic activity; they are distinct from official rewards, are allocated outside the official system and do not appear in official returns. They often involve a higher degree of social satisfaction than is derived from the same activities carried out for formal rewards and located in Box 1. At the same time, the economic component of this reward is often less than would be expected from work derived from Box 1. When people obtain rewards from Box 5 it is likely to involve an element of reciprocity - a doing of favours, a swapping of services - so that high expense or scarcities or bureaucratic complexities inherent in obtaining official provision can be overcome by mutual co-operation. It may also be characterized by an exchange of obligation or increased prestige in return for economic benefit.

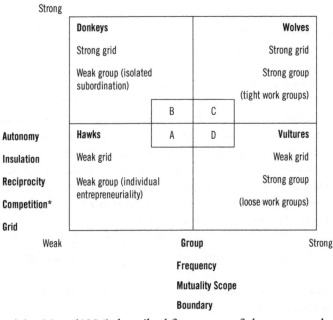

Figure 4.1 Mars (1984) described four types of cheats at work also defined by a two-by-two grid

Type A, Hawks (weak grid and weak group) relate to occupations that emphasize individuality, autonomy and competition. The control that members have over others is greater than the controls exercised over themselves. They emphasize entrepreneurial behaviour, where the individual's freedom to transact on his own terms is highly valued. Individual flair is at a premium. Success is indicated by the number of followers a person controls. Rewards here go to those who find new and better ways of doing things and where the drive for successful innovation is paramount. Hawks are individualists, inventors and small businessmen. They are hungrily 'on the make'.

Hawks are typically entrepreneurial managers, owner businessmen, successful academics, pundits, the prima donnas among salesmen and the more independent professionals and journalists. Hawkish entrepreneuriality is also found in waiters, fairground buskers and owner taxi drivers. Alliances among hawks tend to shift with expediency and that a climate of suspicion is more common than one of trust. They are loners, individualists.

Type B, Donkeys (by strong grid and weak group) are characterized by both isolation and subordination.

A person in a nineteenth-century one-servant family is a good example. Isolated from social contact with others, unable to relate to fellow servants or the family, she was excluded from contact with male admirers. She was tightly scheduled not only over time and space, but also over work and leisure with a programme of activities which minutely controlled all aspects of her life.

Donkeys are in the paradoxical position of being either or both powerless or powerful. They are powerless if they passively accept the constraints they face. They can also be extremely disruptive, at least for a time. Resentment at the impositions caused by such jobs is common and the most typical response is to change jobs. Other forms of 'withdrawal from work' such as sickness and absenteeism are also higher than normal. Where constraints are at their strongest, sabotage is not infrequent as a response, particularly where constraints are mechanized.

Type C, Wolves (strong grid and strong group) are the home of those 'traditional' rapidly disappears working-class occupations such as miners and longshoremen. These are occupations based on groups with interdependent and stratified roles, such as garbage collection crews, aeroplane crews and stratified groups who both live and work in 'total institutions' such as prisons, hospitals, oil rigs and some hotels. Where workers do live in, or close to, the premises in which they work, group activities in one area are reinforced by cohesion in others. Such groups then come to possess considerable control over the resources of their individual members. Once they join such groups, individuals tend to stay as members.

In old traditional docks every man's skill is needed to organize pilferage in almost the same way as it is needed to organize legitimate work. There is no place here for the independent individualist: teamwork is vital and highly valued both for success and for security.

Type D, Vultures (weak grid but with a strong group). These are jobs that offer autonomy and freedom to transact but where this freedom is subject to an overarching bureaucratic control that treats workers collectively, employs them in units. Workers in these occupations are members of a group of co-workers for some purposes only and they can and do act individually and competitively for others. They are not as free from constraint as are hawks, but neither are they as constrained as donkeys; the group is not as intrusive or controlling as are wolfpacks.

Vulture jobs include sales representatives and travellers of various kinds, like driver deliverers, linked collectively by their common employer, common workbase and common task, but who have considerable freedom and discretion during their working day.

Mars (2006) noted that these groups form their own ideology or view of the world and values. They make sense of their situation and their values follow from this. Thus, wolf-packs value control, discipline and order. Hawks value autonomy, freedom and independence. Vultures tend to be suspicious outsiders.

Mars (2006) attempted to update his analysis for issues in the twenty-first century. He notes three major changes that have occurred at work and their possible impact on 'scams, fiddles and sabotage'.

1. **Technical changes**
   Computers can be used to monitor behaviour. Computers can be used to regulate and monitor behaviour but they do offer many new opportunities for sabotage. Angry, disenchanted people can introduce a computer virus; they can destroy, distort and delete databases; they can disseminate confidential information or deny access. Most of these examples are not about increasing opportunities to make money but rather to take revenge on others.

2. **Psycho-social changes**
   Mars (2006) focuses on the growth of individualism and the fact that fewer people seem bound by social groups or group allegiances. This means a reduced respect for hierarchies and the relaxation of group controls, occupational specialization, the flattening of hierarchies and the increase in delegation offering people more autonomy.

3. **Globalization**
Young multinational people, because of their aspiration, education and ideology, seem more divorced from the communities in which they work. This can also marginalize migrant labours who move in search of work. It also means that local companies get bought by large, foreign companies which are associated with thefts.

The crucial point that Mars is making is that the job itself largely dictates what sort of corrupt behaviours are possible and preferable. Further, that some of these are done effectively in groups.

4.8 Conclusion

Clinical, organizational and personality psychologists have frequently and often correctly been accused of a *'simplistic flight to the dispositional'* meaning that they have often tried to explain behaviour, often negative behaviour, in terms of the characteristics, traits and temperaments of individuals. In doing so they neglect to understand, or completely underestimate, the power of situations to influence behaviour.

The organizations for which people work are embedded in a national culture with its own history, laws and morals. These to some extent dictate what sort of organizations exist and thrive in that area. Furthermore all organizations develop a strong corporate culture which dictates how people should and should not behave. Some cultures openly accept bullying and corruption in the form of back-handers and theft. Others turn a blind eye to those engaged in a variety of corrupt practices. Some people seek out places where corruption is rife.

For some workers the only way to 'get on' in a corrupt organization is to 'do as others do'. Many initially wrestle with their conscience but follow well-known processes to get things done.

The crucial issue when trying to understand how leaders fail and derail is to see the extent to which their beliefs, values and behaviours were shaped and influenced by the situation in which they found themselves.

Chapter 5

The criminal personality and criminal gangs

5.1 Introduction

The appetite for crime-fiction and indeed crime-fact books is testimony to fascination with whom, how, when or why people turn to crime. We have blue- and white-collar crime, individual and corporate crime, national and transnational crime. Some people are, for want of a better theoretical and non-psychological term, evil. They are morally corrupt and capable of inflicting physical and mental pain onto others. They are more than difficult or nasty or incompetent. Indeed, they are often more than simply bad. They appear to have criminal and psychopathic tendencies. Their lack of conscience and an absence of a sense of right and wrong make them able to inflict great harm onto others without regret or remorse. Not all criminals are psychopaths, anymore than not all psychopaths are criminals.

There are many studies and books with the title *Criminal Personality*. Some, like Samenow's book *Inside the Criminal Mind*, are very detailed. It could be read as the study of psychopaths, but this is clearly insufficient to describe and explain criminality. The psychiatrists, unlike the criminologists, have sought to understand the criminal in terms of their concepts. Thus, Wulach (1988) saw the criminal as having a heady mix of four personality disorders: antisocial, narcissistic, borderline and histrionic.

Yet, whilst some criminals work alone, most take part in group or organized crime which is business-like and entrepreneurial (Gottschalk, 2010).

This chapter considers what the world of criminology can offer as insight to the dark side of behaviour at work. Are bullies, bastards and backstabbers little more than criminal personalities? Is the personality profile of the criminal really very similar to that of the dark-side manager?

5.2 The criminal personality

Early criminologists like Lambrosso and Sheldon argued for a criminal type, born with an innate disposition to criminality and antisocial behaviour, but these ideas were (and are) angrily dismissed by criminologists, sociologists and others who claim they ignore all important social factors. For some fifty years, the trait position was disregarded (though enthusiastically supported by Eysenck) but had returned especially with the development in behaviour genetics. There is no shortage of theories about the cause of crime and criminality. Early *demonological* theory (criminals are evil, sinners, etc.) was replaced by Marxist *economic* theories (social class inequality, lack of opportunity) then early *biological* theories (mental/moral/physical deficiency) and then *psychological* theories (unconscious processes, peer learning). Most criminology has been dominated by sociological theories that emphasize social processes, labelling and conflict.

For a long time both psychologists and sociologists argued that *crime was learnt*. Early ideas can be expressed thus:

- Criminal behaviour is learned.
- Learning is through association with other people.
- The main part of the learning occurs within close personal groups.
- The learning includes techniques to execute particular crimes and also specific attitudes, drives and motives conducive towards crime.
- The direction of the drives and motives is learned from perception of the law as either favourable or unfavourable.
- A person becomes criminal when their definitions favourable to breaking the law outweigh their definitions favourable to non-violation.

- The learning experiences – differential associations – will vary in frequency, intensity and importance for each individual.
- The process of learning criminal behaviour is no different from the learning of any other behaviour, like altruism, selling or negotiating with others.
- Although criminal behaviour is an expression of needs and values, crime cannot be explained in terms of those needs and values. (e.g. it is not the need for money which causes crime, rather the method used to acquire the money; the method is learned.)

The learning approach advocated by behaviourists is that people develop *a sense of,* and more importantly *behaviours associated with,* right and wrong by the way they are socialized through processes of reward and punishment. Thus, children learn to be good but some learn better, faster and more efficiently than others.

Criminologists have studied the development of antisocial and criminal behaviour and offending patterns as people *learn to become criminals.* They note both certain risk factors for being delinquent and criminal as well as the life events on a criminal career. Thus, the points listed in Table 5.1 have been noted as early risk factors for later delinquency.

Table 5.1 Factors correlated with crime

Individual factors	Early antisocial behaviour (physical aggression, biting, cruelty to animals) poor cognitive development, low intelligence, hyperactivity, impulsivity, ADHD
Family factors	Maltreatment Family violence, parental psychopathology and antisocial behaviours, teenage parenthood
School and community factors	Poor academic performance, Low academic aspirations, living in a poor maladjusted family, disorganized neighbourhoods, delinquent peer groups

There are many risk factors associated with youth crime. The Joseph Rowntree Foundation Social Policy Research Document 93 (1996) lists nine risk factors shown in Table 5.2.

Table 5.2 Personal risk factors

Prenatal and perinatal	Early child-bearing (i.e. young mothers) increases the risks of such undesirable outcomes for children and is associated with low school attainment, antisocial behaviour, substance use and early sexual activity. An increased risk of offending among children of teenage mothers is associated with low income, poor housing, absent fathers and poor child rearing methods.
Personality	Impulsiveness, hyperactivity, restlessness and limited ability to concentrate are associated with low attainment in school and a poor ability to foresee the consequences of offending.
Intelligence and attainment	Low intelligence and poor performance in school although important statistical predictors of offending are difficult to disentangle from each other. One plausible explanation of the link between low intelligence and crime is its association with a poor ability to manipulate abstract concepts and to appreciate the feelings of victims.
Parental supervision and discipline	Harsh or erratic-parental discipline and rejecting parental attitudes have been linked to delinquency and are associated with children's lack of internal inhibitions against offending. Physical abuse by parents has also been associated with an increased risk of the children themselves becoming violent offenders in later life.
Parental conflict and separation	Living in a home affected by separation or divorce is more strongly related to delinquency than when the disruption has been caused by the death of one parent. However, it may not be a 'broken home' that creates an increased risk of offending so much as the parental conflict that leads to the separation.

(Continued)

Socio-economic status	Social and economic deprivation are important predictors of antisocial behaviour and crime, but low family income and poor housing are better measurements than the prestige of parents' occupations.
Delinquent friends	Delinquents tend to have delinquent friends. But it is not certain whether membership of a delinquent peer group leads to offending or whether delinquents simply gravitate towards each other's company (or both). Breaking up with delinquent friends often coincides with desisting from crime.
School influences	The prevalence of offending by pupils varies widely between secondary schools. But it is not clear how far schools themselves have an effect on delinquency (e.g. by paying insufficient attention to bullying or providing too much punishment and too little praise), or whether it is simply that troublesome children tend to go to high delinquency-rate schools.
Community influences	The risks of becoming criminally involved are higher for young people raised in disorganized inner city areas, characterized by physical deterioration, overcrowded households, publicly subsidized renting and high residential mobility. It is not clear, however, whether this is due to a direct influence on children, or whether environmental stress causes family adversities which in turn cause delinquency.

5.3 Eysenck's theory of the criminal personality

Perhaps the most robust and fecund of the theories of the criminal personality is that of Hans Eysenck (1977). Feldman (1993) has noted, 'One of the theory's great merits is that it makes predictions which are clear-cut, testable and refutable' (p. 166).

The idea is beguilingly simple. Eysenck believed that sociological theory has little to offer society on the causes of crime, arguing that psychological theories have more explanatory power (Eysenck & Gudjonson, 1989). Eysenck suggests that criminal behaviour is not the product of either environment *or* biology alone, but rather is an inter-action of *both* (Eysenck & Eysenck, 1973). This extends his original belief that biology played the largest part in determining criminality when he first declared his theory on criminality in his book *Crime and Personality* (1964). Eysenck suggested that some people are born with cortical and autonomic nervous systems that affect their ability to learn from their environment which leads some to be prone to illegal and criminal acts.

There are three biologically based heritable, and distinct, personality factors each of which relates to a conditionability, notably the learning of rules of society (see Table 5.3).

Table 5.3 Eysenck's theory

Extraverts	Social and impulsive. Excitement-seekers interested in novel experiences and venturesome. This leads them to be poorer learners than introverts at many tasks including the acquisition of general social rules. They are often, therefore, naughty children who turn into juvenile delinquents and hence criminals.
Neurotics	Anxious and moody, restless and rigid. React strongly to threat often with great fear to painful stimulation. This means they too don't learn social rules well and are 'inefficient learners' particularly with respect to punishment.
Tough-Minded Psychoticism	Aggressive, egocentric, insensitive, inhumane, uncaring and troublesome behaviour.

Thus, the Eysenckian criminal personality theory is:

- Personality is consistent over time and stable across social situations.
- Personality traits are related to the personality disorders.

- Odd/Eccentric/Psychoticism (Paranoid, Schizoid, Schizotypal); Dramatic/Extraverted (Histrionic, Narcissistic, Antisocial Borderline); Anxious/Fearful/Neurotic (Avoidant, Dependent, Compulsive, Passive-Aggressive). Passive-Aggressive show overlap between traits and disorders.
- There is a significant negative relationship between intelligence and crime but this is mediated by social class, educational attainment, race and gender.
- Prosocial (unselfish, altruistic, law-abiding) behaviour has to be learned. Certain personalities do not learn as well as others.
- Psychoticism is the most important predictor of criminality.
- Different profiles lead to different types of criminals; high P, high E, low N turn into con-men; high P, low E, low N into thieves, etc.
- Personality traits (P, E, N) are biologically based.

Thus, it is the people that score high on all three dimensions that are least conditioned, least socially restrained. They are aggressive, hedonistic, impulsive and reckless.

Eysenck and Gudjonsson (1989) have summarized their position thus:

- There exists a general behaviour pattern of antisocial behaviour and criminality, marking the opposite end of continuum to that is constituted by prosocial altruistic behaviour.
- Within the antisocial and criminal type of behaviour, there is a certain amount of heterogeneity, marked particularly by the opposition between active and inadequate criminals, but probably also including differences according to type of crime committed.
- Criminality is related to certain dimensions of personality, in particular that labelled Psychoticism, which is apparent in all age groups and under all conditions studied.
- There is a strong tendency for extraversion to be linked to criminality, particularly in younger samples and among more active criminals; inadequate older criminals do not show high extraversion and may indeed be below average on this trait.

- Most criminals are characterized by a high degree of neuroticism, but this may not be found as markedly in children and youngsters.
- Scores on the L scale are regarded in these studies as a measure of conformity (rather than of dissimulation) and tend to correlate negatively with antisocial and criminal conduct, both in children and in adolescents and adults.
- The criminality scale, made up of the most diagnostic items of the EPQ, tends to discriminate significantly between criminals and non-criminals.
- Primary personality traits, such as impulsiveness, venturesomeness, risk-taking, empathy and others correlate, in predictable directions, with antisocial and criminal conduct.
- These relationships are observed also in conditions where self-report of antisocial behaviour is the major criterion. Thus, personality – criminality correlations are not confined to legal definitions of crime or incarcerated criminals.
- The observed personality – criminality correlations have cross-cultural validity, appearing in different countries and cultures with equal prominence.
- Personality traits of antisocial and criminal behaviour are also found correlated with behaviour that is not criminal but is regarded as antisocial such as smoking, drug use, whether legal or illegal tend to have higher P, E and N scores. Studies show high P and N scores among drug users, but E scores are elevated only among drug users convicted of other crimes.

One major objection has been from sociologists and educationalists. Life circumstances – that is, poverty, growing up in a criminal family or an unruly (ungovernable) society, economic inequality, opportunities to commit crime – are all most powerful predictors of criminality than an individual's personality.

Eysenck's position did develop and change over time. He placed more emphasis on the role of Psychoticism and admitted more the possibility of the social causes of crime. However, it has been the longitudinal studies that have perhaps offered most, using a large sample followed from birth. Caspi et al. (1994) found replications in the Eysenkian hypothesized personality – crime relationships across country, gender race and method. Poor social control (impulsivity, hyperactivity, etc.) predicted weak social bonds, adolescent delinquency and later criminality.

In a big meta-analytic review Miller and Lynam (2001) note that developments in personality theory and in data analysis have permitted a second look at the criminal personality idea. They concluded:

> From the overall results, it is possible to generate a description of the personality traits that are characteristic of antisocial individuals. Individuals who commit crimes tend to be hostile, self-centered, spiteful jealous, and indifferent to others (i.e. low in Agreeableness). They tend to lack ambition, motivation, and perseverance, have difficulty controlling their impulses, and hold non-traditional and unconventional values and beliefs (i.e. are low in Conscientiousness). It is informative that by beginning with the criminal, we arrived at a description very similar to the one offered by Gottfredson and Hirschi (1990) who began with the crime. Gottfredson and Hirschi (1990) offer that individuals who are low in self control (1) have difficulty delaying gratification and instead respond to tangible stimuli in the immediate environment; (2) lack diligence, tenacity, or persistence in a task; (3) tend to be adventurous, physical, and active rather than cautious, cognitive, and verbal; (4) are little interested in and unprepared for long-term occupational pursuits; (5) are self-centered, indifferent, or insensitive to the suffering and needs of others; (6) are gregarious and social people; and (7) have minimal frustration tolerance. The first four characteristics map on very well to the dimension of Conscientiousness or Constraint. Similarly, the fifth and seventh characteristics are clear indicators of low Agreeableness. The only significant disagreement between our descriptions concerns the sixth characteristic – sociability; we found that dimensions related to Extraversion were not related to ASB. (p. 780)

They believe personality relates to antisocial behaviour in general and crime in particular in distal and proximal ways. Personality predicts how people react to situations, how other people react to them and indeed the situations they find themselves in. Personality also predicts decision making.

They believe criminologists should be less hostile to personality and individual differences because it helps to explain the relative stability of antisocial behaviour as well as prevention of crime.

There have been various reviews of the Eysenckian position including attempts to analysis of the now many studies that have tested his theory. These are studies of adult criminals, adolescent delinquents but also 'normal' non criminal individuals. Most studies look at the relationships between scores derived from Eysenck's famous personality test and some other measure such as self-reported crime (Furnham & Thompson, 1991). Thus, it is possible to give an individual both a personality test and a self-reported measure of delinquent behaviour including everything from traffic violation, acts of 'minor vandalism' as well as petty theft.

Overall the results provide mixed, but largely positive evidence for the criminal personality theory. Certainly when the relationships are significant they show the higher people score on (in this order) Psychoticism, Extroversion and Neuroticism, the more likely they are to have been involved in criminal, antisocial and delinquent behaviour.

5.4 Criminal personality disorder

Can one talk legitimately of a criminal personality disorder? Raine (1993) has provided good evidence in favour of his theory that much criminal behaviour can be seen as a type of individual clinical or personality disorder. He notes:

Based on these findings, it is argued that there are good reasons to believe that a variety of *social and biological factors exist that predispose the individual towards criminal behavior*. In combination with the fact that criminal behavior also meets a number of the definitions of disorder, it is concluded that there is a reasonable evidence either to directly support the view that crime is a disorder or alternatively to give serious consideration to this possibility. At the very least, there is sufficient evidence in favour of the notion that crime is a disorder to place the burden of proof on those wishing to disprove this position. That is, unless there are convincing arguments to the contrary, we should at least consider the possibility that if crime was identified by any other name which was free of all societal connotations placed on it ('crime' for example), then in the light of this substantive body of evidence, it is likely that crime would be more readily considered a disorder (Raine, 1993, p. 292).

He provides various sources of data in support of his theories (see Table 5.4).

Table 5.4 Supportive evidence for the theory

Evolutionary evidence	There are evolutionary explanations both for the development and inhibition of cheating
Genetics	Twin and adoption studies provide strong evidence of the heritability of criminality proneness
Biochemistry	Antisocials have reduced serotonin which supports behavioural disinhibition theory, which, in part explains antisocial behaviour
Neuropsychology	Frontal (front-temporal-lubic) structures characterize antisocial behaviour and it could be assured there are neuropsychological correlates of the criminal personality
Brain imaging	PET scanning supports the idea of frontal dysfunction
Other biological factors	Body build, raised testosterone, minor physical abnormalities characterize the criminal personality
Cognitive factors	IQ (verbal), learning disabilities, poor social information processing, lower moral, reasoning, overt sensitivity to rewards
Familial factors	Parental crime, child abuse, maternal deprivation, divorce/separation, poor parental supervision, erratic and inconsistent punishment, negative affect, marital conflict and neglect
Extrafamilial factors	Negative peer influences, academic failure, bad schools, large family sizes, parental and self-social class, unemployment, urban living, poor housing and overcrowding

The idea that crime can be largely explained in terms of a specific set of disorders or traits does run into problems, especially the concept of *criminal personality disorder*. The following challenges have been made to this position:

- There are major age, gender and ethnic differences in rates of criminal behaviour; such demographic effects are inconsistent with the view that crime is a disorder.
- There have been major changes in crime rates over time, which are inconsistent with viewing crime as a disorder.
- There are important cross-cultural variations in the rates of crime that invalidate crime as a disorder.
- Crime is a heterogeneous concept, so it cannot represent a unitary disorder identified by a discrete cluster of trails.
- Crime is a socio-politico-legal construction that can be changed by changing the law, whereas psychiatric disorders are determined by biological and social forces and as such represent more fundamental, fixed concepts.
- Crime cannot be a disorder because it is so pervasive in society; we all commit crime, and the whole population cannot be viewed as 'disordered'.
- The group of criminals that the disorder argument is being applied to cannot be definitely delineated; the inability to precisely identify the target population rules crime out as a disorder.
- Some research shows that the same factors found to underlie severe criminal behaviour also characterize less severe forms of antisocial behaviour; this suggests that there is no discrete category of offenders to whom the notion of a disorder can be applied.
- Crime is committed by groups and organizations, not by individuals; therefore, crime cannot be a disorder because organizations cannot be psychiatrically disordered.
- Crime cannot be cured, so it probably is not a disorder.
- Criminal behaviour differs from other psychiatric disorders in that criminals pose harm to others; this delimits it from other disorders.

- Crime is an aberration of behaviour, whereas disorders represent aberration of mental functioning; crime, therefore, is not a disorder in the same sense as other disorders.
- Criminal behaviour is voluntary, whereas other disorders are involuntary.

5.5 White-collar crime

In this book, we are essentially concerned, not with petty, violent or organized crime but what has come to be known as white-collar crime. This is nearly always financial crime: fraud, insider-trading, embezzlement, money laundering. It is usually thought of as economic crime. It is committed by someone of higher socio-economic status and education. Typical crimes include insider trading, cybercrime, forgery, copyright infringement and embezzlement.

What crime categories exist within white-collar crime? First, *fraud* – 'intentional perversion of truth for the purpose of inducing another in reliance upon it to part with some valuable thing belonging to him or to surrender a legal right'. These criminals receive significantly longer prison sentences than corruption criminals. Second, *theft* – the illegal taking of another person's, group's, or organization's money, property or goods without their permission. Theft can be combined with other forms of commodity, such as identity. Theft has the lowest taxable income of the crime subgroups.

Third, *manipulation* – gaining illegal control or influence over others' activities, means, and results such as tax evasion. The least amount of white-collar crimes involve manipulation.

Fourth, *corruption* – defined as giving, requesting, receiving or accepting an improper advance related to a position, office or assignment. 'It is to destroy or pervert the integrity or fidelity of a person in his discharge of duty, to induce to act dishonestly or unfaithfully, to make venal, and to bribe.' These criminals received significantly shorter prison sentences than fraud criminals. Corruption criminals have the highest taxable income of the crime subgroups.

It is committed when a person in a privileged business situation abuses that position (Gottschalk, 2014). White-collar crime comprises of various components (Arnulf & Gottschalk, 2013): It's deceitful; it is intentional; it breaches trust; it involves losses; it may be concealed; and there may be an appearance of outward respectability. Bookman (2008) emphasizes that it is committed by non-physical means and by concealment or guile to obtain money or property, to avoid payment or loss, or to obtain business or personal advantage. Perri (2011) documented that even white-collar criminals can resort to violence in order to cover up their crimes, extending as far as murder.

The person is usually a respectable individual and of a higher social status – they are the upper-middle class; the elite. Sutherland's 1940 theory drew attention to the fact that highly educated people with high status, wealth and an outward appearance of respectability also commit crime.

It is usually a business situation, but some argue now that with the rise in technology and access to the Internet means that any person can (relatively easily) commit a white-collar crime.

Brightman (2009) argued that the term 'white-collar crime' should be broader in scope; ignoring social status, it should include virtually any non-violent act committed for financial gain. Individuals of lower social class can now buy and sell stocks online; it is no longer only for the financially well off.

Financial crime, fraud and white-collar crime have been known to be used interchangeably (Pickett & Pickett, 2002). White-collar crime is the use of deception, breaching trust and concealment of true motives to achieve illegal gain. White-collar crime has also been defined as crimes against property; 'the unlawful conversion of property belonging to another to one's own personal use and benefit'. This is also called profit-driven crime done in order to gain access to and use of money and property that belong to others.

Swindlers are white-collar criminals. A swindler is somebody who seeks to get money out of people by selling non-existent or 'dodgy' goods or services, claiming they are winners of prizes and demanding some down payment or deposit as well as offering special deals. Some even pose as charity collectors. Many target older or vulnerable people. Swindlers can be phony salesmen or even fortune tellers. They use face-to-face methods, the telephone and increasingly the web to do their business. People are told they have won, or been left by some 'unknown' relative vast sums of money which they can obtain if they make a payment or give over their bank details.

Factors that contribute to external crime include a lack, and poor perception, of market integrity; market misconduct; a lack of effort to educate, detect, and enforce law regulations, and a poor effectiveness, efficiency, and fairness of market structures.

Benson and Simpson (2009) suggested that unlike common street crime, white-collar criminals will have had no (or very little) interaction with the criminal world or justice system, and will have no previous record. However, research has found that white-collar criminals do often have prior criminal records (Weisburd & Waring, 2001), are repeat offenders (Listwan et al., 2010) and have low self-control/impulse control (Boddy, 2010).

Two main distinguishable characteristics of the white-collar criminal and white-collar workers are irresponsibility and antisociable behaviour (see Table 5.5). Most white-collar criminals are men (92 per cent of the sample).

Table 5.5 Some attempt has been made to differentiate between different types of white-collar criminals

Criminal Entrepreneurs	Whilst most of the entrepreneur literature focuses on the positive side of this ability, little focuses on the notion that not all entrepreneurships are legal endeavours. These criminals create value by offering a product or service in order to obtain large and easy profits. Self-control theory attempts to explain this type of criminal; low self-control, risk-taking and self-centredness are associated with involvement in criminal behaviour. These criminals receive significantly longer jail sentences. Criminal entrepreneurs have the lowest participants in each crime.

(Continued)

Corporate Criminals	Criminals who engage in financial crime for the benefit of the organization rather than themselves. This type is usually committed by higher-ranking members of the organization, who engage in fraud or corruption in order to boost profits. These criminals are usually significantly older than other criminals. Corporate criminals have significantly higher amounts of financial crime (in currency); interesting to note that even though their crime amount is higher, their jail time is still not the longest. Corporate crime is committed in larger organizations.
Criminal Followers	They do not initiate the criminal activities, but trail behind someone else into criminal schemes. They are convinced of their rightness and believe no one can harm them as they feel the leader will take the fall. They follow as a result of a dynamics between their behaviour and the charisma of the leader. Followers may feel three types of pressure to follow: obedience (to superiors), compliance (to peers as well as superiors) and conformity (perceived or societal norms) pressure. Obedience pressure has been noted as especially potent due to the power some superiors have over their underlings. When criminal followers are involved, significantly more individuals participate in the crime.
Female Criminals	Because so few females commit white-collar crimes, and they are found in other categories, they are treated as their own group due to the lack of female opportunity in many business organizations. Traditionally, 'pink-collar' crimes involve embezzlement and fraud. Men greatly outnumber women in terms of standard and white-collar crime offenders (6:1), meaning that gender is the strongest predictor of criminal involvement. Gender theory of female offending focuses on these elements and their interplay: gender norms, biological factors, criminal opportunities (sexism in the criminal underworld, access to skills), gender differences in crime, context of offending and the motivation for the crime. Female criminals have significantly lower amounts of financial crime (in currency). Female criminals have the lowest taxable income among criminals.

Who are the victims of white-collar crime? Victims can be either an organization or an individual. A victim will encounter an agency that is injurious or destructive to them, through either being deceived or cheated. Victims suffer financial loss due to the financial crime committed by the white-collar criminals. Croall (2007) stated that there is a different relationship between the perpetrators and victims of white-collar crimes compared to normal crime: there is less blood or harm to the victims; it is less personal; the victims are usually employers, the public sector, governments or the environment. Victims of these activities are often excluded from crime and victim research due to not being recognized as 'real' victims.

Employers are victims of crimes such as embezzlement and theft (cash or fraud). This is the most frequent category of victim (Gottschalk, 2014). When the organization is the victim as an employer, then the organization is larger than other categories (large organizations associated with employer victims).

5.6 Emerging crimes

Over the past decade there have been a number of 'new crimes' that have attracted the criminal personality.

5.6.1 Hacking and Hacktivism

'Hacking' is a term used to define unauthorized access to a computer device. Hacktivism is a combination of hacking and activism – the use of hacking for political reasons. Cracking, however, is criminal hacking, referring to hacking activities for purely criminal reasons (Conway, 2003).

With the increasing level of technical ability that hackers possess, their skills could potentially enter the free market. However, their social inhibition, isolation and difficulty to locate (or advertise for them without getting caught) seem to stop hackers from teaming up with outside groups (Conway, 2003). Yet, it has been known to happen; in 1989, hackers in Hanover began selling information obtained from NASA and other American governmental bodies to the KPG (Conway, 2003).

Barber (2001) noted there are three groups of hackers: script kiddies, hackers and crackers:

1. **Script kiddies** fit the generic profile of a hacker – 14–16 years old, still at school, tend to be male and spend their time on computers rather than with friends. However, these are not computer 'whiz kids'; they have very limited knowledge of the complexities of computers, and issue simple commands that are freely available on the Internet in order to cause damage and destruction. They often go to chat-rooms to talk about their successes and trade ideas. Due to their lack of knowledge, they often make very large mistakes at first, but are still dangerous because of the powerful tools they use ineptly.
2. **Hackers** are more knowledgeable, highly capable and are able to write their own programmes. Their main motivation is curiosity; they want to use techniques they have developed and have a 'poke around'. Sometimes, this is the equivalent of them trying every door and window on your house for an entrance, coming in and having a look around, but then leaving a calling card on their way out to tell IT staff about the open threats to their system.
3. **Crackers** have made the conscious decision to damage and steal. They act out of personal gain or the love of destruction. There is a fine but distinct line between hackers and crackers; when hackers' motivations are malicious or criminal, they become a cracker.

Extrinsically motivated hackers are thought to attack organizations that have a high degree of digitization; those organizations include banks, casinos and financial institutions that are heavily dependent upon cyberspace in order to operate (Kshetri, 2005). Analysis from the International Data Corporation revealed that 60 per cent of computer hacks in 2003 were attacks on financial institutions (Swartz, 2004; in Kshetri, 2005).

Intrinsically motivated hackers, however, are more inclined to attack organizations and groups of symbolic significance. This can be governmental departments, critical infrastructures and companies that hold national significance (Kshetri, 2005). Other critical infrastructures, such as oil, gas and telecommunications, are thought to be increasingly under threat from cyber-terror (Comité Européen Des Assurances, 2004).

5.6.2 *Piracy*

In 1999, online piracy began with peer-to-peer file-sharing sites, such as Napster, that allowed individuals to go online, search for music files or movies, and download them for free. It was later that year, when the Recording Industry Association of America realized what was happening, that Internet piracy was first documented as being illegal and an issue. Since then, piracy has evolved with law; online sites such as Pirate Bay let users download everything from music, movies, videos and software for free by hosting their sites in foreign domains. However, these sites are short lived; they are always found and shut down within a month or so, when new servers are utilized and piracy begins again.

5.6.3 *'Catfishing'*

A catfish is someone who deliberately steals someone else's identity or creates a fake persona online in order to pursue online relationships (generally romantic). The term derives from a 2010 documentary about a New York photographer, Yaniv Schulman, who had an online relationship with a young, attractive student. It turned out that the girl was actually a mid-40-year-old woman with a husband and two children, who had created multiple online personas to play as. Her husband, clueless to her endeavours, was telling Yaniv about how they moved cod in ships.

Catfishing is technically dating fraud, but closely resembles online identity fraud. Users will often take the photos, names and information of other real people in order to create a false persona online. Some have posited that catfishing represents a form of the somatoform illness, factitious disorder, where individuals feign psychological and/or physical symptoms in order to play the victim, whilst there are no external signs or existence of those symptoms.

5.6.4 *Trolls*

There is now an online world of *Flamer, Hater and Snert Trolls*. These people can cause enormous damage to individuals and organizations.

They often hide behind anonymity and lead to much wasted time, effort and pain. Innocent people can have their reputations seriously damaged. Trolling is aimed at embarrassing, disrupting and angering other users (Dahlberg, 2001). There is an overlap and differing emphases between differing online abusers, such as hackers, hacktivists and criminals.

The deceptive and 'pointless disruption that is associated with troll-actions is different from other types of online antisocial agents, where others have a more clear identity and intention' (Buckels et al., 2014). Trolls will have their own language and methods of communication – they engage in behaviours for the 'lulz' (derived from 'lols', meaning to do it because it is funny; Buckels et al., 2014). Hackers have been compared with trolls in the literature. Hackers have been categorized into three groups: organized crime for financial gain, script kiddie for self-gratification, and hacktivism for political messages and social justice (Falk, 200).

Donath (1999) has suggested that trolling is a form of deception and manipulation, often with tacit consent of community members, but with the potential to disrupt, offend or disseminate bad advice. Bergstrom (2011) defined trolling in relation to the anger, harm or discomfort resulting from its transgressions of particular community norms – to be made a victim and to be caught along in the undertow and be the butt of someone else's joke.

Trolls are a part of a growing internet subculture with fluid morality and a disdain for pretty much anyone else online (Schwartz, 2008). Trolling behaviour entails luring others into pointless and time-consuming discussions, characterized by severe emotions (namely anger) (Herring et al., 2002).

In one study by Buckels et al. (2014), 5.6 per cent of internet users report enjoying trolling other users. These individuals had the highest Dark Tetrad scores, and higher extraversion yet lower agreeableness. Sadism, however, was the most robust association with trolling. The association between sadism and the Global Assessment of Internet Trolling were so strong that it is possible to state online trolls are prototypical everyday sadists. Narcissism was negatively related to trolling enjoyment. Sadists just want to have fun, and the internet is their playground.

Some managers and business leaders are, in effect, criminals of one sort or another. They knowingly commit crimes for their own advantage. This chapter has considered the theories behind the criminal personality and the processes and mechanisms which explain their behaviour. More interesting are white-collar criminals and the many new technology crimes that are appearing.

Chapter 6

Five accounts: Explaining the cause of leadership derailment

6.1 Introduction

The question for both the academic and the practitioner is how is it that business people get promoted to positions of power and influence when they are so fundamentally flawed. How do 'potential derailers' get selected and 'climb the greasy pole' of organizational life only to 'explode' in firework display of failure. Inevitably there are very different theories and approaches. Some are more popular than others; some have considerable empirical support and others very little; some have more explanatory power than others. This chapter will consider these different accounts.

6.2 The personality disorders account

It was due to the brilliant insight of Robert and Joyce Hogan in the 1990s that it is possible to describe, explain and predict a good deal of management derailment in terms of the psychiatric personality disorders. Furthermore, by developing a measure called the Hogan Developmental Survey (HDS) they made research in this area possible. As a result there is now a coherent account and a great deal of emerging literature. Furthermore, their ideas have been borrowed, elaborated upon and extended by others working in the area.

Psychologists are interested in personality traits; psychiatrists in personality disorders. Psychologists interested in personality have made great strides in describing, taxonomizing and explaining the mechanisms and processes in normal personality functioning. Psychiatrists also talk about personality functioning. They talk about personality disorders that are typified by early onset (recognizable in children and adolescents), pervasive effects (on all aspects of life) and with relatively poor prognosis (that is difficult to cure).

Both argue that the personality factors related to *cognitive, affective* and *social aspects of functioning.* In other words, the disorder or traits affects how people think, feel and act. It is where a person's behaviour 'deviates, mark-edly' from the expectations of the individual's culture where the disorder is manifested. The psychiatric manual is very clear that 'odd behaviour' is not simply an expression of habits, customs, religious or political values professed or shown by a people of particular cultural origin.

Over the years psychiatrists have made great strides in clarifying and specifying diagnostic criteria and these can be found in the various *Diagnostic and Statistical Manual of Mental Disorders* (called DSM for short). They have changed over the years and it is now in its fifth edition. Some disorders have 'disappeared' like 'passive aggressive'.

Psychiatrists and psychologists share some simple assumptions with respect to personality. Both argue for the *stability* of personality. The DSM criteria talk of 'enduring pattern', 'inflexible and pervasive', 'stable and of long duration'. The pattern of behaviour is not a function of drug usage or some other medical condition. The personality pattern further-more is not a manifestation or consequence of another mental disorder.

The DSM manuals note that personality orders all have a long history and have an onset no later than early adulthood. Moreover, there are some gender differences: thus the antisocial disorder is more likely to be diagnosed in men, whilst the borderline, histrionic and dependent personality are more likely to be found in women.

The manuals are at lengths to point out that some of the personality disorders look like other disorders: anxiety, mood, psychotic, substance-related, etc. but have unique features. The essence of the argument is, 'Personality Disorders must be distinguished from personality traits that do not reach the threshold for a Personality Disorder. Personality traits are diagnosed as a Personality Disorder only when they are infle-xible, maladaptive, and persisting and cause significant functional impairment or subjective distress.' (p. 633)

One of the most important ways to differentiate personal style from personality disorder is flexibility. There are lots of difficult people at work but relatively few whose rigid, maladaptive behaviours mean they continually have disruptive, troubled lives. It is their *inflexible, repetitive, poor stress-coping responses* that are marks of disorder.

Personality disorders influence the *sense of self* – the way people think and feel about themselves and how other people see them. The disorders often powerfully influence *interpersonal relations at work*. They reveal themselves in how people 'complete tasks, take and/or give orders, make decisions, plan, handle external and internal demands, take or give criticism, obey rules, take and delegate responsibility, and co-operate with people' (Oldham & Morris, 1991, p. 24). The antisocial, obsessive, compulsive, passive-aggressive and dependent types are particularly problematic in the workplace.

People with personality disorders have difficulty expressing and understanding emotions. It is the intensity with which they express them and their variability that makes them odd. More importantly they often have serious problems with self-control.

It was Hogan who developed the Hogan Development Survey (HDS) which 'translates' the personality disorders into dark-side traits often associated with derailment. In the advertising material they note the following:

> Bosses that alienate colleagues and subordinates undermine the commitment and effectiveness of the workforce with inevitable consequences for productivity, retention and the bottom line. Based on research into management derailment, the HDS identifies eleven such patterns of dysfunctional interpersonal leadership behaviour. These 'dark side' tendencies erode trust, loyalty and enthusiasm and are of particular concern in relation to supervisory, managerial and leadership roles. The HDS measures eleven such flawed interpersonal styles that become exaggerated under pressure and are difficult to detect in interviews.

Table 6.1 shows the relationship between the classic DSMIV personality disorders and the HDS.

Table 6.1 The DSM IV and the HDS

PROFILE				HDS	
DSM Labels	Theme	Scale	Theme	Scale	Theme
Borderline	Inappropriate anger; unstable and intense relationships alternating between idealization and devaluation.	Unstable Relationships	Flighty; inconsistent; forms intense albeit sudden enthusiasms and disenchantments for people or projects	Excitable	Moody and hard to please; intense, but short-lived enthusiasm for people, projects or things
Paranoid	Distrustful and suspicious of others; motives are interpreted as malevolent.	Argumentative	Suspicious of others; sensitive to criticism; expects to be mistreated	Sceptical	Cynical, distrustful, and doubting other's true intentions
Avoidant	Social inhibition; feelings of inadequacy and hypersensitivity to criticism or rejection	Fear of Failure	Dread of being criticized or rejected; tends to be excessively cautious; unable to make decisions	Cautious	Reluctant to take risks for fear of being rejected or negatively evaluated
Schizoid	Emotional coldness and detachment from social relationships; indifferent to praise and criticism	Interpersonal Insensitivity	Aloof; cold; imperceptive; ignores social feedback	Reserved	Aloof, detached and uncommunicative; lacking interest in or awareness of the feelings of others

(Continued)

	PROFILE			HDS	
DSM Labels	Theme	Scale	Theme	Scale	Theme
Passive-Aggressive	Passive resistance to adequate social and occupational performance; irritated when asked to do something he/she does not want to	Passive-Aggressive	Sociable, but resists others through procrastination and stubbornness	Leisurely	Independent; ignoring people's requests and becoming irritated or argumentative if they persist
Narcissistic	Arrogant and haughty behaviours or attitudes; grandiose sense of self-importance and entitlement	Arrogance	Self-absorbed; typically loyal only to himself/herself and his/her own best interests	Bold	Unusually self-confident; feelings of grandiosity and entitlement; over-valuation of one's capabilities
Antisocial	Disregard for the truth; impulsivity and failure to plan ahead; failure to conform with social norms	Untrustworthiness	Impulsive; dishonest; selfish; motivated by pleasure; ignoring the rights of others	Mischievous	Enjoying risk-taking and testing limits; needing excitement; manipulative, deceitful, cunning and exploitative
Histrionic	Excessive emotionality and attention seeking; self-dramatizing, theatrical and exaggerated emotional expression	Attention-seeking	Motivated by a need for attention and a desire to be in the spotlight	Colourful	Expressive, animated and dramatic; wanting to be noticed and needing to be the centre of attention

(Continued)

	PROFILE			HDS	
DSM Labels	**Theme**	**Scale**	**Theme**	**Scale**	**Theme**
Schizotypal	Odd beliefs or magical thinking; behaviour or speech that is odd, eccentric or peculiar	No Common Sense	Unusual or eccentric attitudes; exhibits poor judgement relative to education and intelligence	Imaginative	Acting and thinking in creative and sometimes odd or unusual ways
Obsessive-Compulsive	Preoccupations with orderliness, rules, perfectionism and control; overconscientious and inflexible	Perfectionism	Methodical; meticulous; attends so closely to details that he/she may have trouble with priorities	Diligent	Meticulous, precise and perfectionistic; inflexible about rules and procedures; critical of others' performance
Dependent	Difficulty making everyday decisions without excessive advise and reassurance; difficulty expressing disagreement out of fear of loss of support or approval	Dependency	Demand for constant reassurance, support and encouragement from others	Dutiful	Eager to please and reliant on others for support and guidance; reluctant to take independent action or go against popular opinion

Many others have been influenced by the usefulness of the DSM classification of the personality disorders. In order to explain and describe these disorders other writers have changed the names to make them more interpretable to a wider audience. Table 6.2 shows the labels from different authors.

Table 6.2 Different labels for the personality disorders

DSM-IV Personality Disorder	Hogan and Hogan (1997)	Oldham and Morris (1991)	Miller (2008)	Dotlich and Cairo (2003)	Moscosco and Salgado (2004)
Borderline	Excitable	Mercurial	Reactors	Volatility	Ambivalent
Paranoid	Sceptical	Vigilant	Vigilantes	Habitual	Suspicious
Avoidant	Cautious	Sensitive	Shrinkers	Excessive Caution	Shy
Schizoid	Reserved	Solitary	Oddballs	Aloof	Lone
Passive-Aggressive	Leisurely	Leisurely	Spoilers	Passive Resistance	Pessimistic
Narcissistic	Bold	Self-Confident	Preeners	Arrogance	Egocentric
Antisocial	Mischievous	Adventurous	Predators	Mischievous	Risky
Histrionic	Colourful	Dramatic	Emoters	Melodramatic	Cheerful
Schizotypal	Imaginative	Idiosyncratic	Creativity and Vision	Eccentric	Eccentric
Obsessive-Compulsive	Diligent	Conscien-tious	Detailers	Perfectionistic	Reliable
Dependent	Dutiful	Devoted	Clingers	Eager to please	Submitted

Dotlich and Cairo (2003), in *Why CEOs Fail: The 11 behaviours that can derail your climb to the top – and how to manage them*, perhaps wrote the first popular book based on Hogan's ideas. Their descriptions made it easy to interpret the personality disorders. They are described in Tables 6.3 and 6.4.

Table 6.3 The derailers (Dotlich & Cairo, 2003)

Arrogance	Overly confident about one's opinion, to the degree that no learning can take place, others' opinion is ignored and own mistakes are not recognized but rather blamed on the rest of the team.
Melodrama	Shifting focus away from serious problems by exaggerated speeches, even losing sense of reality due to increased dramatic style. However, relatively easy to improve.
Volatility	Unexpected mood swings and frequent explosions. Causes others to be very cautious and to not expressing their true opinion in order not to risk an explosion. May increase creativity but it usually distracts the team.
Excessive Caution	Extreme hesitation to take big steps due to obsession about potential negative consequences, which leads to preventing progress and harming the organization.
Habitual Distrust	Becoming overly suspicious about other people's motives and intentions, causing constant negative criticism and difficulty in making alliances with other companies.
Aloofness	Distant from the rest of the team to a degree that transparency is not possible and crisis cannot be resolved, leading the remaining team members to lose motivation and to become unable to accomplish goals.
Mischievousness	Impulsive breaking of rules and frequent changes in policies resulting to not admitting own mistakes and to team members not being able to follow.
Eccentricity	Providing with a lot of new ideas but failing to prioritize them, causing confusion to team members, being doubted by them and not being able to collaborate effectively.
Passive Resistance	Having a very private agenda, not following initial plans and avoiding involvement in crisis, leading team members to being cynical towards their leader as well as not being able to work in teams.
Perfectionism	Focusing on superficial aspects of a project and being overly stressed to make them perfect to a degree that one is overwhelmed by stress, trusting other team members with the project is hard, team members are not the priority and the original purpose of the project is overlooked.
Eagerness to please	Willing to keep the peace of the company by making sure that everyone is happy even if this means that something else needs to be sacrificed, which results in avoidance of conflict, loss of personal opinion and lack of loyalty towards the leader.

Table 6.4 The three factors (De Haan & Kosozi, 2014)

Movers and Shakers	The Charming Manipulator	*Antisocial* patterns linked with Charming Manipulator: you believe the rules are made to be broken. Do you find it hard to be held accountable for your actions?
	The Playful Encourager	*Passive-Aggressive* patterns linked with the Playful Encourager: what you say is not what you really believe. Do you find it hard to take responsibility for your views and actions?
	The Glowing Gatsby	*Narcissistic* patterns linked with the Glowing Gatsby: You think that you're right, and everyone else is wrong. Do you as a leader often think that others are wrong and not up to their jobs?
	The Detached Diplomat	*Schizoid* patterns linked with the Detached Diplomat: you're disengaged and disconnected. Do you often distance yourself from the everyday running of your business?
Rigorous Thinkers	The Responsible Workaholic	*Obsessive-compulsive* patterns linked with the Responsible Workaholic: you get the little things right and the big things wrong. Do you often fret about minutiae whilst losing focus on the big picture?
	The Impulsive Loyalist	*Borderline* patterns with the Impulsive Loyalist: you're subject to mood swings. Do you find it very hard to hear bad news about how the business is going?
	The Brilliant Sceptic	*Paranoid* patterns linked with the Brilliant Sceptic: you focus on the negatives. Do you often think that people are for or against you, and in particular against you?

(Continued)

	The Creative Daydreamer	*Schizotypal* patterns linked with the Creative Daydreamer: you try to be different just for the sake of it. Is your picture of the future often proven wrong?
Sensitive Carers	The Virtuous Supporter	*Dependent* patterns linked with the Virtuous Supporter: you try to win the popularity contest. Are you looking after everyone and trying to make them all feel happy?
	The Accomplished	*Histrionic* patterns with the Accomplished Thespian: you need to be the centre of attention. Are you obsessed with your public image?
	The Simmering Stalwart	*Avoidant* patterns linked with the Simmering Stalwart: you're afraid to make decisions. Are you concerned or hesitant because of what other people might think or do?

Perhaps the most recent and imaginative attempt to explain derailment in terms of the personality disorders has been the interesting work of De Haan and Kasozi (2014) in their book *The Leadership Shadow: How to recognize and avoid derailment, hubris and overdrive*.

They too used the personality disorders framework. The book develops a theory heavily influenced by psychoanalytic concepts. Their argument goes thus: leaders 'shine their light' on the effectiveness of the organization, they split off other areas which become their own leadership shadows. This is a Jungian idea. The rifts and shadows concern the 'relational' nature of leadership. They suggest three styles of leadership that each cast their own shadow:

- the supporting function, where leadership expresses itself as 'doing' and assertiveness comes to the fore, whilst doubt and vulnerability go into the shadow.

- the inspiring function, where leadership expresses itself as 'thinking' and knowledge comes to the fore, whilst trust and safety go into the shadow.
- the containing function, where leadership expresses itself as 'feeling' and empathy comes to the fore, whilst assertiveness and power go into the shadow.

As every leader participates selectively in those three functions, unique aspects of their personality are asserted whilst other aspects are relegated to their personal shadows. The only way to work with them is through either self-analysis, picking up hints from under the surface or working through what irritates you about others in order to understand your own shadow.

The journeys of leaders are influenced by interlocking virtuous cycles, recovery cycles, cycles of transference and hubristic cycles. Through individuation processes the rifts of leadership can be healed further. All leaders can become more effective by driving for (sometimes painful) upwards feedback from within the organization; driving for (sometimes painful) upwards feedback from their own shadows; working relationally by nurturing their relationships and addressing the parallel process here and now; engaging in active, meaningful and honest (self-)reflection.

The idea is that people have core strengths which paradoxically become pitfalls because they are overused and put in 'overdrive'. This then provides a unique challenge (which is the shadow quality) which can be an 'allergy' if used in shadow overdrive.

The theory is interesting and unusual because it combines standard psychiatric concepts with Freudian and Jungian concepts as well as the new positive psychology and strengths approach. In this sense it is an extension of the classic personality disorders account of management failure and derailment.

Table 6.5 describes in more detail not only what the disorders are like but also what can or should be done to control them and provide an 'antidote'.

Table 6.5 Personality patterns

Personality Pattern	Personality Overdrive	Open Door	Target Door	Trap Door	Working Style and Drivers	Antidote/Permission
The Charming Manipulator	Antisocial	Behaviour	Thinking	Feeling	• You believe the rules are made to be broken • Be strong + Please others	• Respect others more: your rule-breaking strategy is one day going to catch up with you • It's OK to be vulnerable
The Playful Encourager	Passive-aggressive	Behaviour	Feeling	Thinking	• What you say is not what you really believe • Try hard + Be strong	• Just do it, or else be upfront about your resistance
The Glowing Gatsby	Narcissistic	Behaviour	Feeling	Thinking	• You think that you're right and everyone else is wrong • Be perfect + Be strong	• You look pathetic a lot of the time, being the only one not seeing that you cannot and will not be able to know or do it all • Be less dependent others' praise
The Detached Diplomat	Schizoid	Behaviour	Thinking	Feeling	• You're disengaged and disconnected • Be strong	• Try to engage more with others • Feels are helpful and human

(*Continued*)

Personality Pattern	Personality Overdrive	Open Door	Target Door	Trap Door	Working Style and Drivers	Antidote/Permission
The Responsible Workaholic	Obsessive-compulsive	Thinking	Feeling	Behaviour	• You get the little things right and the big things wrong • Be perfect + Be strong + Try hard	• Think big picture as well • It's OK to make mistakes, and it is important for learning too
The Impulsive Loyalist	Borderline	Thinking	Behaviour	Feeling	• You're subject to mood swings	• Try to count to ten and relax
The Brilliant Sceptic	Paranoid	Thinking	Feeling	Behaviour	• Be perfect + Hurry up • You focus on the negatives • Be perfect + Be strong	• Relax: there will always be a more charitable explanation
The Creative Daydreamer	Schizotypal	Thinking	Behaviour	Feeling	• You try to be different just for the sake of it	• Try to listen and connect with other stakeholders
The Virtuous Supporter	Dependent	Feeling	Behaviour	Thinking	• Be strong + Try hard • You try to win the popularity contest • Please others + Be strong	• Try instead to look after yourself more • It's OK to want something for yourself and it is OK to disagree
The Accomplished Thespian	Histrionic	Feeling	Thinking	Behaviour	• You need to be the centre of attention • Please others	• Relax about how other people see you
The Simmering Stalwart	Avoidant	Feeling	Behaviour	Thinking	• You're afraid to make decisions • Try hard	• Worry less about what people will think

There have been various attempts to categorize these ten to twelve disorders in a 'higher order' system. There are various tripartite systems. Hogan, the concepts for Karen Horney and this have become very popular:

It should be pointed out that various other personality systems can be fitted into this categorical system. Thus, Eysenck's PEN model could be thought of as:

- **Moving Against**: Psychoticism which measures the extent to which people are tough-minded, non-conformist, risk-taking and antisocial.
- **Moving Away**: Neuroticism which measures negative emotionality, sensitivity to punishment and proneness to anxiety and depression
- **Moving Towards**: Extraversion which measures desire for stimulation, optimism, sociability and excitement seeking.

Indeed the psychiatric system has a threefold classification based both on theory and research. This makes things a little easier as one can concentrate on three rather than ten to thirteen disorders. Furthermore, the results suggest that it is one of these groups or clusters that is the most problematic namely Cluster B or Moving Against People. It is types in this group who, if they are talented and skilled, may get picked for leadership and which often derail (Table 6.6).

Another way of marrying classic personality theory with the psychiatric system is by using the three personality trait factors identified by Eysenck. This would mean ten disorders would be classified thus:

- **Psychoticism**: Paranoid, Schizoid, Schizotypal
- **Extraversion**: Antisocial, Borderline, Histrionic, Narcissistic
- **Neuroticism**: Avoidant, Dependent, Obsessive-Compulsive

Table 6.6 The higher order classification of the personality disorders

DSM	Horney	Hogan	
Cluster A (odd disorders)	**Moving Away from People**	**Moving Away from People**	
• *Paranoid personality disorder:* characterized by a pattern of irrational suspicion and mistrust of others, interpreting motivations as malevolent	• The need for **self-sufficiency** and independence; whilst most desire some *autonomy*, the neurotic may simply wish to discard other individuals entirely.	Excitable	Moody and hard to please; intense but short-lived enthusiasm for people, projects or things
• *Schizoid personality disorder:* lack of interest and detachment from social relationships, apathy and restricted emotional expression	• The need for **perfection**; whilst many are driven to perfect their lives in the form of well-being, the neurotic may display a fear of being slightly flawed.	Sceptical	Cynical, distrustful and doubting others' true intentions
• *Schizotypal personality disorder:* a pattern of extreme discomfort interacting socially, distorted cognitions and perceptions	• Lastly, the need to **restrict life practices** to within narrow borders; to live as inconspicuous a life as possible.	Cautious	Reluctant to take risks for fear of being rejected or negatively evaluated
		Reserved	Aloof, detached and uncommunicative; lacking interest in or awareness of the feelings of others
		Leisurely	Independent; ignoring people's requests and becoming irritated or argumentative if they persist

(Continued)

DSM	Horney	Hogan
Cluster B (dramatic, emotional or erratic disorders)	**Moving Against People**	**Moving Against People**
• *Antisocial personality disorder:* a pervasive pattern of disregard for and violation of the rights of others, lack of empathy, bloated self-image, manipulative and impulsive behaviour	• The need for **power**; the ability to bend *wills* and achieve control over others – whilst most persons seek strength, the neurotic may be desperate for it.	Bold — Unusually self-confident; feelings of grandiosity and entitlement; overvaluation of one's capabilities
• *Borderline personality disorder:* pervasive pattern of instability in relationships, self-image, identity, behaviour and affects often leading to self-harm and impulsivity	• The need to **exploit others**; to get the better of them. To become *manipulative*, fostering the belief that people are there simply to be used.	Mischievous — Enjoying risk-taking and testing the limits; needing excitement; manipulative, deceitful, cunning and exploitative
• *Histrionic personality disorder:* pervasive pattern of attention-seeking behaviour and excessive emotions	• The need for **social recognition**; *prestige* and limelight.	Colourful — Expressive, animated and dramatic; wanting to be noticed and needing to be the centre of attention
	• The need for **personal admiration**; for both inner and outer qualities – to be valued.	
• *Narcissistic personality disorder:* a pervasive pattern of grandiosity, need for admiration and a lack of empathy	• The need for **personal achievement**; though virtually all persons wish to make achievements, as with No. 3, the neurotic may be desperate for achievement.	Imaginative — Acting and thinking in creative and sometimes odd or unusual ways

(Continued)

DSM	Horney	Hogan	
Cluster C (anxious or fearful disorders)	**Moving Towards People**	**Moving Towards People**	
• *Avoidant personality disorder*: pervasive feelings of social inhibition and inadequacy, extreme sensitivity to negative evaluation	• The need for **affection and approval**; pleasing others and being liked by them.	Diligent	Meticulous, precise and perfectionistic, inflexible about rules and procedures; critical of others
• Dependent personality disorder: pervasive psychological need to be cared for by other people	• The need for **a partner**; one whom they can *love* and who will solve all problems.	Dutiful	Eager to please and reliant on others for support and guidance; reluctant to take independent action or to go against popular opinion
• Obsessive-compulsive personality disorder (not the same as obsessive-compulsive disorder): characterized by rigid conformity to rules, perfectionism and control			

Still others have been influenced by Hogan and tried a different classification. Since the 1930s it has been claimed there were three classic behaviour patterns displayed when individuals were faced by anger and frustration; disappointment and failure. They were:

- **Extrapunitiveness**: the habit, tendency or preference to unfairly and unreasonably (but skilfully) blame others.
- **Impunitiveness**: this is to simply deny one's role in the failure or indeed to challenge whether the failure is one at all.
- **Intropunitiveness**: this is the tendency to both exaggerate failure but also to blame themselves too harshly with excessive guilt.

In an original piece by Dattner and Hogan (2011) the personality disorders were arranged around this model. Again, they have tried to provide different labels for the personality disorders making them more memorable and hopefully easier to understand by non-experts.

As one may expect there is a considerable overlap between these various descriptions. Table 6.7 illustrates their theory.

Table 6.7   The Dattner and Hogan model

A. Blames Others (Extrapunitive)	
Excitable: 'Volatile Guardian':	Overreacts to minor mistakes; Determines failure prematurely
Cautious: 'Sensitive Retirer':	Expects failure to occur; Is too defensive to learn from feedback
Sceptical: 'Wary Watcher':	Believes he will be unfairly blamed; Sees only criticism in constructive advice
Leisurely: 'Rationalizing Blamer':	Looks for and offers up excuses; Often blames whoever assigned the task
B. Denies Blame (Impunitive)	
Bold: 'Big Person on Campus':	Becomes angry or hurt when blamed; Ingratiates herself with her superiors in the hope of avoiding blame

(Continued)

Mischievous: 'High-Wire Walker':	Denies his role in failure; may deny that failure has even occurred; Distorts information to avoid blame
Reserved: 'Indifferent Daydreamer':	Ignores potentially helpful feedback : Seems not to care about failure or blame
Colourful: 'Thespian':	Expects forgiveness for any and all failures; Would rather be blamed than ignored
Imaginative: 'Assertive Daydreamer':	Offers complex explanations for failures; Seems anxious about being blamed in the future but indifferent in the present
C. Blames Oneself (Intropunitive)	
Diligent: 'Micromanager':	Criticizes himself for even minor issues and problems
Dutiful: 'Martyr'	Accepts more blame than she deserves in order to preserve work relationships. Blames herself so harshly that others typically refrain from criticising her

The eleven personalities above have dysfunctional reactions to blame.

6.3 Supportive evidence: The research

There is now a growing research base using the HDS and investigating dark-side factors at work (Furnham & Trickey, 2011). A number of writers have pointed out the paradox that whilst dark-side traits may help you up the greasy pole of management, they do, in the end, derail people. Thus, Furnham et al. (2013a) found that Bold, Mischievous and Colourful (Narcissistic, Psychopathic and Histrionic) (Moving Against) types tended to get more quickly promoted than others. Another study found those who scored high on Sales Potential scored high on Mischievous, Colourful and Imaginative; whilst managerial potential was associated with high scores on Bold, Imaginative and Diligent (Furnham et al., 2012).

There is certainly evidence that a person's dark-side profile relates, independently of their skills and values, to the jobs they are attracted to and thrive in. Some studies have looked at those who are attracted to the private vs the public sector (Furnham et al.,

2014b; Oldham & Skodol, 1991). The pattern is predictable: those in the public sector tend to score highly on the Moving Away (Sceptical, Reserved) and Moving Toward (Diligent, Dutify) but lower on Moving Against (Bold, Mischievous, Colourful) than those in the private sector.

There have been some interesting, small scale studies, in this area. One of the very first papers in this area was by Moscoso and Salgado (2004) who tested eighty-five Spanish adults on a Dysfunctional Personality Style questionnaire. They were rated by their supervisors eight months into the job on issues like quality of performance, learning ability, support for colleagues, rules accomplishment, effort, initiative and global performance. These ratings were combined into three scores. There results were interesting and can be seen in the adapted table below (see Table 6.8). Three observations can be made:

1. First, nearly all the correlations were negative indicating the higher one scored on the dark-side factors the lower the performance.
2. Second, the correlations were modest though a third were around $r = .30$.
3. Some dark-side factors like Passive-Aggressive and Schizotypal were much more clearly correlated with job performance than others (Borderline and Histrionic).

Table 6.8 Correlations between the personality styles and overall, task and contextual performance (N = 85)

Personality Disorder	Task	Contextual	Contextual
Narcissistic	−.06	−.22*	−.18
Paranoid	−.25*	−.32**	−.33**
Sadistic	.09	−.11	−.12
Avoidant	−.31**	−.27*	−.31**
Depressive	−.30**	−.27*	−.31**
Passive-Aggressive	−.32**	−.34**	−.37**
Schizotypal	−.35**	−.45**	−.45**
Borderline	−.15	−.15	−.17

(*Continued*)

Personality Disorder	Task	Contextual	Contextual
Schizoid	.19	.17	.20
Compulsive	.10	.05	.07
Histrionic	−.04	.07	.03
Antisocial	−.31**	−.21**	−.27**
Dependant	.24*	−.12	−.18

Another small scale study looked at 117 New Zealand CEOs and the relationship between their dark side and leadership. They found three significant correlations: Those who were rated high on transformational leadership tended to be low of the Cautious and Reserved but high on the Colourful scale. They also found that being Bold was associated with Inspirational Motivation which they argued was the result of dramatization of issues used by those with charisma.

One study looked at the dark-side correlates of innovation. Zibarrass et al. (2008) looked at dark side correlates of motivation to change (persistence and ambition), challenging behaviour (risk-taking and non-conformity), adaptation (evolution not revolution) and consistency of work styles (methodological and systematic). They found that Cautious people who scored low on everything but that four dark-side traits (Arrogant/Bold; Manipulative/Mischievous; Dramatic/Colourful; Eccentric/Imaginative) were positively associated with the first two measures that were both linked to innovation, but negatively related to the last two which were not. Their conclusion from further analysis was that people who score high on the 'Moving Against People' cluster tend to be more innovative.

In a much bigger study, Carson et al. (2012) looked at 1796 employees in a global retail organization. They were particularly interested in how two of the higher order dark-side factors namely Moving Against and Moving Away related to such things as job tenure, being fired and leaving the organization. The results showed, as predicted, that those managers with dysfunctional Moving Against tendencies were more likely to leave either being fired or twitting. They concluded thus:

Our findings thus support the contention that derailment potential is related to the presence of 'moving against' tendencies and not merely the absence of functional or effective personality traits (i.e., conscientiousness and extraversion). In contrast, our results showed that "moving away" tendencies evidenced a slight negative correlation with the behaviors characteristic of the potential to derail. Managers who exhibit the tendency to "move away from people" express needs for self-sufficiency, independence, and perfection (Horney, 1950). Such needs may interfere with the ability to work collaboratively in the workplace; however, managers' who exhibit these needs may be perceived as maintaining rigorous performance standards and expecting a great deal from themselves and their subordinates. These qualities may help managers to overcome some of the derailment potential behaviors, including failing to deliver results and failing to take a stand. Our results also indicate that dysfunctional interpersonal tendencies relate to involuntary turnover directly. (p. 301)

One central question is when, why and how (if ever) dark-side traits are associated with Leadership. Many have made the point that 'moderate' scores on the dark-side traits tend to be associated with leadership success, whilst extreme scores predict failure and derailment (Kaiser et al., 2014). Thus, extremes were related to Enabling, Strategic and Operational leadership. The Moving Against Leaders are therefore good at making bold moves, setting direction and supporting innovation but weak at monitoring performance, focusing resources and getting the details right. There is a cost benefit analysis with dark-side traits.

In an important meta-analysis Gaddis and Foster (2013) looked at the relationship between the dark-side factors and eight managerial behaviours including trustworthiness, work attitudes, leading others, decision making and problem solving, achievement orientation, dependability, adaptability/flexibility and interpersonal skills. They summarized their findings (see Table 6.9) thus:

The Excitable, Sceptical, Cautious, Reserved and Leisurely scales comprising Horney's (1950) 'moving away from others' factor were responsible for 26 of 43 statistically significant outcomes across criteria. All five scales negatively predicted overall managerial performance and leading others, and a majority of these scales negatively predicted work attitude, making effective decisions, and being perceived as a dependable leader. The Bold, Mischievous, Colorful and Imaginative scales comprising Horney's (1950) 'moving against others' factor accounted for 13 statistically significant outcomes, with all four scales negatively predicting managerial trustworthiness and individual scales negatively predicting work attitude, achievement orientation, dependability, adaptability and interpersonal skills. However, these tendencies showed mixed results for overall managerial performance and positively predicted leading others. Finally, the Diligent and Dutiful scales comprising Horney's (1950) 'moving toward others' factor predicted only 4 of 43 statistically significant outcomes. Scores on the Diligent scale negatively predicted dependability and interpersonal skills, with Dutiful scores showing mixed findings for trustworthiness and leading others. However, neither of these scales predicted overall managerial performance. (pp. 18–19)

Table 6.9 Dark Side Traits at Work

Job Performance	There is a negative relationship for most traits
Citizenship Behaviour	With few exceptions (Dependent Personality) dark-side traits are associated with low communal, citizenship behaviour
Counterproductive Behaviour at Work	This is positively related to many traits
Creative Performance	There is often a positive relationship though the relationship is non-linear
Training	Many dark-side traits are associated with overconfidence but low learning and development
Interviewing	Many dark-side traits are associated with interviewing success
Leadership	They can play a role in both success and failure
Managerial Derailment	There are many cases of this
Abusive Supervision	This is clearly linked to callous, malicious and destructive traits

They conclude:

> Dark personality represents a naturally intriguing aspect of day-to-day functioning, as evidenced by the cursory review of popular coverage on the topic at the beginning of this article. These characteristics seem to be helpful in explaining a wide range of work behavior, some dark and some normal. Additionally, there could be dividends paid from investing in this area. It is clear that dark personality is only sometimes negative; understanding how dark personality characteristics' effects are moderated could help us to build more effective theories of individual differences, generally. That is, attempting to understand when dark personality characteristics have the good or more-expected bad consequences may help us to understand specific work contexts more clearly. (p. 20)

As the data gets bigger and more sophisticated so the results are more complex. In an important study of nearly 1000 American cadet soldiers over time Harms et al. (2011) looked at dark-side correlates of various ratings (i.e. communication, conduct, courage, sense of duty) over three years. There results were not entirely as they expected. They pondered their findings thus:

Debates over the personality disorders continue. However what has been most useful is the observation that underlying *all* the personality disorders are a very limited number of issues. The first is the ability to initiate and maintain healthy, happy, productive and long-term relationships both inside and outside the workplace. Given that leadership and management is a 'contact sport' it seems clear why that is so important.

The second issue concerns is self-awareness. It is self-evident that people do better if they are aware of their strengths and limitations; how and when they 'buckle' under stress and what sort of situations help and hinder their work.

Using the DSM framework, try to explain why and how people with particular dark-side profiles have problems with relationships and self-awareness.

Finally, in an important and neglected paper entitled 'Disordered Personalities at Work', Board and Fritzon (2005) suggested that it was possible to understand all the personality disorders on two dimensions: Friendly-Hostile and Dominant-Submissive. In their study they compared the profiles of three groups: Forensic Patients imprisoned in a Maximum Security prison in the UK; a psychiatric sample and a smaller group of British senior managers. What, of course, was most interesting is where there were *no differences* between the three groups. There were no differences on Narcissistic or Compulsive disorders between the four groups. Interestingly the business managers were also no different from the psychiatric patients on Borderline and Passive-Aggressive disorders. They conclude: 'The reason why people with a PD profile such as that of the business manager sample progress to positions of legitimate power and authority, rather than some socially deviant alternative remains perplexing' (p. 28)

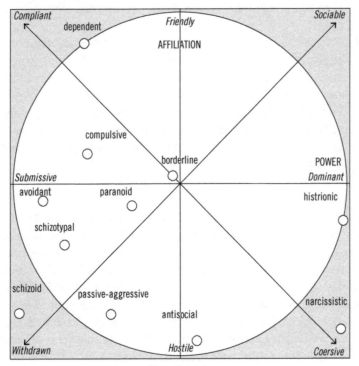

Figure 6.1   DSM-IV personality disorder.

6.4 The dark triad account

A second account can, to some extent, be seen as a short-version of the personality disorders account as it uses two of the personality disorders to attempt to explain the cause of derailment. There is a relatively new area of research into a concept called the 'Dark Triad' which is an individual differences construct proposed by Paulhus and Williams (2002). The use of the term 'dark' reflects the idea that these traits, independently and together, have interpersonally aversive qualities. They are described as follows:

- Narcissism is characterized by a vanity, arrogance egotism and a lack of empathy. People who score highly on this trait want others to admire them, pay attention to them. They expect special favours from others and they are very hungry for prestige and personal status.
- Machiavellianism is characterized by manipulative exploitation of others, a cynical disregard for laws and morals and a focus on self-interest and deception. They use flattery and lies to get what they want and almost revel in their skill at duping others,
- Psychopathy is characterized by antisocial behaviour, impulsivity, selfishness, callousness, and remorselessness. They seem totally insensitive to the feelings of others and deeply cynical about human nature.

When Paulhus and Williams (2002) introduced the Dark Triad into individual differences research they did so because they noticed an overlap of similar features, specifically 'all three entail a socially malevolent character with behaviour tendencies toward self-promotion, emotional coldness, duplicity, and aggressiveness' (p. 557). They did not give a specific theoretical reason for why the three should or would be related or studied together. Their reasoning was based on the observed similarities between the triad. There are two areas of research which do give some substance to the dark triad.

It should be pointed out that although there is an extensive literature on co-morbidity in the personality disorders there is little actual clinical data on the co-morbidity of psychopathic and narcissistic disorder. They however both belong in Cluster B. There are many attempts to make distinctions between different types of psychopaths (i.e. distempered, charismatic) and narcissists but the only data available is where scholars have measures of both variables. The most convincing literature on the relationship of these two disorders lies in two types of data. First, factor analytic studies where both disorders load similarly highly on the same factor (Furnham & Crump, 2005; Furnham & Trickey, 2011; Hogan & Hogan, 1997). Second, others that show when correlated with other self-, other-report and behavioural measures the results are similar (Moscoso & Salgado, 2004; Khoo & Burch, 2008) in that both psychopathic and narcissistic traits have similar correlates.

Paulhus, in his presentation titled 'The Dark Tetrad of Personality: Relevance to Nefarious Groups', suggests that Narcissists, Machiavellians and Psychopaths all have a high degree of callousness therefore making it a key feature of the Dark Triad. Those that are callous feel no emotion and/or feel or show no sympathy for others. Perhaps this is a function of low levels of the Big Five factor Agreeableness. To not feel emotion or show or feel sympathy for someone else may be because their characteristic disagreeable nature, branded by cold egocentrism and realism, makes it logical to not have or show emotion or be moved by pleas of pity so that they can more easily manipulate those around them and their environments.

Jonason et al. (2010) gave three explanations for how those beliefs would be functionally adaptive and related to the triad, each corresponding to a particular triad construct. They *first* proposed that because those who score higher on the Dark Triad are conceptualized as more *agentic* (Jonason, Li & Teicher, 2010), meaning proactive in the manipulation of their environments, they are more successful in the control of outcomes, and therefore more accurate in their perceptions. Machiavellianism may be the contributor to this situation with their characteristic manipulative nature. The *second* proposition is that narcissism facilitates *social exploitation* through high degrees of self-confidence because of previous findings that communicating confidently increases persuasiveness (London, 1973). This may be true when conceptualizing the Dark Triad as a 'frequency-dependent, "cheater" strategy' (Mealey, 1995). The *third* alternative is related to those who score higher on the Dark Triad and their exploitation of high-risk, high-payoff niches like 'gambling for high stakes'. In their study, Jonason, Koenig and Tost (2010) incorporate this gambling question as part of their conceptualization of psychopathy, thus relating the exploitation of the niche to the individual difference. However, though plausible, these claims require further research to support them.

There is plenty of evidence to suggest people with elevated Dark Triad scores will have problems at work. They tend to be impulsive, sensation-seeking, risk-takers (Jonason, 2014). They tend to revel in schadenfreude, the experience of pleasure at another's misfortune.

There have been attempts to describe why the Dark Triad is related to derailment and work problems. Social Exchange theory suggests that employees work in exchange for direct, specific rewards such as pay, as well as indirect, socioemotional rewards such as status and admiration. You give and you get. 'These exchanges create relationships among employees and employers, which are strengthened when (a) the rewards are valued ones and any costs created by the relationships are minimized; (b) exchange partners trust each other to fulfil their obligations over the long term; (c) the exchange is judged to be a fair one, with fairness defined primarily by mutual adherence to the norm of reciprocity; and (d) both parties develop a psychological commitment to the relationship, as indicated by increased affective attachment, a sense of loyalty, mutual support, and a authentic concern for the other's well-being' (O'Boyle et al., 2012, p. 559).

Because 'People of the Dark Triad' are selfish and self-serving, their valuation of rewards and costs, willingness to overlook obligations and reciprocity, and lack of emotional commitment to others likely undermine work relationships. Machiavellians are cynical and distrustful, and less likely to assume that they will be paid reciprocally for any extra effort they put in on the job. Narcissists feel they always outperform their fellow co-workers so that rules about reciprocity and obligation do not apply to them. Psychopaths' celebrated insensitivity to others' means they are less likely to act in ways that will please or help others.

In a big and important meta-analysis of over 40,000 people O'Boyle et al. (2012) were able to show that the Dark Triad was associated with Counter-Work Behaviour. However they found very little relationship between the Dark Triad and work performance because of the power of two moderating factors. The first was authority and showed the more power a DT person had because they were in higher positions of authority, the more dangerous they were and likely to cause problems. The second was organizational culture which showed the more the corporate culture was collectivistic and stressed organizational commitment and citizenship behaviour the less the influence of those with DT. More interesting perhaps they concluded, as have others that although the three DT traits are positively related they are sufficiently distinctive 'to warrant theoretical and empirical partitioning'. (p. 557)

Of these three constructs Machiavellianism is the only one that is not traditionally seen as a clinical syndrome (i.e. a personality disorder), but rather, a 'normal' personality belief dimension or personal philosophy characterized by cynical, manipulative behaviour, expedient and self-interested rather than principled behaviour and cold affect. A measure was derived from a selection of statements from Machiavelli's original books and experimental and correlational work by Christie and Geis (1970) called the Mach-IV inventory.

Psychological work in the area goes back to the early work of Christie and Geis (1970) who in their first chapter noted four characteristics of people who had this style (trait, syndrome, disorder). They are as follows:

- A relative lack of affect in interpersonal relationships, low in empathy, little concern for moral, task oriented.
- A lack of concern with conventional morality. They are often amoral as well as immoral with a utilitarian perspective.
- A lack of gross psychopathology. They have good reality checks and do not fit into any other established category.
- Low ideological commitment: short-term, tactical goal achievement is their major task.

Christie and Geis (1970) end their groundbreaking book with a chapter called 'implications and speculation'. They start off by admitting concern about the exclusively negative connotations surrounding the concept. Are all Machs shadowy and unsavoury manipulators? They seem self-insightful, more willing to admit unsavoury traits and impressive negotiators. Certainly high and low Machs see each other differently. The former see the latter as naïve, out-of-touch and unrealistic, whilst the low Machs see their high Mach brethren as immoral, inhuman and both lacking in compassion and faith in others.

This model leads the authors to ask under what conditions would a Mach show better or worse leadership behaviour. They believe it has to do primarily with the structure of the organization. They note:

> In general, our observations and theoretical position suggest that anyone extremely low on Mach would make a poor administrator. He would be too likely to become affectively involved with those whom he was presumably supervising and lack the detachment necessary to depersonalise his relationships with them when a cognitive analysis of the situation was necessary. In almost any organisation hard decisions have to be made which have negative consequences for some of its members – decisions such as not promoting or even firing an ineffective worker who is a nice guy, knowing when to tell people to shape up and being able to do so, and a host of other contingencies which demand taking a hard line for the benefit of the organisation. The problem with extremely high-Mach administrators is that their cool cognitive analysis of the needs of the organisation coupled with a disregard for the individual needs of those within it could quite easily lead to disaffection and problems or morale which can cripple the organisation. (p. 243)

Various researchers have looked at Machs at work. Graham (1996) argued that political skill was essential for many jobs like project management. They need to be highly task oriented; they need tight and efficient controls and they need to resist social influence. They need to be energetic and self-assured, focused on results and have good communications, negotiation and problem solving ability. In fact he found Machs' scores did not relate to project management success, though he did speculate that this may be due to all project managers needing decent, guile and manipulation to do their job well.

Becker and O'Hare (2007) looked at Machs' organizational good citizen behaviour or the frequency of going above or beyond the call of duty to help their employer or co-workers. It concerned the extent to which Machiavellianism was related to acts of altruism, co-operation and helpfulness as well as gestures of goodwill. Inevitably they expected Machiavellianism to be associated with little of the above but paradoxically to try hard to give the impression that they did. They were likely to try to cultivate a good impression especially with the boss. Their 'latitude for improvization' makes them good impression managers.

The work on the Dark Triad has really taken off. There are now commercial measures available which purport to be able to measure the dark triad in a work setting.

6.5 The maladaptive personality account

There have been many attempts to 'marry' the classic personality models from psychology and the work of the psychiatrists on the personality disorders. The idea was to express the one in terms of the other. The result is a fivefold model where Negative Affect is Low Emotional Stability (high Neuroticism), Detachment (Low Extraversion), Antagonism (Low Agreeableness) Disinhibition (Low Conscientiousness) and Psychoticism (High Openness).

Moreover, what has proved to be very attractive is to describe a personality type or category that applies to derailment in the workplace. This has led a group of work psychologists to attempt to describe what has been titled 'The Maladaptive Personality'. Indeed an entire issue of the journal *Industrial and Organizational Psychology (Vol. 7)* was dedicated to this concept.

The researchers on this topic have recently tried to spell out distinctive traits that are most clearly manifest in the maladaptive personality (Dilchert et al., 2014) (Table 6.10).

Table 6.10 The most maladaptive behaviours

Antagonism	This is defined as manifesting behaviours that put people at odds with others. It has various components, such as manipulativeness (using seduction, charm, glibness, ingratiation), deceitfulness (dishonesty, fabrication, fraudulence), grandiosity (self-centredness, entitlement, superiority), attention-seeking (seeking admiration) and callousness (lack of guilt, remorse).
Disinhibition	This is defined as manifesting behaviours that lead to immediate gratification with no thought to the past or future. It has various components, such as irresponsibility (no honouring of obligations or commitments), impulsivity (spur of the moment, immediate responses), sloppiness (no quality control), distractibility (inability to concentrate) and risk-taking (looking for dangerous, self-damaging activities).
Detachment	This is defined as showing behaviours that are associated with social avoidance and lack of emotion. It has various components, such as social withdrawal (preference for being alone), anhedonia (inability to experience pleasure), depressivity (feeling down, miserable, hopeless), intimacy avoidance (social and sexual avoidance) and suspiciousness (mild paranoia).
Negative affect	This is defined as experiencing anxiety, depression, guilt, shame, anger and worry. It has components such as emotional liability (intense and unstable emotions), anxiety (prone to nervousness, tension, panic), restricted affectivity (constricted emotional expression), hostility (persistent anger and irritability) perseveration (repeating dysfunctional behaviour), and submissiveness (subordinating oneself to others).
Psychoticism	This is about displaying odd, unusual and bizarre behaviours. It includes having many peculiar beliefs and experiences (telekinesis, hallucination-like experiences), eccentricity (in looks, dress, speech), cognitive and perceptual dysregulation (odd thought processes). Some may see them as creative, others in need of therapy.

Dilchert et al. (2014) were at pains to distinguish between maladaptive traits and maladaptive behaviours in work settings. This refers to whether the behaviour is maladaptive for the individual vs the organization. If the individual manifests maladaptive behaviour that does not impede their work this is more likely to be the manifestation on a trait.

They note:

> Behaviors should be considered maladaptive when they hinder positive personal occupational behavior such as job performance, as well as extrinsic success (e.g. achievements in career progression, compensation growth) or intrinsic success (e.g. personal growth, satisfaction). For example, maladaptive behaviors such as self-injurious behaviors (e.g. self-biting, cutting, hair pulling), ritualistic behaviors (e.g. obsessive hand washing), and aberrant behaviors can affect personal success and well-being at work but cannot reasonably be included among CWB. When such behaviors do not prevent the employee from fulfilling essential functions of their job, screening for traits at the root of these behaviors becomes problematic On the other hand, inappropriate interpersonal behaviors (e.g. swearing, screaming), property destruction, and aggression (e.g. hitting others) are both maladaptive and counterproductive at work, and organizations have legitimate reasons for predicting and preventing them. Maladaptive traits can be expected to predict appropriately matched maladaptive behaviors in the workplace.
>
> Maladaptive traits can also relate to job performance at the global and facet levels. The DSM-5 maladaptive personality constructs antagonism and disinhibition predict CWB. Some maladaptive range traits (e.g., risk-taking, distractibility) can give rise to poor task performance. Others can impact employability as in the case of psychotic incapacitation (e.g. due to cognitive and perceptual dysregulation) or severe interpersonal problems. (pp. 106–107)

Guenole (2014) suggested that the conception was particularly useful for work psychologists to explore the darkness. However, he spelt out five reasons why people seem reluctant to use these tests (Table 6.11).

Table 6.11 Reasons why people are reluctant to use dark side tests

Litigation	The essence of the issue is whether it can be shown that the test (of aptitude or attitude) measures something that is clearly predictive of relevant job performance. Tests that are designed to measures darkness, deviance and disorders perhaps do not always qualify. Legal constraints may require you to show how these tests are job related in a very specific situation. This can be done, but the cost and effort put people off.
Social Responsibility	Is a personality disorder a disability, like a physical disability? Is this another way of punishing people with mental disorders such as depression? The law says that you cannot discriminate on anything that is unrelated to job performance.
Too small gains	Whilst it is possible to show empirically that the dark side is related to poor performance the effects are quite small. That is, given how relatively deep the dark-side problems are, their effects are too trivial to worth getting excited about. There may be relatively few people who derail at senior levels, but they can seriously rock the boat.
Value for money	In psychometric jargon the terms used are 'incremental validity' and 'construct redundancy'. 'Brightside' normal personality questionnaires on their own can be used to indicate dark-side issues. This is usually done by a combination of using extreme scores and particular profiles. So you can see darkness when looking at the light and might think it is pretty redundant to use more different tests. But the data suggest otherwise. If you choose to use a dark-side measure you get much more clarity.
Faking	All tests are transparent and the applicants can easily see through them. Worse, it is the deviants who fake most and come out looking adapted, whilst the nice guys who respond honestly tend to get tarred by the dark-side pathology.

There have been various comments on the Maladaptive Big Five (MB5) as it has been called (Desimone, 2014; Wille & DeFrugt, 2014). Some were concerned about how much the Maladaptive Personality approach adds (Christiansen et al., 2014), whilst others are more concerned with the application of the theory to the workplace.

It is the case that this account of derailment is not radically different from the personality disorders account though it probably relies as much on the bright-side normal personality scheme. Furthermore, it remains to be empirically tested.

6.6 The Freudian account

Inevitably those with a psychodynamic orientation have been interested in the dark side (Vince & Mazen, 2014). They often see the motives of people to respond to unwelcomed and often unconscious fears and obsessions like fear of failure, fear of intimacy and fear of rejection. They also tend to stress the tension between intra-psychic forces like Hogan's 'Get Along' and 'Get Ahead' tensions.

The most articulate and productive psychoanalytic account of leadership failure has been called the *Inner Theatre* Approach pioneered by Manfred Kets de Vries. The concept of inner theatres relates to questions that we ask about individuals: 'what are the things that motivate you?' or 'what do you feel most passionately about?' He believes it is deeply important to answer these questions as if you do not know what you are thinking, what you are doing or what you are all about, it is hard to be effective in many ways.

In 'The Leader on the Couch', Kets de Vries (2006a) defines our inner theatre as 'the stage on which the major themes that define the person are played out' (p. 12). The concept of inner theatres relates to questions that we ask about individuals: *'what are the things that motivate you?'* or *'what do you feel most passionately about?'* He argues that to get a better understanding of ourselves, we must explore our inner theatre, and pay attention to our wishes, desires, and fantasies. It is important to focus on human unconsciousness and how it impacts our perception of reality and the reasons behind our own actions in regards to the tripartite personality. The impact of unconscious drivers on our everyday life is profound, and it has an important role to play in the work environment.

Beyond the 'curtain of our inner theatre' is a 'vibrant tragicomic play' being acted upon our inner stage, with the key characters representing our loved ones, those we have feared, hated and admired. These internal figures have a strong influence on the development of our values, beliefs and attitudes which create the foundation of our personality, preferred leadership styles and actions. The inner play has a large impact on how we form friendships, our artistic expressions, and also how we form relationships with our bosses, colleagues and subordinates as well as how we make decisions.

Kets de Vries suggests that our inner theatres develop through nature–nurture interactions, generating a genetic predisposition to behavioural patterns. These patterns are not fixed, but 'rewiring' occurs throughout our lifetime in response to developmental factors we are exposed to, especially our early experiences.

Motivational needs systems (MNS) determine the uniqueness of our internal theatre; these are the rational forces behind perceivably irrational behaviours. It is the interaction between our MNS and environmental factors (especially human factors) that define our uniqueness, manifesting mental schema that guide our relationships with others. These mental representations of ourselves, others and relations help us understand all aspects of reality. MNS are determined by three forces: innate learned response patters, role of significant caretakers and the extent to which the individual attempts to recreate positive emotional states experienced in infancy/childhood. Mental schema or 'templates' emerge through their interactions throughout life. These create symbolic model scenes and are the 'scripts' of our inner production.

Two other higher-level systems influence the work situations more profoundly: the attachment/affiliation need system and the exploration/assertion need system:

(a) **Need for affiliation**/attachment derives from the humanness revealed in seeking relationships. This need for attachment can be extrapolated to groups, where we desire affiliation. Both serve an emotional balancing role and attribute to a person's self-worth and self-esteem.

(b) **The Need for exploration**/assertion is manifested soon after birth where prolonged states of arousal occur in infants with the discovery of novelty and its consequences. This continues into adulthood because striving, competing, and seeking mastery are fundamental characteristics of the human personality.

Whilst the person's inner script is determined by MNS, the themes of it develop over time and reflect the pre-eminence of our inner wishes that contribute to our unique personality style. These are known as Core Conflict Relationship Themes (CCRT). CCRT develop over time with our MSN and take a prominent role inside us. They make a vital contribution to who we are and how we respond to others. Our basic wishes are reflected in our life scripts, and the CCRT adds the nuances and shading to make us unique. We bring our rose-tinted glasses, shaded by the CCRT, to work which govern our reactions and expectations, which can differ from reality.

Our basic wishes influence our scripts, our scripts shape our relationships which determine the way we believe others will respond to us and how we should respond to others. These wishes include being loved, noticed, understood, etc. We take these wishes to our workplace and project them onto others, then anticipate their reactions. In turn, we react to the perceived reaction, not the actual one. A leader's dominant style derives from his primary CCRT. The life-scripts drawn as children are not applicable to adults and thus cause a dizzying merry-go-round that takes affected leaders into a self-destructive cycle of repetition.

The leader who embraces introspection is one that will be more successful; the journey into the dark of their inner theatre may be frightening, but it will reveal where they want to go, what they want to achieve, and (most likely) how they wish to proceed. By using a 360°

feedback instrument, executives can answer the important, unanswered questions of *'what are your strengths and weaknesses?'*. However, without exploring the inner theatre, without an understanding of the dramas and scripts that play continually, it is impossible to understand behaviour and character traits holistically, let alone how these impact on leadership style and how to change them.

Whilst everyone has an inner theatre, the books, research and literature on this topic are generally concerned with the theatre of the executives due to the power and influence of their wields. Dysfunctional behaviour thus occurs when we try to keep the curtain closed; the show must go on after all.

To be an effective leader, you need to know what you are doing and what you are all about: what are you good and bad at? If you are not good at something, how can you work on that or find someone who can complement you? It is generally understood that a certain degree of narcissism is necessary for leadership success. Therefore to understand life in organizations, it is essential to understand narcissism.

Basic group assumptions, social defences and toxic organizational ideals don't materialize from nowhere; they have a history. Repetition of phenomena such as neurotic organizations imply the existence of shared scripts in the inner theatre of power holders.

Organizations tend to reflect their leaders as they externalize and act out their production on the stage that is the organization. These inner dramas develop into corporate culture, structures, and specific patterns of decision-making. Through this, they 'institutionalize' their inner theatre, allowing it to play out even after they're gone.

Successful leaders help companies become effective; dysfunctional ones live out their fantasies and contribute to a dysfunctional organizational culture. Though each organization is unique, there are 5 dominant organizational 'constellations' with its own leadership style, executive personality, corporate culture and underlying theme.

Kets de Vries (2012, 2013) has written many interesting papers about specific issues and syndromes. In all his work he stresses the importance of self-knowledge and insight. For instance in a paper entitled '*What do executives want out of life?*' he suggests people ask themselves some searching questions:

What do you want out of life? What does success actually mean to you? Do you have an idea where this desire to be successful comes from? List what you perceive as important to feeling successful in order of priority. What do you need to do in order to be successful? Do you feel that you have to pay a price in order to be successful? What would you be willing to give up in pursuing what you have defined as success? How far are you prepared to go to acquire wealth? Would you be prepared to do things you hate in order to make tons of money? Would you be prepared to sacrifice your health and/or your principles in order to be successful? Do you need an audience to recognize your success? Who would that audience be? What would you do in life if you couldn't fail?

6.7 The strengths (overused) as weakness account

A number of scholars have tried to explain management derailment in terms of what is sometimes called the overdrive, shadow or overused strengths. The idea is that strengths become weaknesses because they are essentially overused. Rather than confront weaknesses or learn new skills the potentially derailing manager relies on, and overuses their strengths which may be inappropriate for the situation.

Scholars in the area of Strengths Psychology have identified twenty-four strengths which can be classified into six Virtues. People are encouraged to try to identify and use their strengths, rather than confront their weaknesses.

Pendleton and Furnham (2012) had a similar approach sometimes called the incomplete manager approach. It is based on two dimensions: Competence and Personality. There are four components:

1. A **natural strength** where a person has a competency which is helped by their personal makeup/ the idea is **WORK WITH** this ability.
2. A **potential strength** where they do not have a competency but their personality would help them acquire and express it of they had it. They are therefore encouraged to **WORK ON** it.
3. A **fragile strength** where a potential leader has relevant competency but their personality hinders the expression of it. Again, the advice is the **WORK ON** this topic.
4. A **resistant limitation** where person does not have a competency nor the personality profile to support it. They are advised to **WORK AROUND** the issue.

The overuse of strengths has now been identified as one of the causes of leadership derailment, as well as of diminished effectiveness. The basic premise of positive psychology is the focus on what makes life good and not what it makes it unbearable, such as mental illness, which is the basic focus of mainstream psychology. It is 'strength-based' and it aims in making leaders aware of their strengths in order to take advantage of them and effectively apply them in their workplace. Recently, however, it has become notable that doing too much of what is considered a strength, can result in harmful effects on the team and its efficiency and therefore on the overall productivity.

The general pattern suggests that leaders should use what comes naturally to them – their strengths – and apply them in order to guide their team and encourage them to progress in order to ultimately increase the quality and quantity of their results. There are now a number of papers that challenge the strength based approach suggesting that overdoing or overusing strengths leads to derailing and lopsided leadership (Kaplan & Kaiser, 2009; Kaiser & Overfield, 2011).

Effectively (over) applying one's strengths is unwise for two reasons. First, most managers are often unaware of their strengths. This can be due to the fact that they are not open to affirmation of their positive qualities because they focus more on criticism as effective but also because they might consider it mere flattery. Another reason of ignoring one's strengths is the lack of self-awareness which is not a rare phenomenon. Personality scale, or coach feedback, is often necessary in order for one to exactly spot a real strength since very few people seem able to accurately assess their positive strengths by themselves. The second reason why strengths become weaknesses is because they are overused. This is when strengths become weaknesses.

Most researches assume a *linear positive relationship* between strengths and overall outcomes such as job satisfaction, performance, results, morale and others. However, it has been shown that the function is rather represented by *an inverted-U*, with the left side indicating 'too little', the peak point 'the right amount' and the right side 'too much' of the investigated behaviour. This behaviour represents one strength of the manager and is rated by their colleagues and subordinates.

It is often the case that managers will rate themselves as doing too little of a behaviour that their peers rate them as overdoing, which is another indication that they are not self-aware. A similar pattern is observed when measuring the overall effectiveness of the four major leadership styles – Enabling, Forceful, Strategic and Operational – in relation to two basic of performance of the manager's team, team vitality and team productivity. *Team vitality* addresses the way team members feel about the other team members as well as about the performance of the team. This aspect is measured in engagement, solidarity, individual's morale and other means of indicating the right functioning of a team. The second factor *team productivity* refers to the more tangible facets of a team and includes the results of the team's performance. It is measured in quantity and quality of the team's overall outcomes. These two factors are tightly interconnected with the four styles of leadership. It has been shown empirically by Kaiser and Kaplan that despite the type of leadership, team vitality and productivity are always optimal when the leadership style is also at the peak of the inverted-U shape, which represents the 'right amount' of the display of this style.

All management behaviours can be rated on a variety of scales. Some scales used to rate behaviours are: 'too little', 'right amount' and 'too much'. Many studies have shown that the optimal is in the middle of the shape. However, in many cases most managers are rated as displaying 'too much' of one specific leadership style and this is when it becomes a weakness. This happens because, when the manager over-does a behaviour that they consider strong, they are unable to accept criticism and unaware that this may actually prove harmful for their organization. Moreover, the strength becomes a weakness because it prohibits the manager from engaging in contrasting but complementary behaviours.

So finding and exploiting a strength can be a weakness. Being very kind can result in a leader not talking about poor performance; being very optimistic can make a leader insufficiently vigilant about problems ahead.

The four leadership styles identified by Kaiser and Kaplan come in opposing pairs: Forceful vs. Enabling and Strategic vs. Operational. Managers usually fall in the trap of viewing one type of each pair as the correct, best or optimal one. They tend to try to be one or the other depending on which suits their personality and skills. Then so-called lopsided leadership occurs. This happens when managers lean too much towards one leadership approach/style to the degree that they simultaneously ignore doing the opposing one.

Thus, a leader can display excellent technical skills but completely lack human skills. On the other side, someone who is too focused on execut-ing operational details is predestined to lose the bigger picture and lack strategic ability.

The goal of lopsided leaders and even of those who have not reached the extreme of derailment yet should be to add versatility to their skills and strengths. That is, work on the opposite. Yet, as ratings of colleagues have indicated, very few leaders are versatile and eager enough to try to 'balance' their approach.

Studies have shown that the most effective way to encourage versatility is the rating scale that follows the pattern of *'what should I stop doing, what should I continue doing and what should I start doing?'*. This three-phase question can clearly indicate to the managers the key aspects of their personalities that they overdo, and consequently those that they ignore. One can also prevent strengths becoming weaknesses by comparing self-evaluation with those of their colleagues. That way, they are also able to increase their self-awareness by viewing where they really stand in terms of whether what they think of themselves agrees with what others think of them.

The paradox of overused strengths relates to the spectrum hypothesis discussed earlier where extremes of anything are considered undesirable. Optimal is better than maximal.

6.8 Conclusion

This chapter looked at five accounts, or theoretical descriptions/explanations, for derailment: the personality disorders, dark triad, maladaptive personality, Freudian and Strengths overused account. Clearly there was great deal of overlap between these accounts, particularly the first three. All of these accounts are in some sense individualistic and pathologizing. They all see the major cause of derailment in the makeup of the leader themselves. They all underplay the role of the corporate and national environment (see Chapter 4) which equally plays an important role.

Chapter 7

The successful psychopath at work

7.1 Introduction

There is an extensive, compulsive and fascinating literature on the psychopaths among us. Films have made people think psychopaths are all deranged, axe-murderers and serial killers. They are also convicts and mercenaries; con artists and corporate executives.

This chapter will look at what Hare (1999) called 'White Collar' psychopaths and what are now often referred to as *successful psychopath*. If they are educated, good looking and intelligent, they can be lethal in the business world. They usually charm superiors, tolerate and manipulate peers and use and abuse juniors.

Boddy (2011) attempted to explain the rise in corporate psychopaths.

Before the last third of the twentieth century, large corporations were relatively stable and the idea of a job for life was evident, with employees slowly rising through the corporate ranks until they reached a position beyond which they were not qualified by education, intellect or ability to go. In such a stable, hierarchical, slowly changing environment employees got to know each other very well, and Corporate Psychopaths would have been noticeable and identifiable as undesirable managers because of their personality and ethical defects which would gradually be noticed over longitudinal periods of time by other employees. Changing companies mid-career was seen as questionable and inadvisable, and their rise would therefore have been blocked both within their original company and with external employers, who would question their reasons for changing jobs. However, once corporate takeovers and the resultant corporate changes, involving such activities as asset stripping, corporate streamlining and the shedding of non-core business activities, started to accelerate, exacerbated by globalisation and rapidly changing technological environment, corporate stability began to disintegrate. Jobs for life disappeared, stability lessened, job security decreased and not surprisingly, employees' commitment to their employers also lowered accordingly. Job switching first became understandable and acceptable, and then even became common, and employees increasingly found themselves working for unfamiliar organisations and with other people they did not know very well. (p. 164)

Babiak (1995) found five characteristics in the many studies of industrial psychopathy and various case studies. He has reported case studies of individuals and began to describe how they succeed despite their predisposition. He has noted from a series of case studies:

Comparison of the behaviour of the three subjects observed to date revealed some similarities: each a) began by building a network of one-to-one relationships with powerful and useful individuals, b) avoided virtually all group meetings where maintaining multiple facades may have been too difficult, and c) created conflicts which kept co-workers from sharing information about him. Once their power bases were established, d) co-workers who were no longer useful were abandoned and e) detractors were neutralised by systematically raising doubts about their competence and loyalty. In addition, unstable cultural factors, inadequate measurement systems, and general lack of trust typical of organisations undergoing rapid, chaotic change may have provided an acceptable cover for psychopathic behaviour. (pp. 184–185, emphases added)

In his book titled *Corporate Psychopaths: Organisational Destroyers*, Boddy (2011) noted: Once inside organisations, psychopaths identify a potential support network of patrons who can be flattered and befriended to help the Corporate Psychopath ascend to senior levels. They also identify pawns who can be used and manipulated as necessary and they identify potential opponents (auditors, security personnel, human resources personnel) who may try to block their rise if these people are not previously undermined, disenfranchised and emasculated. Corporate Psychopaths, then, manipulate their way up the corporate ladder, using pawns and shedding patrons as these people are superseded and no longer needed. According to Hare, two factions typically develop in the organisation: the network of supporters, pawns and patrons of the Corporate Psychopath, and the group of their detractors and those pawns who realise they have been used and abused or that the organisation is in danger. (p. 101)

Babiak and Hare (2006) believe that psychopaths are indeed attracted to today's business climate. They devised a questionnaire to help people at work spot them. There are, according to the authors, ten markers of the problem. The successful, industrial psychopath is characterized by the following. He or she:

1. Comes across as smooth, polished and charming.
2. Turns most conversations around to a discussion of him- or herself.
3. Discredits and puts down others in order to build up own image and reputation.
4. Lies to co-workers, customers or business associates with a straight face.
5. Considers people he or she has outsmarted or manipulated as dumb or stupid.
6. Opportunistic; hates to lose, plays ruthlessly to win.
7. Comes across as cold and calculating.
8. Acts in an unethical or dishonest manner.
9. Has created a power network in the organization and uses it for personal gain.
10. Shows no regret for making decisions that negatively affect the company, shareholders or employees.

Are corporate psychopaths more likely to be found in the public or private sector? Boddy (2011) has noted:

> However, other organisational research has found that public sector organi-
> sations are more political in terms of internal behaviour than commercial
> organisations are. Such political environments would seem ideal for smooth,
> conning and manipulative talents of Corporate Psychopaths. It may be that
> it is also easier for Corporate Psychopaths to hide their lack of effort in public
> sector organisations, as performance appraisals in such organisations are
> less objective in that they are not directly linked to external and objective
> performance indicators such as profits, as they often are in commercial
> organisations. This means that organisational politics can potentially play a
> bigger part in performance appraisals and promotions, and this gives advan-
> tage to those who are able to influence and manipulate others, as Corporate
> Psychopaths are able to do. On the other hand, ministerial control and
> public scrutiny in the public sector may serve as barriers to Corporate
> Psychopaths gaining the promotions and power that they crave and seek
> within public sector organisations. (p. 114)

Psychopaths can easily look like ideal leaders: smooth, polished, charming. They can quite easily mesh their dark side – bullying, amoral,
manipulative. In the past, it may be politics, policing, law, media and
religion that attracted psychopaths, but more and more it is the fast-
paced, exciting, glamorous world of business.

The issue with the psychopathic boss is whether they are subclinical vs.
clinical psychopaths and what in fact 'pushes' them over the limits. The
term 'psychopath' or 'sociopath' was used to describe antisocial personality types whose behaviour is amoral or asocial, impulsive and lacking
in remorse and shame. Once called 'moral insanity', it is found more
commonly among lower socio-economic groups, no doubt because of
the 'downward drift' of these types. However, it should be pointed out,
at the onset, that there are inevitably competing conceptualizations
and disagreements among experts.

Comparatively recently a number of popular books have appeared on
psychopaths (Ronson, 2011). There are also many websites, some

well researched, which help describe the symptoms of psychopathy as well as related terms like sociopath and antisocial personality disorder (ASPD). They mention memorable lines like the fact that whilst psychopaths are antisocial, many antisocial people are not psychopaths. Sociopaths are usually considered less abnormal but very aggressive and manipulative. Some try to make distinctions between different types of psychopaths like the charismatic, distempered or primary psychopath. Some of these popular books provide excellent summaries of the issues whilst other inevitably sensationalize and distort.

In a book entitled *Corporate Psychopaths: Organisational Destroyers*, Boddy (2011) describes corporate psychopaths thus:

> They seem to be unaffected by the corporate collapse they have created. They present themselves as glibly unbothered by the chaos around them, unconcerned about those who have lost their jobs, savings and investments, and lacking any regrets about what they have done. They cheerfully lie about their involvement in events, are very persuasive in blaming others for what has happened and have no doubts about their own continued worth and value. They are happy to walk away from the economic disaster that they have managed to bring about, with huge payoffs and with new roles advising governments hoe to prevent such economic disasters. (p. 1)

Boddy (2011) suggested that there are six identifiable outcomes of having corporate psychopaths: a heightened level of conflict; commitment to employees plummet dramatically; heavier than necessary organizational constraints; poorer communication and a blame culture; reduced employee job satisfaction; organizational withdrawal of many good employees. He suggests that:

> Corporate Psychopaths prefer to implement their self-serving plans unnoticed, but when they fear being found out, their strategy is to create chaos so that in the confusion they can avoid scrutiny and detection as the people around them in the organization concentrate on bringing order to the mess created. (p. 78)

Over the past twenty-five years there has been a sudden and dramatic rise in interest in psychopaths in the workplace where they go under various names like 'corporate destroyers' or 'snakes in suites'. There are many stories of 'ruthless bullies who rise to the top echelons of organisations, lying in wait to destroy not only companies and lives, but also economies' (Smith & Lilienfeld, 2013, p. 3). There are studies that have shown ASPD is associated with all sorts of counter-work behaviours like theft and aggression at work (Scherer et al., 2013) as well as low well-being and job satisfaction of those who work for corporate psychopathic supervisors (Mathieu et al., 2013). Studies have demonstrated that, self-evidently, corporate psychopaths respond unethically to business ethical dilemmas and seem very good at moral disengagement which portrays their behaviour as less harmful than it is, as well as diffusing responsibility and distorting consequences (Stevens et al., 2012). Indeed it is through the clever process of moral disengagement that so many psychopaths seem to get away with their unethical decision making.

However, a theme has been developing in this literature. It is that psychopathy at work is a double-edged sword in the sense that it can predispose to both positive and negative outcomes. If one considers just two dimensions that have been isolated: fearless dominance and self-centred impulsivity it seems clear that the former may really help people 'climb the greasy pole of business life' whilst the latter is associated with poor leadership.

The idea that a psychopath could be (highly) successful in business settings is based on the spectrum concept which suggests that one can have degrees of psychopathy. Thus, one can have a mild expression of behaviours in the form of a subclinical manifestation where certain behaviours like fearlessness, self-confidence and charm can be highly adaptive. Some of the ideas coming out of this literature are that psychopathic traits seem over-represented in certain groups like senior business people. Also, it is asserted that in business psychopathic traits are associated with lack of integrity, aggression and counter-productive behaviours. One study of American presidents concluded:

These findings indicate that the boldness associated with psychopathy is an important but heretofore neglected predictor of presidential performance, and suggest that certain features of psychopathy are tied to successful interpersonal behavior. (Lilienfeld et al., 2012)

Various studies have been done in these areas and many strong assertions made yet careful scholarship has shown that the evidence and the results are weak suggesting that we need to get better data before making simply minded statements (Smith & Lilienfeld, 2013).

7.2 Background

In his famous book *The Mask of Insanity*, Cleckley (1941) first set out ten criteria: superficial charm and intelligence; absence of anxiety in stressful situations; insincerity and lack of truthfulness; lack of remorse and shame; inability to experience love or genuine emotion; unreliability and irresponsibility; impulsivity and disregard for socially acceptable behaviour; clear-headedness with an absence of delusions or irrational thinking; inability to profit from experience; and lack of insight. The book is indeed a classic in psychology and psychiatry because of its insight. Cleckley noted the slick but callous business person, the smooth-talking and manipulative lawyer and the arrogant and deceptive politicians as psychopaths.

Cleckley identified sixteen personality traits that, through his work with such individuals, he believed captured the essence of the psychopathic personality. The following are Cleckley's sixteen traits:

1. Superficial charm and good 'intelligence'
2. Absence of delusions and other signs of irrational thinking
3. Absence of 'nervousness' or psychoneurotic manifestations
4. Unreliability
5. Untruthfulness and insincerity
6. Lack of remorse or shame

7. Inadequately motivated antisocial behaviour
8. Poor judgement and failure to learn by experience
9. Pathologic egocentricity and incapacity for love
10. General poverty in major affective reactions
11. Specific loss of insight
12. Unresponsiveness in general interpersonal relations
13. Fantastic and uninviting behaviour with drink and sometimes without
14. Suicide rarely carried out
15. Sex life impersonal, trivial and poorly integrated
16. Failure to follow any life plan

Cleckley stressed the personality dimensions of this disorder, and clearly believed that most psychopaths are not violent. Whilst he acknowledged that a substantial proportion of incarcerated individuals exhibit psychopathic traits, he asserted that the majority of psychopaths are not incarcerated. According to Cleckley, the psychopath...

is not likely to commit major crimes that result in long prison terms. He is also distinguished by his ability to escape ordinary legal punishments and restraints. Though he regularly makes trouble for society, as well as for himself, and frequently is handled by the police, his characteristic behaviour does not usually include committing felonies which would bring about permanent or adequate restrictions of his activities. He is often arrested, perhaps one hundred times or more. But he nearly always regains his freedom and returns to his old patterns of maladjustment. (p. 19)

7.3 Definitions

Various writers have tried to distinguish between subtly different types of psychopaths. These include: Primary psychopaths; Secondary [neurotic] psychopaths; Dissocial (antisocial) psychopaths; Inadequate psychopaths; Schizoid psychopaths; White-collar ('successful psychopaths'); Unsuccessful Psychopaths (individuals who get caught); Sexual psychopaths; 'Mild' psychopaths or 'subcriminal psychopaths'.

As with all psychiatric illnesses, there have been discussions and debates about definitions and terms. Babiak and Hare (2006) clarified the distinction between three overlapping terms:

Psychopathy is a personality disorder described by the personality traits and behaviours. Psychopaths are without conscience and incapable of empathy, guilt or loyalty to anyone but themselves. Sociopathy is not a formal psychiatric condition. It refers to patterns of attitudes and behaviours that are considered antisocial and criminal by society at large, but are seen as normal or necessary by the subculture or social environment in which they developed. Sociopaths may have a well-developed conscience and a normal capacity for empathy, guilt and loyalty, but their sense of right and wrong is based on the norms and expectations of their subculture or group. Many criminals might be described as sociopaths.

Anti-social personality disorder (APD) is a broad diagnostic category found in the American Psychiatric Association's Diagnostic and Statistical Manual of Mental Disorders, 4th edition (DSM-IV). Antisocial and criminal behaviours play a major role in its definition and, in this sense, APD is similar to sociopathy. Some of those with APD are psychopaths but many are not. The difference between psychopathy and antisocial personality disorder is that the former includes personality traits such as lack of empathy, grandiosity and shallow emotion that are not necessary for a diagnosis of APD. APD is three or four times more common than psychopathy in the general population and in prisons. The prevalence of those we would describe as sociopathic is unknown but likely is considerably higher than that of APD. (p. 19)

The new DSM-5 (APA, 2014) manual notes seven clear factors that identify those with ASPD (p. 659):

1. Failure to conform to social norms with respect to lawful behaviours, as indicated by repeatedly performing acts that are grounds for arrest.
2. Deceitfulness, as indicated by repeated lying, use of aliases, or conning others for personal profit or pleasure.

3. Impulsivity or failure to plan ahead.
4. Irritability and aggressiveness, as indicated by repeated physical fights or assaults.
5. Reckless disregard for safety of self or others.
6. Consistent irresponsibility, as indicated by repeated failure to sustain consistent work behaviour or honour financial obligations.
7. Lack of remorse, as indicated by being indifferent to or rationalizing having hurt, mistreated or stolen from another.

It was originally thought that the defining characteristics of psychopathy tend to fall on two dimensions. The *first* is socio-emotional where the psychopath is superficial and lacking in empathy, guilt or remorse. They are also deceitful and manipulative whilst being prone to egocentricity and grandiosity. The *second* is their social deviance associated with boredom susceptibility, impulsivity and lack of self control. In children they show evidence of behaviour problems and in adulthood antisocial behaviour.

More recently, it has been suggested that there are three themes that seem to characterize all psychopaths (Smith & Lilienfeld, 2013) (Table 7.1).

Table 7.1 Three features of all psychopaths

Disinhibition	Problems with impulse control leading to irresponsibility, unreliability and untrustworthiness
Boldness	Fearless, tolerant of ambiguity, able to deal with stress and become dominant
Meanness	Emotionally detached, defiant, competitive and rebellious

7.4 Popular descriptions

Oldham and Morris (2000) call these types '*Adventurous*'. Hogan and Hogan (2001) call the antisocial person '*Mischievous*'. They note that these types expect that others will like them and find them charming and they expect to be able to extract favours, promises, money and other resources from other people with relative ease. However, they see others as merely to be exploited, and therefore have problems maintaining commitments and are unconcerned about social, moral and economic expectations. They are self-confident to the point of feeling invulnerable and have an air of daring and sang-froid that others can find attractive and even irresistible. In industries where bold risk-taking is expected they can seem a very desirable person for senior management position.

Their self-deception, self-confidence and recklessness lead to lots of conflicts, but they have almost no ability to learn from experience. According to Hogan and Hogan (1997):

> They tend to be underachievers, relative to their talent and capabilities; this is due to their impulsivity, their recklessness and their inability to learn from experience. These people handle stress and heavy workloads with great aplomb. They are easily bored, and find stress, danger and risk to be invigorating – they actively seek it. As a result, many of these people become heroes – they intervene in robberies, they rush into burning buildings, they take apart live bombs, they volunteer for dangerous assignments and they flourish in times of war and chaos. Conversely, they adapt poorly to the requirements of structured bureaucracies. (p. 49)

Miller (2008) calls psychopathic bosses 'predators'. He claims they think 'It's a dog-eat-dog world. Look out for number one. Rules are for losers. I'm smarter than all these suckers...My needs come first. I can get over anyone.' (p. 58). Miller (2008) notes that psychopathic bosses are prototype cut-throat, chainsaw type entrepreneurs. The interpersonal inquisitiveness is more about getting to know how to manipulate people than befriend them. They joy in outsmarting 'suckers', reinforce their personal sense of cleverness and powerfulness. They can easily become experts, cheats, embezzlers or harassers. Curiously they often risk a lot for a little because of their love of thrill and excitement.

Miller (2008) notes two types of psychopathic bosses. First is the bright devious, cunning conning natural manipulator. This is the plotting smooth operator. The less bright psychopathic boss is more likely to use bullying and intimidation.

The psychopathic boss is not loyal or grateful but will humour staff that fulfils his or her needs and purposes. They will disregard people once they have served their purpose. They steal credit but hand out blame.

7.5 Measuring psychopathy

There are many questionnaires and checklists which attempt to measure whether a person is a psychopath. Assuming they answer reasonably honestly and have enough insight into their behaviour there are tests available. Without doubt the most famous are the various versions of the Hare Psychopathy Checklist which has recently been revised. It consists of 20 items which are rated 0 to 2, 0 meaning 'does not apply', 1 'applies somewhat' and 2 'applies fully'. The checklist is done by an expert after an interview with the person and then attempts to corroborative information such as criminal history, medical history, school history, etc.

A great deal of work has been done on this checklist which is recognized to be a good psychometric instrument. However, there are many others like the self-report scale developed by Levenson et al., (1995). It has some simple questions that one can agree or disagree with like: 'I often admire a really clever scam'; 'Love is overrated' and 'For me, what's right is whatever I can get away with'.

There have been many attempts to develop good multidimensional measures. In one important study Lynam et al. (2011) isolated four factors called Interpersonal manipulation, callous affect, erratic lifestyle and antisocial behaviour. In second study they identified eight factors labelled Machiavellian egocentricity, social potency, fearlessness, cold-heartedness, impulsive non-conformity, alienation, carefree non-planfulness and stress immunity.

Some instruments have been devised specifically to look at psychopaths at work. One is the Business-Scan 360 (Babiak & Hare, 2012). Business-Scan (B-SCAN) (B-SCAN 360) is an instrument that screens for psychopathic tendencies in managers. The B-SCAN instrument is designed to identify developmental needs in management and assesses the degree to which a person responds to challenges to organizational responsibility and effectiveness as expressed in his or her behaviours, attitudes and judgements.

7.6 Possible causes

Babiak and Hare (2006) summarize the issue neatly.

> Are psychopathic features the product of nature or nurture? As with most other things human, the answer is that both are involved. A better question is 'To what extent do nature and nurture influence the development of the traits and behaviours that define psychopathy?'

The answer to this question is becoming much clearer with the application of behavioural genetics to the study of personality traits and behavioural dispositions.

Several recent twin studies provide convincing evidence that genetic factors play at least as important a role in the development of the core features of psychopathy as do environmental factors and forces. Researchers Blonigen et al. (2003) stated that the results of their study of 271 twin pairs provided 'substantial evidence of genetic contributions to variance in the personality construct of psychopathy'. Subsequently, researchers Larrson et al., (2006) arrived at a similar conclusion in their study of 1090 adolescent twin pairs: 'A genetic factor explains most of the variation in the psychopathic personality.' Viding et al., (2005) studied 3687 seven-year-old twin pairs and also concluded that 'the core symptoms of psychopathy are strongly genetically determined'. They reported that the genetic contribution was highest when callous unemotional traits were combined with antisocial behaviours.

Evidence of this sort does not mean that the pathways to adult psychopathy are fixed and immutable, but it does indicate that the social environment will have a tough time in overcoming what nature has provided. As noted in *Without Conscience*, the elements needed for the development of psychopathy – such as a profound inability to experience empathy and the complete range of emotions, including fear – are provided in part by nature and possibly by some unknown biological influences on the developing foetus and neonate. As a result, the capacity for developing internal controls and conscience and for making emotional 'connections' with others is greatly reduced. To use a simple analogy, the potter is instrumental in moulding pottery from clay (nurture) but the characteristics of the pottery also depend on the sort of clay available (nature). (pp. 24-25).

One obvious question is how common psychopathic traits are in the average population. One recent big study found it affects less than 1 per cent of the population but it is more common among prisoners, homeless people and psychiatric patients. Psychopaths tend to be violent, young males. It is argued that of the prison population around 8 per cent of males and 2 per cent of females are psychopaths (Cold et al., 2009)

However, the biological psychologists have a different model. Goa and Raine (2010) in a paper on the neurobiological differentiators of successful and unsuccessful psychopaths note: We postulate that intact or enhanced neurobiological processes, including better executive functioning, increased autonomic reactivity, normative volumes of prefrontal gray and amygdala, and normal frontal functioning, may serve as factors that protect successful psychopaths from conviction and allow them to attain their life goals, using more covert and nonviolent approaches. In contrast, brain structural and functional deficits, alongside with reduced autonomic reactivity, impaired executive functioning, and risky decision making, predispose the unsuccessful psychopaths to more extreme forms of antisocial behavior utilizing more overt and aggressive methods of manipulation. (pp. 194-195)

7.7 Psychopaths at work

Hare (1999) in a chapter of white-collar psychopaths noted how many were 'trust-mongers' who, through charm and gall, obtained, then very callously betrayed, the trust of others. He notes how they make excellent imposters and how they frequently target the vulnerable. They target and exploit people's gullibility, naivety and Rousseauian view of the goodness of man.

He calls them *subcriminal psychopaths* who can thrive as academics, cult-leaders, doctors, police officers and writers. They violate rules, conventions and ethical standards always just crossing legal boundaries. He also gives a rich case study description of what he calls a *corporate psychopath*. He notes that there is certainly no shortage of opportunities for psychopaths who think big. It's lucrative. 'They are fast talking, charming, self-assured, at ease in social situations, cool under pressure, unfazed by the possibility of being found out, and totally ruthless' (p. 121).

Babiak and Hare (2006) believe most of us will interact with a psychopath every day. But their skills and abilities make them difficult to spot. Often they tend to be charming, emotionally literate and socially skilled. Next they are often highly articulate. Third, they are brilliant chameleon-like in their impression management. They note:

> Not all psychopaths are smooth operators, though. Some do not have enough social or communicative skill or education to interact successfully with others, relying instead on threats, coercion, intimidation and violence to dominate others and to get what they want. Typically such individuals are manifestly aggressive and rather nasty and unlikely to charm victims into submission, relying of the bullying approach instead. (p. 19)

The successful psychopath has, essentially, a manipulative approach to life. Their sole aim is to get what they want with effort, emotion or fear and whether they deserve it or not. Hence the importance of various groups that may be called 'the organisational police', auditors, human resources, quality controllers whose job it is to ensure compliance with standards.

There is a small but growing literature on the successful, that is, non-institutionalized psychopath. Successful non-incarcerated psychopaths seem to have compensatory factors that buffer them against criminal behaviour like higher social class and intelligence. In this sense the successful psychopath has a wider set of coping mechanisms than less privileged and able psychopaths who soon get caught. It is the articulate, good-looking, educated psychopath that is most dangerous at work.

Self-report measures of the psychopathic personality give a clear indication of the sort of behaviours that are relevant (Benning et al., 2005): Impulsive non-conformity (reckless, rebellious, unconventional); Blame externalization (blames others, rationalizes own transgressions); Machiavellian egocentricity (interpersonally aggressive and self-centred); Carefree non-planfulness (excessive present orientation with lack of forethought or planning); Stress immunity (experiencing minimal anxiety); fearlessness (willing to take risks, having little concern with potentially harmful consequences) and general cold-heartedness (unsentimental, unreactive to others' distress, lacking in imagination). These seem to factor into *two* dimensions: one related to high negative emotionality and the other low behavioural constraint. Further research by Benning et al. (2005) led these authors to think about two distinct facets of the psychopath: *fearless dominance* (glib, grandiose, deceitful, low stress) and *impulsive antisociality* (aggressive, antisocial, low control). This suggests that within the psychopath population one may be able to distinguish between these two groups.

It is an interesting question to try to understand in what sorts of jobs psychopathic traits might be, at least for a time, advantageous. This may refer both to the type of job but also a particular situation such as when an organization is changing rapidly, in decline, or under investigation. They like outwitting the system – opportunistically exploiting who and what they can. They usually hate routine and administration, which are seen as drudgery. No wonder people who work for them feel so demoralized.

They make bad bosses and bad partners because they are egocentric and only continue on in a relationship as long as it is good for them. They rarely have long-lasting, meaningful relationships. They have two human ingredients missing which are pretty crucial to a fully functioning person: *conscience* and *compassion*. They score very low on agreeableness and conscientiousness. Hence they can be cruel, destructive, malicious and criminal. They are unscrupulous, and are exploitatively self-interested with little capacity for remorse. They act before they think and are famous for their extreme impulsivity.

Dotlich and Cairo (2003) note that the mischievous psychopath knows that the rules are really 'only suggestions'. They are rebels without a cause, rule breakers who believe rules, laws and other restrictions are tedious and unnecessary. They clearly have destructive impulses and a preference for making impulsive decisions without considering any consequences. They can, and do, speak their mind, use their charms and creativity but for no clear business goal.

They document five signs and symptoms. Staff questions the mischievous leaders' commitments and projects they have initiated but subsequently neglected; they frequently never take time or effort to win people over; everything rates as a challenge to them. Also they are easily bored and they have to spend a lot of effort covering up cock-ups and mistakes.

Kets de Vries (2014) succinctly calls these people SOB executives or 'lite' psychopaths. He notes:

> These 'lite' psychopaths are a particular kind of SOB – not the kind usually associated with that acronym but what I term Seductive Operational Bullies. Compared to 'heavy' psychopaths, most of whom can be found in prisons or mental hospitals, SOBs are much better at keeping up a consistent guise of normality. Their behavior may even be so adapted to certain organizations that some of them will reach top executive positions. (p. 18)

He reports how difficult it is to deal with a senior person who is a psychopath.

7.8 Corporate culture and psychopathy

Once corporate psychopaths have been identified, the question always arises how did they get through the net? Why were they rarely challenged? Indeed why were the promoted? Do bullies get away with it because they hide their performance incompetence? Is it possible that many modern organizations actually reinforce pathological management which reinforces task performance over anything else? If people get the message that the ends rather than the means are important, that rewards are entirely dependent on output and the organization turns a blind eye towards the 'abuse' of staff and customers, it is perhaps not at all surprising that psychopaths thrive in certain cultures.

Pech and Slade (2007) attempted to build a model to explain the apparent success of organizational sociopaths/corporate psychopaths. They start with the concept of organizational complexity which can encourage a rather devious process of delegation which psychopaths can use to build a network and absolve themselves of responsibility. They talk of 'mate-ocracy' and a great deal of goal abstraction. Complexity also can be used to distort information. Moreover people are rewarded by their aggressiveness and disinhibition to 'kick arse'.

The idea is that people notice that in effect deviant behaviours are rewarded and hence adopt them and recommend them to others. Those with psychopathic tendencies can therefore thrive and legitimize their managerial behaviours. Hence there are pathological cultures. So how to prevent this (from) occurring? The answer lies in part in recruitment and selection but also in putting in controls that inhibit and punish aberrant behaviours whilst reinforcing values of integrity, openness, cooperation and accountability. To start is to consider the control systems of organizations: what behaviours do they really reward and how is performance management done? Next do they have subtle and sophisticated recruitment, selection and promotion policies? Finally are there really open channels of communication and genuine transparency?

Clearly people need to gather good evidence to build a case. However he argues that it is better to prevent them getting into the organization in the first place: to bring these issues to light. To weed out any SOB who has managed to gain entry to the organization, a culture needs to be in place where it is easy for rank-and-file employees to express concerns about their colleagues and bosses. Because many SOBs don't act up in front of their bosses, it is important for leaders to collect feedback from colleagues or subordinates to identify inappropriate behaviors. There should be processes in place so that employees can bring up concerns and complaints. In a culture where multi-party feedback is par for the course, this process is easier to facilitate. Feedback systems are good ways to signal the presence of psychopathic executives and detect dysfunctional behavior before it has graver consequences. Because SOBs are often included among high potentials, organizations should be on their guard for incongruities at an early career phase and insist on rigorous cross-checking with previous and current colleagues. A red flag should go up if there are glaring discrepancies between how direct reports and junior employees perceive an executive, and how their peers or boss perceive them. Lower-level employees are often on the receiving end of an SOB's psychopathic behavior and usually spot a problem much sooner than senior management. Organizations should ensure that they have clear means of communication for signaling inappropriate behavior – for example, the presence of an ombudsman, an anonymous tip line, or specific whistleblower provisions. One very straightforward indicator that something is wrong is a worrying exit rate of good people from a specific project group, department, or division. This denotes the need for a closer look at that part of the organization. Another obvious signal is converging complaints received by HR. (p. 23)

Others, from a business ethics perspective, have come to a similar conclusion. Thus, den Nieuwenboer and Kaptein (2008) have suggested there are three factors that lead to corporate corruption. The first they call the spiral of divergent norms where organizations psychologically split into groups with all the consequences for in-group favouritism and out-group discrimination. This leads to detachment and particular groups 'closing off' from the wider organization and environment. Second, there is the spiral of pressures where people get trapped into protecting their status and group acceptance and allegiance by committing more and more corrupt acts. Third, there is the spiral of opportunity where corruption grows because of the diminishing sanctioning power of managers who do not object to corrupt behaviour.

7.9 Dealing with psychopaths

How to deal with the psychopath? Easier said than done; however, Dotlich and Cairo (2003) offer four pieces of advice for what is, no doubt a successful psychopath, shown in Table 7.2.

Table 7.2 Advice to offer psychopaths

Encourage them to take ownership for their actions and interrogate their rule breaking, consequence-ignoring behaviours.

Encourage them to think clearly about which rules they will really follow as opposed to break.

They may benefit from being on the receiving end of the sort mischief they dish out.

They may benefit from confiding in a coach.

Oldham and Morris (2000) offer 'tips on dealing with the adventurous person in your life':

First have fun but be careful: your partner seeks excitement through charming, disarming, adventurousness. Next, have no illusions about changing him or her: they won't or can't so you have to be the flexible one. Third don't crowd them or try to keep them on the traditional 'straight and narrow' path. Fourth, you have to be responsible for ones' safety, others welfare...because they won't be. Next know your limits for excitement, risk, drugs, etc. because he/she will draw you into their world. Sixth, don't expect much support and help because you are not going to get it so you need to be strong, resilient, tough. Finally stay as sexy as you are. Keep your sexual relationship interesting and lively. Toss your inhibitions and be ready and willing to experiment. (p. 243)

Babiak and Hare (2006) offer lots of advice to people dealing with psychopaths. The following is their advice if the psychopath is the client:

1. Get paid up front. If you lose the case, you will be blamed and unpaid. If you win the case, the client will take the credit and you will still be unpaid.
2. Be very careful about boundaries. The client is not your friend, and will collect and use against you whatever information is obtained. (This includes information related to the case and related to you personally.)
3. Remain in charge. A psychopathic client will attempt to run the show and to manipulate you and the system, making your job much harder.
4. Don't take at face value the client's description of events or interactions with others. Check everything out.
5. Be aware that the client will distort and minimize his or her criminal history. When confronted with the inaccuracies, the client will offer excuses that place the blame on defence attorney, a corrupt system or others.
6. The client will flatter you as long as things are going smoothly. If the case goes sideways, often because of the client's tendency to take charge and to ignore advice, you will become the enemy.
7. Keep copious notes on everything. (p. 314)

It is difficult to estimate the number of successful 'industrial' psychopaths. It is also sometimes difficult to explain why they 'get away with it' for so long. However, it is no mystery when enquiring from those who do or have worked with a successful psychopath how much misery or dysfunctionality they can bring to the workplace. The idea is that psychopaths easily get hired using charm and blatant lies. Next they soon identify, befriend, woo and 'sweet-talk' all the powerful 'key-players' in the organization. They build these people into a support network aimed both to establish their own reputation but more importantly undermine their potential opponents. Next they abandon those who have been useful to them.

The issue with the psychopathic boss is whether they are subclinical vs. clinical psychopaths and what in fact 'pushes' them over the limits.

Hare (1999) in his clinical study of psychopaths asks 'can anything be done?' He says nothing seems to work precisely because psychopaths see no reason to change. Further therapy can make them worse because it teaches them more effectively how to deceive, manipulate and use people. They learn therapy language (getting in touch with their feelings) without ever actually changing.

However, he does offer a survival guide that comes under two headings: Protect Yourself and Damage Control. The former is a warning to be on your guard; disregard their clever acting; beware of their flattery; and tall stories; and know yourself because psychopaths are skilled at detecting vulnerability. He also warns those who deal with psychopaths to be very aware of who the victim is. That is, psychopaths like to portray themselves as victims yet you are likely to be it.

Hare (1999) warns those who associate with psychopaths to be aware of their power struggles and to set firm ground rules to prevent manipulation. He also advises to cut your losses: the psychopath's appetite for power and control knows no bounds and is best left to their own devices.

In their practical, popular and work oriented book on successful psychopaths, Babiak and Hare (2006) note how psychopaths attempt to ruin others' reputation in terms of their competence and loyalty. They operate as brilliant manipulators and puppeteers to destroy your reputation. Because they try to create conflict in work teams through 'divide and conquer', it is important to build and maintain relationships at work. They offer seven pieces of advice if your boss is a psychopath.

1. Build, nurture and maintain your (true) reputation as a good performer.
2. Keep records of everything and put it in writing.
3. Make use of and be very wary of the performance appraisal process.
4. Avoid confrontation by minimizing contact and never responding to bait.
5. Be very wary about making a formal complaint as anonymity is not always assured and retribution very likely to follow.
6. If you have to (by transfer, resignation), do so on good terms.
7. Move on remembering the lesson.

They offer similar advice for the psychopathic co-worker, subordinate or client.

Babiak and Hare (2006) suggest that there is a common pattern when psychopaths join a company. They charm at assessment and go through their honeymoon period. Soon they become manipulative and disparaging to others and start doing flagrant-image enhancement. Then they confront others by trying to neutralize enemies and abandoning those of little use to them. Finally, if successful, they tend to abandon their patrons as they move ever upward and onward. To be alerted to the possibility of this pattern may help identify psychopaths before it is too late.

7.10 Conclusion

The term 'psychopath' is much used but more misunderstood. Psychopathy lies on a continuum from low to high. Successful, subclinical, industrial psychopaths can be very successful at work. If they are clever and presentable, their superficial charm and boldness may suit them well particularly in business situations that are rapidly changing. Furthermore, it is stress that may push people 'over the line' from people with 'weak conscience' and taste for excitement into subclinical and even psychopathic behaviour.

One test of whether a person is a subclinical psychopath lies in their biography. From the age of adolescence onwards it may be possible to detect early signs of delinquency, brushes with the law and a string of people lining up to testify, quite happily, about the way they were lied to, cheated and 'conned' by a particular individual they trusted. Hence the importance of a thorough biographical check when selecting senior managers.

It is important to end on a more cautious note. In a very important and relevant review of what we know and do not about psychopaths in the workplace, Smith and Lilienfeld (2013) conclude:

There is no question that the construct of psychopathy bears potentially important implications for the workplace. A better understanding of how psychopathy manifests itself in the workplace is critical for both pragmatic and theoretical reasons. Pragmatically, this question may provide crucial information for employee selection and monitoring. Theoretically, this question may help us to understand the potentially differential manifestations, both adaptive and maladaptive, of psychopathy across settings. In addition, it may shed light on the still controversial and poorly understood construct of successful psychopathy.

Nevertheless, the study of business psychopathy has languished in a state of neglect from researchers for some time. This neglect stems largely from the fact that until the 1980s, most research on psychopathy was based on criminal and, to a lesser extent, psychiatric populations. In this regard, the recent increase in attention accorded to workplace psychopathy is encouraging. With the development of business-specific and self-report psychopathy measures (bypassing reliance on file information) that can be used in nonclinical samples, workplace psychopathy has begun to receive more attention from investigators, leading to a modest but growing body of research.

Chapter 8

Arrogance, hubris and narcissism: The overconfident leader

8.1 Introduction

Most leadership books paint the 'Heroic' school of management. In successful businesses, military and political leaders are Great Saviours. Their abilities and skills, alone, account for the great success of institutions. Higgs (2009) has called them 'managers on steroids' and 'lone he-men'.

There are various aspects to narcissistic leadership. Ouimet (2010) has identified five:

1. **Charisma**: The ability to seduce others in their entourage through various mechanisms.
2. **Self-interested influence**: With a sense of entitlement, the relentless striving to construct, and protect a (false) strict self-image, and the attribution of humanizing traits to oneself as opposed to others.
3. **Deceptive motivation**: Using bold actions and a sensationalism (attention getting acquisitions) trying to cover up their real motives of aggrandizement.
4. **Intellectual inhibition**: The hypersensitivity to criticism, the exaggerated need for admiration and the remorseless perceived threats to integrity leading to very poor decision making.
5. **Simulated consideration**: The callous and superficially charming manipulation and exploitation of employees and colleagues.

As will be noted, there have been various attempts to make differentiations in the narcissism literature which spans psychiatry and psychology. It has been conceived as a type and a trait, even a psychological process (Morgan & Richardson, 2001). There have been studies on overt (more exhibitionistic and aggressive) versus covert (anxious, defensive, vulnerable) narcissists (Otway & Vignoles, 2006) and many attempts to differentiate 'healthy', 'productive' narcissism from 'unhealthy', 'destructive' narcissism. Indeed there appears to be some differences when there is a 'clinical' versus 'non-clinical' account of narcissism (Campbell, 2001). This problem may be resolved by the trait concept whereby it is possible to locate everybody on the self-esteem – narcissistic trait. Clinicians may see only extreme cases that are recommended for therapy, while personality and organizational psychologists see less 'extreme cases' who appear 'relatively' well adjusted.

There is a Business, Freudian, Psychological and Psychiatric literature on this topic. Interestingly, the relevant literature seems to use three related concepts: hubris, narcissism and overconfidence. The latter is used mainly by cognitive psychologists who have noted the causes and consequences of judgemental overconfidence which causes people to overestimate their actual ability, their past and future performance, and also their level of control over events and their chances of success.

Several versions of the myth of Narcissus survive. They are warnings about hubris and pride. Poets, painters and moralists have been intrigued with the myth seeking to interpret its meaning. The Freudians found the myth beguiling and sought intrapsychic and psychopathological interpretations. There have also been various illuminating psychological accounts of famous plays like Miller's (1949) *Death of a Salesman* as being a prototypic story of narcissism (Tracy & Robins, 2007).

At the heart of the myth is the caution of misperception and self-love: the idea that inaccurate self-perceptions can lead to tragic and self-defeating consequences. There appears to be a moral, social and clinical debate about narcissism. The moral issues concern the evils of hubris; the social issue the benefits or otherwise of modesty; the clinical debate is about the consequences of misperceptions. This chapter focuses on how narcissism 'plays out' in the workplace.

Psychologists have also attempted to measure narcissism and to distinguish it from simply being a form of 'high self-esteem'.

8.2 Harmful effects of high self-esteem

For nearly thirty years, it has been an accepted fact in psychology that low self-esteem was the root cause of many social problems particularly among young people. Thus, everything from teenage pregnancy to suicide and delinquency to school failure was due to low self-esteem. Hence the development and proliferation of the self-esteem movement which attempted through a variety of crypto-clinical and educational interventions set out to raise the esteem of various targeted groups. The assumption was because self-esteem has such powerful causal power it was the most efficient way to improve the lot of various groups that experienced a variety of social problems.

However, over the past few years, social psychologists have challenged many of these assumptions and found them wanting. One challenge came from Emler (2005), who did a careful, critical evaluation of the literature. His conclusion was essentially that there is little evidence for the *causal power* of low self-esteem causing social problems or for that matter, of the efficacy of programmes that attempted to raise it. The research drew a number of specific conclusions:

- Relatively low self-esteem is not a risk factor for delinquency, violence towards others (including child and partner abuse), drug use, alcohol abuse, educational under-attainment or racism.
- Relatively low self-esteem is a risk factor for suicide, suicide attempts, depression, teenage pregnancy and victimization by bullies. However, in each case it is only one among several related risk factors.
- Although the causal mechanisms remain unclear, relatively low childhood self-esteem also appears to be associated with adolescent eating disorders and, among males only, with low earnings and employment problems in young adulthood.

- Young people with very high self-esteem are more likely than others to hold racist attitudes, reject social pressures from adults and peers and engage in physically risky pursuits, such as drink-driving or driving too fast.
- The most important influences on young people's levels of self-esteem are their parents – partly as a result of genetic inheritance and partly through the degree of love, concern, acceptance and interest that they show their children. Physical and sexual abuse are especially damaging for children's feelings of self-worth.
- Personal successes and failures also influence self-esteem. But despite the attention given to the effects on high or low achievement in school, the degree of influence of self-esteem is relatively small.
- Children's self-esteem can be raised by parenting programmes and other planned interventions, but knowledge of why particular interventions are effective is limited.

Emler, in fact, argued that low self-esteem could have beneficial motivational characteristics while high self-esteem could lead to arrogant, conceited, self-satisfied behaviour rather than provide specific benefits.

In addition to reviews, experimental studies began to show the negative effects of high self-esteem. That is, they appeared to show that people with high self-esteem pose a greater threat to themselves and others than those with low self-esteem.

Baumeister's (Bushman & Baumeister, 1998; Baumeister et al., 2003) imaginative studies have probably provided the best empirical evidence that there is no causal relationship between low self-esteem and life success though this conclusion has been disputed. Some recent longitudinal studies suggest otherwise (Trzesmewski et al., 2008c). In fact, if anything, the opposite is true. Still others have shown that self-esteem can have both positive and negative consequences. If people derive their self-esteem from external factors like physical appearance, they may be prone to eating disorders (Crocker & Wolfe, 2001).

The essence of the argument is that we need to be accurate in self-evaluation which is about our competencies with both a spirit of acceptance and realism. To be self-accepting, we need to take responsibility for our actions. Hence, there is a difference between authentic or genuine self-esteem and external or false self-esteem. The former is internal and under our control, the latter external and under the control of others which may be insecure and fickle.

8.3 Narcissistic personality disorder

Dotlich and Cairo (2003) list narcissism-arrogance in their terms as the first (probably major) cause of why CEOs fail. It is a case of you're right but everybody else is wrong, a blinding belief in your own opinions. They note four common symptoms:

- A diminished capacity to learn from others or previous experience.
- An off-putting (inferiority) outright refusal (ever) to be accountable and hence responsible.
- Resistance to change because they know 'my way' is best.
- An inability to recognize their (manifold) limitations.

Oldham and Morris (2000) have noted that narcissists seem never defensive or embarrassed about their ambition and supremely confident in the ambitions. However, because they are so aware of, comfortable with and grateful for their strengths they are easily and profoundly wounded by any suggestion that they have serious weaknesses or shortcomings.

At work they tend to be high-energy, outgoing and competitive. They seem instinctively drawn to office politics and how to find and use power. They will charm those in authority or those from whom they believe they have something to gain.

Oldham and Morris (1991) summarize the psychiatric diagnostic criteria thus:

A pervasive pattern of grandiosity (in fantasy or behaviour), lack of empathy, and hypersensitivity to the evaluation of others, beginning by early adulthood and present in a variety of contexts, as indicated by at least five of the following:

1. reacts to criticism with feelings of rage, shame or humiliation (even if not expressed)
2. is interpersonally exploitative: takes advantage of others to achieve his or her own ends
3. has a grandiose sense of self-importance, e.g. exaggerates achievements and talents, expects to be noticed as 'special' without appropriate achievement
4. believes that his or her problems are unique and can be understood only by other special people
5. is preoccupied with fantasies of unlimited success, power, brilliance, beauty or ideal love
6. has a sense of entitlement: unreasonable expectation of especially favourable treatment, e.g., assumes that he or she does not have to wait in line when others must do so
7. requires constant attention and admiration, e.g., keeps fishing for compliments
8. lack of empathy; inability to recognise and experience how others feel, e.g., annoyance and surprise when a friend who is seriously ill cancels a date
9. is preoccupied with feelings of envy. (pp. 93–94)

The DSM-IV manual has nine diagnostic features. Narcissists are boastful, pretentious and self-aggrandizing, overestimating their own abilities and accomplishments while deflating others. They compare themselves favourably to famous, privileged people believing their own discovery as one of them is long overdue. They are surprisingly secure in their beliefs that they are gifted and unique and have special needs beyond the comprehension of ordinary people. Paradoxically, their self-esteem is fragile, needing to be bolstered up by constant attention and admiration from others. They expect their demands to be met by special favourable treatment. In doing so, they often exploit others because they form relationships specifically designed to enhance their self-esteem. They lack empathy being totally self-absorbed. They are also envious of others and begrudge them their success. They are well known for their arrogance and their disdainful, patronizing attitude. As managers, their difficult-to-fulfil needs can lead them to have problematic social relationships and make poor decisions.

The manual points out that they are exceptionally sensitive to setbacks feeling both degraded and humiliated. They mask this with defiant counter-attacks and rage. They may withdraw from situations that lead to failure or try to mask their grandiosity with an appearance of humility. Those diagnosed with narcissistic personality disorder (NPD) tend to be male.

There are also many issues with differential diagnosis, that is, distinguishing what is unique about the disorder. The most useful feature in discriminating NPD from histrionic, antisocial and borderline personality disorders, which are characterized by interactive styles is the *grandiosity* characteristic of NPD.

> The relative stability of self-image as well as the relative lack of self-destructiveness, impulsivity and abandonment concerns also help distinguish NPD from borderline personality disorder. Excessive pride in achievements, a relative lack of emotional display and disdain for other's sensitivities help distinguish NPD from histrionic personality disorder. Although individuals with borderline, histrionic, and NPD may require much attention, those with NPD specifically need that attention to be admiring. Individuals with antisocial and NPD will share a tendency to be tough-minded, glib, superficial, exploitative and unempathetic. However, NPD does not necessarily include characteristics of impulsivity, aggression and deceit. In addition, individuals with anti-social personality disorder may not be as needy of the admiration and envy of others, as persons with narcissistic personality disorder. (p. 661)

At work, narcissistic individuals have a grandiose sense of self-importance (e.g. they exaggerate their achievements and talents, expect to be recognized as superior without commensurate achievements). Inevitably, they believe they rightly deserve all sorts of markers of their specialness: bigger offices and salary; inflated job titles, a bigger budget dedicated to their needs; more support staff; and greater liberty to do as they wish.

Narcissists are super-self-confident: they express considerable self-certainty. They are 'self-people' – self-asserting, self-possessed, self-aggrandizing, self-preoccupied, self-loving – and ultimately self-destructive. They seem to really believe in themselves: they are sure that they have been born lucky. At work they are outgoing, high energy, competitive and very 'political' depending of course on their normal (big five) trait profile. Thus, the extraverted conscientious narcissist may be rather different from those more neurotic and open. They can make reasonable short-term leaders as long as they are not criticized or made to share glory. They seem to have an insatiable need to be admired, love and be needed. This can appear amusing or pathetic to outside observers. They are often a model of the ambitious, driven, self-disciplined, successful leader or manager. The world, they believe and demand, is their stage.

But narcissism is a *disorder* of self-esteem: it is essentially a cover-up. People with NPD self-destruct because their self-aggrandizement blinds their personal and business judgement and managerial behaviour. At work they exploit others to get ahead yet they demand special treatment. Worse, their reaction to any sort of criticism is extreme, including shame, rage and tantrums. They aim to destroy that criticism, however well-intentioned and useful. They are poor empathizers and thus have low emotional intelligence. They can be consumed with envy and disdain of others, and are prone to depression as well as, manipulative, demanding and self-centred behaviours; even therapists don't like them.

Many researchers have tried to 'unpick' the essence of the paradoxical, fragile, self-esteem of the narcissist. The narcissist's self-esteem is at once unstable and defensive. It seems their self-esteem is utterly contingent on others' feedback. Furthermore, it is dissociated between explicit (overt) and implicit (covert) views (Tracy & Robins, 2007).

Hogan and Hogan (2001) call these types 'Arrogant' 'the lord of the high chair' a two- year-old, sitting in its high chair demanding food and attention, and squealing in fury when his or her needs are not met. Narcissists expect to be liked, admired, respected, attended to, praised, complimented and indulged. Their most important and obvious characteristic is a sense of entitlement, excessive self-esteem and quite often an expectation of success that often leads to real success. They expect to be successful at everything they undertake, they believe that people are so interested in them that books will be written about them, and when their needs and expectations are frustrated, they explode with 'narcissistic rage'.

What is most distinctive about the narcissists is their self-assurance which often gives them charisma. Hogan and Hogan (1999) note that they are the first to speak in a group and they hold forth with great confidence, even when they are wrong. They so completely expect to succeed and take more credit for success than is warranted or fair, that they refuse to acknowledge failure, errors or mistakes. When things go right it is because of their efforts; when things go wrong, it is someone else's fault. This is a classic attribution error and leads to problems with truth telling because they always rationalize and reinterpret their failures and mistakes usually by blaming them on others.

Narcissists can be energetic, charismatic, leader-like and willing to take the initiative to get projects moving. They can be relatively successful in management, sales and entrepreneurship, but usually only for short periods. However, they are arrogant, vain, overbearing, demanding, self-deceived and pompous yet they are so colourful and engaging that they often attract followers. Their self-confidence is attractive. Naively people believe they have to have something to be so confident about.

Narcissists handle stress and heavy workloads badly but seemingly with ease; they are also quite persistent under pressure and they refuse to acknowledge failure. As a result of their inability to acknowledge failure or even mistakes and the way they resist coaching and ignore negative feedback, they are unable to learn from experience. In a more accessible, almost self-help book written as a collaboration between psychiatrist and a journalist Oldham and Morris (1991) chose the more neutral term 'self-confidence'.

Oldham and Morris (1991, 80) note nine characteristics of these types they call 'Self-Confident':

1. **Self-regard**: Self-confident individuals believe in themselves and in their abilities. They have no doubt that they are unique and special and that there is a reason for their being on this planet.
2. **The red carpet**: They expect others to treat them well at all times.
3. **Self-propulsion**: Self-confident people are open about their ambitions and achievements. They energetically and effectively sell themselves, their goals, their projects and their ideas.
4. **Politics**: They are able to take advantage of the strengths and abilities of other people in order to achieve their goals, and they are shrews in their dealings with others.
5. **Competition**: They are able competitors, they love getting to the top and they enjoy staying there.
6. **Dreams**: Self-confident individuals are able to visualize themselves as the hero, the star, the best in their role, or the most accomplished in their field.
7. **Self-awareness**: These individuals have a keen awareness of their thoughts and feelings and their overall inner state of being.
8. **Poise**: People with the self-confident personality style accept compliments, praise and admiration gracefully and with self-possession.
9. **Sensitivity to criticism**: The self-confident style confers an emotional vulnerability to the negative feelings and assessments of others which are deeply felt, although they may be handled with this style's customary grace.

More importantly, they note four tips for working with narcissists:

1. Be absolutely loyal. Don't criticize or compete with them. Don't expect to share the limelight or to take credit. Be content to aspire to the number-two position.
2. Don't expect your self-confident boss to provide direction. Likely he or she will expect you to know what to do, so be sure you are

> clear about the objectives before you undertake any tasks. Don't hesitate to ask.
> 3. You may be an important member of the boss's team, but don't expect your self-confident boss to be attentive to you as an individual. Don't take it personally.
> 4. Self-confident bosses expect your interest in them, however. They are susceptible to flattery, so if you're working on a raise or a promotion or are trying to sell your point of view, a bit of buttering up may smooth the way. (Oldham & Morris, 1991: 85)

This is advice for those working with narcissists. It clearly takes an optimistic perspective never considering that a narcissistic boss could be both abusive and deeply incompetent.

Miller (2008) in another popular book about the personality disorders describes narcissistic bosses and employers as 'preeners' and gives advice to those who may be either. For bosses, he suggests documenting your credentials, being realistic about what you can be proud of and to treat all employers with respect. He suggests to the potentially narcissistic employee to take an honest self-inventory (to gain insight); to emulate the successful and to present your ideas appropriately. Similarly Dotlich and Cairo (2003) offer three pieces of advice for this leadership type. Determine if you fit the arrogance profile (i.e. try a little self-awareness), find the truth-tellers in the organization and ask them to level with you (i.e. get real feedback); use setbacks as an opportunity to cross back over the line before big failure hits.

There remains considerable debate about the treatment of, and prognosis for, each of the personality disorders. Until relatively recently it was argued that they were particularly difficult to treat and that prognosis was therefore poor.

The business world often calls for and rewards, arrogant, self-confident, self-important people. They seek out power and abuse it. They thrive in selling jobs and those where they have to do media work. But, as anyone who works with and for them knows, they can destabilize and destroy working groups by their deeply inconsiderate behaviour. Management and self-help books stress how to cope with clinical or subclinical narcissism. Few take a very negative view or report case studies where narcissists personally destroy whole organizations.

8.4 The two sides of narcissism

Paunonen et al. (2006) have identified two strands in the narcissistic leadership literature. The first is that although many narcissists are described as charismatic, their egotistical Machiavellianism derails them in the end. But in contrast to this *dark* view there is a *bright* view. This suggests that narcissists have low depression and anxiety, and high subjective wellbeing. Furthermore, their obviously strong needs for achievement, control, power and status serve them well to obtain leadership positions, but their inward focus usually leads in the long term to self-destruction.

Clearly, the exploitative, entitlement-obsessed narcissist who manipulates those around him or her for his or her own ends is unlikely to be successful in the long run. However, Paunonen et al. (2006) are happy to distinguish between the benign and pathological narcissist. Furthermore, they are happy to think of narcissism as a trait (not a type) which consists of a constellation of distinct intercorrelated traits on a continuum.

In their study of narcissism and leadership, Paunonen et al. (2006) measured egotism which they took to represent the bright side of narcissism and Machiavellianism as the dark side. They also measured two aspects of impression management: the conscious version and the less conscious delusion version. Their study was a peer-rating study of military cadets who rated five factors: leadership, popularity, benevolence, aggression and honesty. Their results supported their theory notably that the highest rated leaders had the bright-side narcissism profile, high in egoism and self-esteem but low in manipulativeness and impression management. Indeed, they conclude by arguing that they are 'hard pressed' to think of any situation where dark-side narcissism would not threaten the leader–followership relationship to lead it to soon collapse.

Many writers on leadership narcissists contrast the upside-bright or downside-dark traits of narcissistic leaders. This helps resolve the apparent conflict of ideas that narcissistic managers can (perhaps only in the short term) be good managers. Rosenthal (2007) notes a number of the problematic intercorrelated dark-side traits and the leaders with whom they are most associated:

- **Feelings of inferiority**: The need to be surrounded by flattering sycophants (Mao Tse-Tung, Krushchev).
- **An insatiable need for recognition and superiority**: Unrelenting quest to gain power to show potency (Saddam Hussein).
- **Hypersensitivity and anger**: Intense, vengeful, hostile rage when crossed (Kennedy, Castro).
- **Lack of empathy**: Idiosyncratic, self-centred, hubristical behaviour (Bush).
- **Amorality**: Cruel acts justified to others (Saddam Hussein).
- **Irrationality and inflexibility**: Overconfident, fantasy thinking and decision making.
- **Paranoia**: Seeing enemies everywhere.

It may well be that certain organizations at certain points in their history attract narcissists who do well. Those that consistently court attention through public relations, those in crisis or those that crave 'strong leadership' may seek out those dangerously narcissistic.

On the other hand, Rosenthal (2007) sees narcissism as being crucial in a crisis. Narcissists can have great vision and take dramatic action. They not only appear to be but are larger than life figures described as 'productive narcissists'. These are the public relations hungry CEOs driven to gain power, glory and the admiration of others. They can be visionaries and risk-takers seeing the big picture while down playing rules, laws and conventions which handicap them. When they have some insight and self-awareness into their preferences and abilities and which organization forces are in place to restrain them they can act as great forces for positive change and advancement.

One way to resolve the two sides of narcissism argument is to note two things. First, if narcissism is trait like then one can obtain identical scores from both bright and dark side factors. This implies variability within the narcissism dimension itself. Second, one has to consider other factors like cognitive ability, social conscience and conscientiousness. Thus, a highly able, hard-working bright-side narcissist could do very well in organizational settings, while a less able, less-hardworking dark-side would inevitably fail.

8.5 The narcissistic leader

It should not be assumed that narcissism is necessarily a handicap in business. Indeed, the opposite maybe true. If a manager is articulate, educated and intelligent as well as good looking, his or her narcissism maybe seen to be acceptable.

Bright-side narcissists can be good delegators, good team builders and good deliverers. They can be good mentors and genuinely help others. However, subordinates soon learn things go wrong if they do not follow certain rules.

- Everyone must acknowledge who is boss and accept rank and hierarchical structure.
- They must be absolutely loyal and never complain, criticize or compete. They should never take credit for something but acknowledge success is primarily due to the narcissists talent, direction or insights.
- They should not expect the narcissist to be very interested in their personality, issues or ambitions but they must be very interested in the narcissist's issues.
- They have to be attentive, giving and always flattering. They need to be sensitive to the whims, needs and desires of the narcissistic manager without expecting reciprocity.
- Narcissistic managers can be mean, angry or petulant when crossed or slighted and quickly express anger, so subordinates have to be careful when working with them.
- They must ask for help, directions and clarity about objectives when they need it.

- They need to watch out that a narcissistic manager's self-preoccupation, need for approbation and grandiosity do not impede their business judgement and decision making.
- They need to find ways of giving critical feedback in such a way that the manager both understands it but does not get offended.

The dark-side narcissistic manager tends to have shallow, functional uncommitted relationships. Because they are both needy and egocentric they tend not to make close supportive friendship networks in the workplace. They can often feel empty and neglected as a result.

Narcissistic leaders may have short-term advantages but long-term disadvantages because the narcissist's consistent and persistent efforts are aimed at enhancing their self-image which leads to group clashes. Campbell et al. (2005) note that narcissistic leaders often maintain positive feelings around the self with high positive and low negative affect, as well as high self-esteem. However, they bring 'costs' because of their need to distort reality into a form conducive to self-enhancement. They also have the need to seek out positive social feedback while attacking or disparaging negative feedback. Furthermore, they experience long-term performance deficits because their illusion of success interferes without obtaining real success. Narcissists also trade interdependence and closeness for individual status and esteem. Finally, they adopt strategies that while showing gains at the individual level they show losses at the group level. That is, they may gain themselves short-term advantage by looking skilful or tough or insight while these decisions actually have long-term disastrous consequences. Thus, radical re-engineering may improve short-term profitability but lead to long-term chaos and collapse.

One of the more important explanations for the failure of narcissistic leaders is their poor decision making. There are many traits that explain this, such as impulsivity, the inability to learn from one's mistakes, high approach and low avoidance motivation, considerable risk-taking based on performance hopes and expectations rather than hard data, and the insensitivity to social constraints (i.e. breaking the rules).

Most of all, it seems that narcissistic leaders have a special belief in their intuition and gut feel. They seem to favour big, rapid, holistic decisions. They believe that they can see patterns and have insights that others do not have.

Indeed, it is their preferences for System 1 thinking (fast, automatic, frequent, emotional, stereotypic, subconscious) and decision making which often, in time causes most problems. They favour judgement over analysis. They often seem to have little time for careful analysis, and 'mulling' over a decision. They do not have a habit of rational analysis, prolonged contemplation or regular dialogues with others. They do not do 'doubt' which they see as a sign of weakness or dithering. For them decision is more about the heart than the head; and their 'special ability' to have insight into complex problems and get optimal solutions.

Narcissists, like many other bad leaders, have a very low capacity of introspection and reflection. More than that, the way they react to success and failure means they seem never to get good self-insight. They seem dramatically emboldened by social praise but relatively unresponsive to objective indicators of failure (Chatterjee & Hambrick, 2011). This is often manifested in the early phase of a narcissist's 'reign' where they make dramatic changes, acquire other companies and pioneer new methods and products. They are particularly dangerous when 'on a roll' and prone to amazing risk-taking. Acclaim, applause and flattery only make things worse.

It could be argued that many organizations have the need, at times, for some of the characteristics of narcissistic leaders like the way they often provide a string sense of vision and the courage to make bold decisions. They can (temporarily) energize and invigorate faltering organizations.

8.6 New ideas

In a well-reviewed and thoughtful article, Bollaert and Petit (2010) suggested that business researchers have become obsessed with the hubris and narcissism description and explanation for business failure despite obvious problems with the measurement and definition of the concepts. They point out, correctly, that there is a great deal of imprecision in this area.

Kets de Vries (2006a, b) argued that a certain degree of narcissism is an essential, prerequisite for leadership. He offers a psychoanalytic interpretation for the aetiology of narcissism, which is inevitably bad parenting. It is seen as problems associated with two related issues – how they perceive themselves as well as salient others; more specifically how they come to cope with reality that one is neither omnipotent or omniscient nor that parents are powerful and perfect. The child's life-long quest for admiration and approbation is often a mask for self-doubt or hatred or feeling one is never properly loved for one's own sake alone.

Inevitably, with psychoanalysis, both the neglected and the pampered child (too much and too little of a good thing) can lead to the development of narcissism. The indulgent, all praising, pampering parents lead to exactly the opposite of what they want or expect. Excessive praise leads to feelings of superiority and destined greatness which whilst being beneficial for really talented individuals only serves to undermine those who cannot understand why the world does not react like their doting parents. The narcissist does a lot of transference – the unconscious redirection of early feelings (to the parent) to other people. The psychological imprints of early care-givers are thus manifest throughout adult life.

While a 'touch' of narcissism can be good for leaders it can be problematic in the long run particularly if the problem is severe. Because of their selfishness and egocentrism, narcissistic managers are more committed to their own welfare than that of their team or indeed the whole organization. Kets de Vries (2006a, b) also distinguishes between constructive and reactive narcissism.

The healthy constructive narcissist (that is the person with high self-esteem) does take advice, accepts feedback and responsibility for both success and failure. His or her energy, zeal and larger-than-life enthusiasm and theatrics can be precisely what it takes to transform organizations. On the other hand, the reactive narcissist has got a defective sense of identity and self-esteem. He or she can be troubled by feelings of anger and inadequacy as well as lingering but intrusive thoughts of both deprivation and emptiness. His or her whole aim is to compensate for this sense of inadequacy and insecurity. Hence the constant, pervasive and insistent need for praise. The childhood memories of being ignored, belittled or maltreated can, it seems, only become overcome by success in adulthood.

To some extent we can see the narcissistic urges as highly motivational. If narcissistic managers have a very high need for praise and recognition, this may well drive them to work hard to achieve worthy goals. In this sense they can learn to earn recognition. But that need can turn to envy, spite, greed and vindictiveness.

When things are going well, the narcissistic manager can be good news. They can be upbeat and their sense of well-being spreads to others. However, even slight and temporary setbacks can cause disproportionate negative reactions. This might lead to outbursts of rage followed by feelings of dejection, depression and lethargy. However, the narcissist is a master at finding others to blame. They rationalize, project and explain away problems. Some get vindictive attempting to 'get even' with those who they perceive to have slighted them. The major problem is that they do not learn from their mistakes.

Kets de Vries (2006a, b) uses political and business examples because both business and power provide a wonderful stage to see the vicissitudes of narcissism acted out. The short-term expediency, the opportunism, the self-righteousness and self-centredness of narcissists lead to bad business decisions, poor problem-solving and low morale.

However, one really important feature in the narcissism-at-work scenario is the complicity of followers. It is said that we get the leaders we deserve. That is, if our expectations are unrealistic, we tend to get very disappointed. Often, particularly in situations of difficulty or crisis, people at work have unrealistic expectation of their leaders. They want them to be superhuman and to ensure success and continuity.

Followers, according to Kets de Vries (2006a, b), encourage two types of behaviours in narcissistic leaders, which are very bad for both leader and follower. First, there is the process of *mirroring*, where followers use leaders to reflect what they want to see. Narcissists get the admiration they crave and there occurs mutual admiration. The problem is that managers can take their eye off the ball being more concerned with policies and procedures which make them look good rather than serving the best interests of all stakeholders. Second, there is idealization in which followers project all their hopes and fantasies onto the leader. Thus, leaders find themselves in a hall of mirrors which further decreases their grip on reality.

Where narcissistic leaders become aggressive and vindictive, Kets de Vries (2006a, b) claims some followers, in order to stave off their anxiety, do identify with the aggressor. Followers impersonate the aggressor becoming tough henchman of the narcissistic manager. Inevitably, this only exacerbates the problem and begins to explain the vicious cycle of narcissistic management failure.

The central question for the work psychologist is how they can set up processes, apart from careful selection, that help prevent occurrences of narcissistic-induced management failure.

Can one reduce the possibility of appointing, promoting or encouraging narcissistic managers? Clearly, this has a great deal to do with selection policies. However, Kets de Vries (2006a, b) offers three other strategies which may help to 'downsize the narcissist'.

- Ensure distributive decision-making to ensure checks and balances. Thus, do not combine roles like CEO and chairman.
- Educate the CEO and board to look out for signs of narcissism and to have strategies to put in place when they do spot the signs. This involves clear systems of accountability involving shareholders in crucial decisions.
- Offering coaching and counselling to those clearly identified as reactive narcissists although few seem willing to accept help because they by definition rarely take personal responsibility for their failure.

Perhaps certain organizations attract narcissists more than others. It, therefore, is highly recommended that these organizations become aware of the psychological processes associated with narcissism and willing and able to do something about them.

8.7 Hubris and nemesis in politicians

A British politician (once a foreign secretary) and a trained doctor, Lord David Owen, has paid particular interest to narcissism in politicians (Owen, 2006, 2009a, b). Rather than use the term 'narcissism' or 'megalomania', he used the word 'hubris' (overconfidence and exaggerated pride and a shaming and contempt for others).

Perhaps the unique features of the hubris idea are fourfold: first, a very strong identification with a group ('my people'), be they an institution, nation or organization. Second, a related conspicuous tendency to speak in the (royal) third person. Third, an unrealistic but yet unshakable belief that any (dodgy) action will be vindicated in any court. Finally, a strong assertion that their moral rectitude should and does override mundane, trivial and often legal considerations.

The idea is this:

> Charisma, charm, the ability to inspire, persuasiveness, breadth of vision, willingness to take risks, grandiose aspirations and bold self-confidence – these qualities are often associated with successful leadership. Yet there is another side to this profile, for these very same qualities can be marked by impetuosity, a refusal to listen to or take advice and a particular form of incompetence when impulsivity, recklessness and frequent inattention to detail predominate. This can result in disastrous leadership and cause damage on a large scale. The attendant loss of capacity to make rational decisions is perceived by the general public to be more than 'just making a mistake'. While they may use discarded medical or colloquial terms, such as 'madness' or 'he's lost it', to describe such behaviour, they instinctively sense a change of behaviour although their words do not adequately capture its essence. (p. 1396)

Later:

> We believe that extreme hubristic behaviour is a syndrome, constituting a cluster of features ('symptoms') evoked by a specific trigger (power), and usually remitting when power fades. 'Hubris syndrome' is seen as an

acquired condition, and therefore different from most personality disorders which are traditionally seen as persistent throughout adulthood. The key concept is that hubris syndrome is a disorder of the possession of power, particularly power which has been associated with overwhelming success, held for a period of years and with minimal constraint on the leader. (p. 1396)

Because a political leader intoxicated by power can have devastating effects on many people, there is a particular need to create a climate of opinion that political leaders should be held more accountable for their actions. The most important constraint on a Head of Government is fear of not being able to win re-election. Another is fixed-term limits, such as the two 4-year terms for US Presidents. Cabinets, which are appointed by the Head of Government, have not been very successful in constraining hubris syndrome, in part because they owe their appointment to the Head of Government, also because they find it difficult to detect the development of hubris. Single resignations of members of the Cabinet have often been important triggers for alerting people to what is going on behind closed doors. In the US, a threat of impeachment is a constraint and in the UK a withdrawal of support by Members of Parliament has been a crucial element in forcing all the four Prime Ministers, Lloyd George, Chamberlain, Thatcher and Blair – diagnosed here as having hubris syndrome – to resign. Parliamentary revolts would not have happened if Thatcher and Blair had only stayed 8 years in office. Hubris syndrome in politicians is a greater threat than conventional illness to the quality of their leadership and the proper government of our world. (p. 1404)

In his writings he has provided a long list of behaviours considered typical of the hubris syndrome.

The behaviour is seen in a person who:

1. Sees the world as a place for self-glorification through the use of power
2. Has a tendency to take action primarily to enhance personal image

3. Shows disproportionate concern for image and presentation
4. Exhibits messianic zeal and exaltation in speech
5. Conflates self with nation or organization
6. Uses the royal 'we' in conversations
7. Shows excessive self-confidence
8. Manifestly has contempt for others
9. Shows accountability only to a higher court (history or God)
10. Displays the unshakable belief that he will be vindicated in that court
11. Loses contact with reality
12. Resorts to restlessness and impulsive actions
13. Allows moral rectitude to obviate consideration of practicality, cost or outcome
14. Displays incompetence with disregard for the nuts and bolts of policy-making

Among the fourteen behaviours, five are called 'unique' (5, 6, 10, 12 and 13) in the sense that they do not appear among the criteria of personality disorders in DSM-IV (Russell, 2011).

Owen and Davidson (2009a) have argued that at least three of the fourteen defining behaviours should be present, of which at least one should be among the five unique components, to satisfy the diagnostic criteria of the hubris syndrome.

In one study of the American presidents, Watts et al. (2013) showed that gradiose (but not vulnerable) narcissistic presidents were rated in polls as persuasive and good in agenda setting and crisis management. They tended, at least initially, to win the popular vote and to initiate a lot of legislation. However, over time, this narcissism leads to several negative outcomes, and in one case congressional impeachment. They note, as have many others, the double-edged sword of grandiose narcissistic leadership.

8.8 Unanswered questions

Rosenthal (2007) has suggested that the topic of the narcissistic leader is well worth exploring and identified seven areas to examine:

1. The line between narcissism and healthy, optimal self-confidence and self-esteem. This differentiates between the so-called 'bright side', 'charismatic', 'constructive' or 'productive' narcissists and those 'dark side', 'destructive' narcissists. This is about drawing the line between confidence and arrogance, healthy and unhealthy, normal or abnormal. The question is whether those demarcations can be made accurately and whether they are situationally appropriate.

2. Whether there are optimal conditions for narcissistic leadership. That is are there times in organizational life when narcissistic leadership is both desirable and effective. Thus, in times of crisis, or rapid growth this style of leadership may be highly efficient while in steady state times when building sustained relationships and trust is important, it is much less so. Indeed it is very debatable as to whether the narcissist is really capable of building sustained, trusting relationships.

3. Whether narcissistic leadership is effective only in the gaining, but not the maintaining, of power. That is, are they prone to a rapid rise-and-fall scenario because their self-defeating behaviour soon overwhelms their supposed charisma? In this sense are they, from a stakeholder perspective, only very superficially attractive and desirable?

4. What is it about followers that they choose narcissistic leaders? Is the aggressive, confident charismatic type exactly what people want and expect from their leaders? Is it because of their superhuman confidence that they appear so appealing? It has been suggested that a mirroring takes place in that narcissistic followers choose narcissistic leaders. Thus, organizations, indeed nations, may choose leaders to 'sooth their own narcissistic insecurities' and even create other narcissistic enemies. However, it is likely that followers soon rebel against those they have elected and

blame them for living up to their quite obviously unrealistic expectations. Indeed for both parties – narcissistic leaders and followers – self-loathing is projected onto the other with highly negative consequences.

5. Whether a criterion of productive or destructive narcissistic leaders is the extent to which they sacrifice all personal relationships (home and work) for 'success'. Many successful leaders have impaired personal relationships (multiple divorces; fractured broken families), but a central question is whether this is necessarily a sign of narcissism.

6. What can or should be done to prevent productive narcissists' destructive leading to serious 'organisational damage'. Thus, one may have a stable, non-narcissistic deputy or 'side-kick' or one might encourage coaching for the narcissistic leader. Other possibilities include having various procedures which act as checks and balances to the narcissist's power hungry and sometimes rash decision making.

7. Most importantly a good deal of this research is justified by finding historical examples to justify ideas. The better test is that of predictive validity namely being able to accurately make predictions about individuals that can be verified by research data.

8.9 Conclusions

It has only been comparatively recently that work psychologists have begun to take an interest in the personality disorders. Of all the personality disorders, it is no doubt the antisocial or psychopath is of most interest.

Many researchers have pointed out that the paradox of narcissism at work is that many traits and processes associated with narcissism can seem positive and beneficial, while others are the precise opposite. This paradox has been 'solved' by trying to distinguish between the adaptive and maladaptive narcissist, though it is not clear whether this is merely a linguistic tautology. Could one call a constructive narcissist a narcissist? It is an oxymoron in this sense.

Conceiving narcissism as a self-esteem trait disorder does imply, as many personality psychologists have argued, that there is a clear continuum between healthy and unhealthy. The issue remains, however, where to draw the line.

It is also important to bear in mind the perspective of social and work psychologists who stress how situational and cultural variables moderate narcissism. That is, organizations may unwittingly reinforce narcissism thus leading to their own destruction. They may indeed encourage or discourage certain processes (like performance appraisals), which make the problems of narcissists much worse. They may agree to disband committees and allow narcissistic managers to make decisions on their own. They may allow and encourage expensive privileges for people once they achieve certain levels. They may inhibit upward or negative feedback reaching senior managers.

Certainly, narcissists create friends and enemies in organizations and are a major contributing factor to the dysfunctional workplace (Langan-Fox et al., 2007). They certainly provide a serious management challenge to ensure their pathology works for, as against the fortunes of the organization.

Chapter 9

The paranoid, schizotypal, histrionic and obsessive-compulsive leader

9.1 Introduction

The dark-side thesis of Robert Hogan is that under stress a person's dark side is manifested. This dark side can cause great distress to them and their colleagues. This has been discussed in some length in the previous two chapters that have dealt with perhaps the 'disorders' or dark sides that are most closely related to leadership failure and derailment, namely psychopathy and narcissism.

Many researchers have taken up the ideas and tried to show how often beneficial characteristics, such as carefulness, creativity and colourfulness, can have a very dark side or shadow (de Haan & Kasozi, 2014). This chapter concerns four other types – or more strictly dimensions – related to derailment.

As noted in Chapter 4, the various and overlapping personality disorder accounts of derailment have a higher order classification of the disorders. In the DSM system, these are called clusters A, B and C, whereas Hogan describes Moving Toward, Away From and Against people. In each system, there seems to be a collection or grouping of types associated with people-related problems. In this chapter, four personality disorders are discussed. Any leader exhibiting these characteristics is likely to cause considerable problems for people with whom they work.

9.2 Paranoid (argumentative, vigilant)

It is believed that between 0.5 and 2.5 per cent of the population have this disorder, which must not be confused with the paranoid delusions of schizophrenics or the behaviour of refugees and migrants whose personal history leads to widespread distrust.

Paranoid people are *super-vigilant*: nothing escapes their notice. They seem tuned into mixed messages, hidden motives and secret groups. They are particularly sensitive to authority and power and obsessed with maintaining their own independence and freedom. Many have organization-specific conspiracy theories about others in that organization.

Distrust and suspiciousness of others at work are their abiding characteristics. The motives of all sorts of colleagues and boss are interpreted as malevolent, all the time. They often suspect, without much evidence that others are exploiting, harming or deceiving them about almost everything both at work and at home. They are usually preoccupied with unjustified doubts about loyalty or trustworthiness of subordinates, customers, bosses, shareholders, etc., on both big and small matters. They are reluctant to confide in others (peers at work) because of the fear that the information will be used against them: kept on file; used to sack them.

They often read hidden or threatening meanings into most benign remarks or events from emails to coffee-room gossips, and then remember them. They are also certainly *hypersensitive* to criticism. They persistently bear grudges against all sorts of people going back many years and can remember even the smallest slight. They perceive attacks on their character or reputation that others do not see and are quick to react angrily or to counterattack. They seem *hyper-alert and sensitive*. They have recurrent suspicions, without justification, regarding fidelity of their sexual or business partners and can be pretty obsessed with sex.

Paranoid managers are slow to commit and trust but once they do so they are usually loyal friends. They are very interested in others' motives and prefer 'watch-dog' jobs. They like being champions of the underdog, whistle-blowers on corruption. They are courageous because they are certain about their position. They are on the side of right: idealists striving for a better world. But they can be overly suspicious or fearful of certain people, which can manifest itself in an irrational hatred to certain race, religious or political groups.

They are not compromisers but attackers. Many of their characteristics make them excellent managers: *alert, careful, observant* and *tactical*. But they can have problems with authority and in dealing with those who hold different opinions from their own. However, they are more sensitive to the faults in others than the faults in themselves. The business world, they believe (sometimes correctly), is full of danger, dishonest people and those who are untrustworthy and will let them down. Because they believe others are out to harm them they can be overargumentative, bellicose, belligerent, hostile, secretive, stubborn and consumed with mistrustfulness. They are not divulging, suspicious of others and experts in projecting blame onto others.

Psychoanalysts believe that the paranoids feel weak and dependent but are sensitive to weakness in others and disclaim them for it. They yearn for dependency but fear it. Instead of showing personal doubt, they doubt others. Their self-righteousness, morality and punitiveness can be very attractive to some people.

Hogan and Hogan (2001) call this disorder *'Argumentative'*. These types, they argue, expect to be wronged, to be betrayed, to be set up, to be cheated on or to be deceived in some way. They see the world as a dangerous place, full of potential enemies, and they enjoy conspiracy theories; they are keenly alert for signs of having been mistreated. When they think they have been unfairly treated, they retaliate openly and directly. This may involve physical violence, accusations, retaliation or litigation. Retaliation is designed to send the signal that they are prepared to defend themselves. They are known for their suspiciousness, their argumentativeness and their lack of trust in others. They are hard to deal with on a continuing basis because you never know when they are going to be offended by something (unpredictability), and because they are so focused on their own private agenda, they don't have much time for others (unrewarding).

At their best they are very insightful about organisational politics and the motives of their counter players, and they can be the source of the good intelligence regarding the real agendas of others, and the real meaning of events. Although they are very insightful about politics, they are often not very good at playing politics. This is because they are true believers, they are deeply committed to their worldview, and they tend to be unwilling to compromise, even on small issues. Nonetheless, with their passionate commitment to a theory about how the world works, they can be visionary and charismatic, and people may be drawn to them…Because they are unpredictable and not regarding to deal with, they have trouble maintaining a team over a long period. (p. 48)

Paranoids mishandle stress by retreating, by withdrawing into their ideology and then attacking that which is threatening them. They are very persistent and tend to accumulate enemies. They are self-centred and ideology centred – all information and experience is filtered through their odd world view and evaluated in terms of the degree to which it fits with, or threatens that view, which somehow reflects on them.

In order to work with them, reports have no alternative but to agree with them, because they will defeat their objections in a way that makes sense only to them. Reports won't be able to persuade them that they are wrong and risk alienating them by challenging them, and once they decide people can't be trusted, the relationship will be over. Reports are either for them or against them.

De Haan and Kasozi (2014) talk of the adaptive brilliant sceptic and the suspicious neurotic. They provide an interesting case study:

Privately, even in the best of times, the Brilliant Sceptic is not what she seems. She is constantly scrutinizing herself and others for any errors or weaknesses, and she is privately much more anxious than she gives off. When tensions increase she may do overtime with double-checking other people's motives, and she may imagine all sorts of failings and disasters.

This is precisely why she is so brilliant, loyal and humble at the same time: her immense suspicion and sensitivity help her to see a problem long before others do. Under still more tension or under criticism she may imagine much worse scenarios than are realistic, and her nightly nightmares may take over her waking life. A Brilliant Sceptic appears to be little bothered by criticism or tensions, but in fact the opposite is true. She takes criticism extremely personally and adds insult to injury. She may envisage secret plots, she may be fearful of the envy of her colleagues, and she may persist in thinking that her 'bank' will go under. It takes no time for her to become argumentative with any suspected parties. This happens even when there appears to be very little evidence of perfidy or wrong doing. As a consequence the Brilliant Sceptic could start spying on her own employees, or become anxiously fearful of unrealistic dangers. She remains greatly sensitized to signs of betrayal or manipulation so that under pressure she almost 'expects' to be mistreated. She may even become a plotter herself, in order to retaliate and counter insurgencies that are in fact mainly imaginary. (p. 163)

According to Oldham and Morris, the following six traits and behaviours are clues to the presence of what they call the vigilant style. A person who reveals a strong vigilant tendency will demonstrate more of these behaviours more intensely than someone with less of this style in his or her personality profile.

1. **Autonomy**: Vigilant-style individuals possess a resilient independence. They keep their own counsel, they require no outside reassurance or advice, they make decisions easily and they can take care of themselves.
2. **Caution**: They are careful in their dealings with others, preferring to size up a person before entering into a relationship.
3. **Perceptiveness**: They are good listeners, with an ear for subtlety, tone and multiple levels of communication.
4. **Self-defence**: Individuals with Vigilant style are feisty and do not hesitate to stand up for themselves, especially when they are under attack.

5. **Alertness to criticism**: They take criticism very seriously, without becoming intimidated.
6. **Fidelity**: They place a high premium on fidelity and loyalty. They work hard to earn it, and they never take it for granted. (pp. 151–152)

Some jobs suit these people well: security, the military, perhaps pharmaceuticals. But the hyper-vigilant, argumentative, wary manager can be very difficult to live with. Whilst vigilance may be considered a virtue in some situations, the paranoid leader can be very difficult to deal with. Furthermore, they can make very bad decisions about people they work with and for.

9.3 Schizotypal (imaginative, idiosyncratic)

This disorder, more common in males than females, has been estimated to affect about 3 per cent of the population. They all appear to be pretty idiosyncratic and often creatively talented and curious. They often hold very strange beliefs enjoying the occult. They have odd habits, eccentric lifestyles and a rich inner life.

The schizotypal manager is marked by acute discomfort with, and reduced capacity for, close relationships. They show many eccentricities of behaviour. They may look odd and have a reputation for being 'peculiar'. They often have very odd ideas about business: how to succeed, whom to hire, what controls what. They can have very odd beliefs or magical thinking that influence behaviour and are inconsistent with business norms (e.g. superstitions, belief in clairvoyance, telepathy). They may get into crystals, feng shui, etc., in a very big and serious way.

They can have odd thinking and speech styles being vague or elaborate. They can seem 'other-worldly' and maybe very difficult to follow. They can have unusual perceptual experiences... seeing things that are not there, smell and taste things differently. Some are very suspicious or paranoid around the home and office. They show inappropriate or constricted affect: they react oddly emotionally in various contexts. That is, they may become very emotional around some trivial issues but strangely and unpredictably cold at others.

Many organizations do not tolerate the odd behaviours of these idiosyncratic types. They dress oddly and work odd hours. They are not very loyal to their companies and do not enjoy the corporate world. They don't 'connect' with staff, customers and their bosses. Their quirky quasi-religious beliefs estrange them yet more from the normal world of the other people. They are often loners.

Hogan and Hogan (2001) call these types Imaginative and describe them thus:

> They think about the world in unusual and often quite interesting ways. They may enjoy entertaining others with their unusual perceptions and insights. They are constantly alert to new ways of seeing, thinking, and expressing themselves, unusual forms of self-expression. They often seem bright, colourful, insightful, imaginative, very playful, and innovative, but also as eccentric, odd, and flighty.

The schizotypal leader can be curiously interesting and maybe fun to be around. But they are distractible and unpredictable and as managers they often leave people confused regarding their directions or intentions. They tend to mis-communicate in idiosyncratic and unusual ways. At their best, these people are imaginative, creative, interesting and amazingly insightful about the motives of others, but at their worst, they can be self-absorbed, single-minded, insensitive to the reactions of others and indifferent to the social and political consequences of their single-minded focus on their own agendas.

Under stress and heavy workloads, they can become upset, lose focus, lapse into eccentric behaviour and not communicate clearly. They can be moody and tend to get too excited by success and too despondent over failure. They do want attention, approval and applause, which explains the lengths that they are willing to go in order to attract it.

To work with the imaginative reports, one needs to be a good audience, to appreciate their humour, creativity and spontaneity, and to understand that they do not handle reversals very well. They will not mind suggestions and recommendations regarding important decisions, and, in fact, may even appreciate them. Reports should study their problem solving style, listen to their insights about other people and model their ability to 'think outside the box'.

De Haan and Kasozi (2014) described the bright side of the schizotypal person as the creative day-dreamer and the negative side as the absent professor. They noted:

> The Creative Daydreamer becomes the Absent Professor when his attention to new initiatives and new ideas is focused away from his team and organization. When not nurtured or responded to from within the organization he may get carried away towards unpractical solutions or hobbyism. At unpredictable moments an emotional cooling and detachment can set in and he stops being aware of the needs of those he works with. His pattern of shift into overdrive is often triggered when ideas and initiatives from colleagues and internal sources are poor and insufficient to deal with the challenges that are being faced. The Absent Professor may then get bored, humorous or even flippant. As a leader he will feel tempted to engage more with his own or outsiders' ideas to find new and vibrant sources of attention. He can then get rather caught up in his own flights of imagination rather than staying in touch with the situation. Consequently the Absent Professor puts more energy in seeking new initiatives outside than in paying attention to possible initiatives inside. Despite that, in relations with others within the organization he continues to put forward quirky ideas whilst offering very little direction as to why or what should be done. At his worst therefore he is experienced as holding the team or organization to ransom with his own absences and unpractical demands for creativity. When it comes to giving direction or implementation he remains unavailable, inaccessible or confusing. As if he lacks interest in or even awareness of the feelings or agendas of those around him. In addition he is often seen as being physically absent or going off on a tangent. This means that despite his authentic brilliance he is not around to engage with others in a way that can help them or himself make the potential come to fruition. (p. 171)

Oldham and Morris (1991), who call these types idiosyncratic, note:

The following six traits and behaviours are clues to the presence of the Idiosyncratic style. A person who reveals a strong Idiosyncratic tendency will demonstrate more of these behaviours more intensely than someone with less of this style in his or her personality profile.

1. **Inner life**: Idiosyncratic individuals are tuned in to, and sustained by, their own feelings and belief systems, whether or not others accept or understand their particular worldview or approach to life.
2. **Own world**: They are self-directed and independent, requiring few close relationships.
3. **Own thin**: Oblivious to convention, Idiosyncratic individuals create interesting, unusual, often eccentric lifestyles.
4. **Expanded reality**: Open to anything, they are interested in the occult, the extrasensory, and the supernatural.
5. **Metaphysics**: They are drawn to abstract and speculative thinking.
6. **Outward view**: Though they are inner-directed and follow their own hearts and minds, Idiosyncratic men and women are keen observers of others, particularly sensitive to how other people react to them. (pp. 242–243)

They also provide five tips for working with these odd-balls:

1. The Idiosyncratic person is one-of-a-kind. Accept, tolerate and treasure this person for his or her uniqueness, not despite it...
2. Do not pressure the Idiosyncratic person to conform to the Real World – and do not be pressured into conforming to his or her world either...
3. To widen your life together and to bring you closer, share the interests of the Idiosyncratic person in your life...
4. Help the Idiosyncratic person to have more time for his or her spiritual or otherwise special interests...
5. To deal with a very Idiosyncratic person, accept that you are the one who is more attached to conventional reality; take charge of meeting the fundamental responsibilities of life. (pp. 256–257)

The imaginative, idiosyncratic person is unlikely to reach very high position in organizations though they may be promoted in advertising or academia. The absent-minded, nutty professor and the creative advertising genius may share many schizotypical behaviours. If talented, they may do well but rarely as managers of others.

9.4 Histrionic (colourful, dramatic)

The term histrionic is derived from the Latin to mean actor, but the original term was hysterical from the Latin root to mean uterus. This disorder is found more frequently in women. They are attracted to 'lime light' jobs and strive for attention and praise but setbacks can lead easily to serious inner doubts and depression.

Histrionics are certainly emotionally literate: they are open with all their emotions. But these emotions can change very quickly.

These managers have excessive emotionality and attention seeking. They are the 'drama-queens' of the business world.

Most are uncomfortable in situations in which they are not the centre of attention and try always to be so. They delight in making a drama out of a crisis. Their interaction with others is often characterized by inappropriate sexually seductive or provocative behaviour. Needless to say, this causes more of a reaction in women than men. They display rapidly shifting and shallow expression of emotions. They are difficult to read. Most use physical appearance (clothes) to draw attention to self, and this may include body piercing or tattooing. They certainly get a reputation in the office for their 'unique apparel'. Many have a style of speech that is excessively impressionistic and lacking in detail. They always show self-dramatization, theatricality and exaggerated expression of emotion, usually negative. Even the dullest topic is imbued with drama. They are easily influenced by others or circumstances ... and therefore both unpredictable and persuadable. Many consider relationships to be more intimate than they actually are. Being rather dramatic they feel humdrum working relationships more intensely than others.

Histrionics do not make good managers. They get impatient with and anxious about details, routine administrative functions. They prefer gossip to analysis and tend not to be good at detail. They are highly sociable and have intense relationships. They live to win friends and influence people and can do so by being very generous with compliments, flattery and appreciation. They hate being bored: life with them is never staid and dull. They don't like being alone.

Interestingly, the definition of themselves comes from the outside: they see themselves as others say they see them. They therefore lack a consistent sense of who they are. They need constant reassurance and positive feedback from others. And as their heart rules their heads, they can be impulsive, impetuous and impatient. They live not in the real world but in a storybook world.

At work they can be persuasive and insightful. They enjoy the world of advertising, PR, sales and marketing but need strong back-up for things such as plans, budgets and details. At work they are volatile and are known for being moody. They can be effusive with both praise and blame. But everything is an emotional drama and emotionally they can be both childlike and childish. They don't have stable relationships. At work, they need to be the star, the centre of attention else they can feel powerless or desperately unworthy. They are not introspective. It is important not to overreact to their overreactions.

Hogan and Hogan (2001) call this type colourful and seem persuaded that others will find them interesting, engaging and worth paying attention to. They are good at calling attention to themselves – they know how to make dramatic entrances and exits, they carry themselves with flair, they self-consciously pay attention to their clothes and to the way others react to them.

Histrionics are marked by their stage presence or persona, their self-conscious and distinctive aura – they perform extremely well in interviews, in assessment centres and other public settings.

They are great fun to watch, but they are also quite impulsive and unpredictable; everything that makes them good at sales (and selling themselves) makes them poor managers – they are noisy, distractible, over-committed, and love to be the centre of attention. They are not necessarily extraverted, they are just good at calling attention to themselves. At

> their best, they are bright, colourful, entertaining, fun, flirtatious, and the life of the party. At their worst, they don't listen, they don't plan, they self-nominate and self-promote, and they ignore negative feedback. (Hogan & Hogan, 2001, p. 49)

Histrionics deal with stress and heavy workloads by becoming very busy, enjoying high-pressure situations when they can then be the star. Breathless with excitement, they confuse activity with productivity and evaluate themselves in terms of how many meetings they attend rather than how much they actually get done. A key feature of these people that others may not appreciate is how much they need and feed off approval, and how hard they are willing to work for it. And this explains why they persist in trying to be a star after their lustre has faded. To work with them, reports have to be prepared to put up with missed appointments, bad organization, rapid change of direction and indecisiveness. This will never change, although they can be planned for. Yet, by watching reports, you can learn how to read social clues, how to present your views effectively, forcefully, dramatically and how to flatter and quite simple dazzle other people.

De Haan and Kasozi (2014) have talked about the healthy and unhealthy sides of the schizotypal person. They call the former (healthy schizotypal person) the Accomplished Thespian and the latter (unhealthy schizotypal person) the Prima Donna. They provide a short sketch of a typical person who is the latter:

> The Accomplished Thespian becomes the Performing Prima Donna when his focus is more on the performers than on the reason for the performance. Instead of paying attention to doing what is needed, instead of listening to his counterparts, his energy goes into holding his own performance and ensuring that he is looking good in it. In that sense the performance becomes the purpose and the reward, and the wider function or organizational requirement is increasingly missed. The Accomplished Thespian's tough resolve tips over into being unhelpful when his performances no longer elicit the longer-term outcomes and achievements that

the organization seeks. Experiencing the challenge and criticism of others, he becomes less connected with their needs and becomes more concerned with showing that he is delivering or at least doing his best. Paradoxically his attention to performance per se and ignorance of wider circumstances can create a situation where he's seen as irascible and self-absorbed. He is then experienced as being closed off to reality and not open to constructive feedback. At his most challenged, the Performing Prima Donna is experienced as a self-obsessed and unpredictable loose cannon, a superficial talking shop, and an organizational liability. Those who work with him try to avoid his worst excesses of showing off, and to protect others from his most embarrassing outbursts. (pp. 190–191)

Oldham and Morris (2000) noted seven characteristics of this type, which they call dramatic.

A person who reveals a strong dramatic tendency will demonstrate more of these behaviours more intensely than someone who has less of this style.

1. **Feelings**: Dramatic men and women live in an emotional world. They are sensation orientated, emotionally demonstrative and physically affectionate. They react emotionally to events and can shift quickly from mood to mood.
2. **Colour**: They experience life vividly and expansively. They have rich imaginations, they tell entertaining stories and they are drawn to romance and melodrama.
3. **Spontaneity**: Dramatic individuals are lively and fun. Their joie de vivre leads them to act on impulse to take advantage of the moment.
4. **Attention**: Dramatic people like to be seen and noticed. They are often the centre of attention, and they rise to the occasion when all eyes are on them.
5. **Applause**: Compliments and praise are like food and water to persons with Dramatic style: they need them to go on.

6. **Appearance**: They pay a lot of attention to grooming, and they enjoy clothes, style and fashion.
7. **Sexual attraction**: In appearance and behaviour, Dramatic individuals enjoy their sexuality. They are seductive, engaging, charming tempters and temptresses. (pp. 126–127)

They also offer six tips on dealing with them.

1. You are attracted to the Dramatic person's spontaneity, passion, sensuality and ability to have a good time... Allow the Dramatic person his or her emotional freedom, and enjoy the range of experience that will result.
2. Appreciate, praise, flatter and give feedback. The Dramatic person needs you react openly and verbally, especially about your positive feelings, at all times. Don't hold back; there's no such thing as too much of a good thing with this personality style. But be sure to be honest...
3. Be romantic... Even the Dramatic person in your life is a friend, relative, or parent, these sentimental attentions will delight and thrill him or her.
4. Be realistic about this person's relative inability or reluctance to handle certain responsibilities, including money. Handle the finances or the financial planning yourself, if need be. Better, supervise or double check essential details...
5. Don't hold grudges. Dramatic persons don't hold things in, and the Dramatic person in your life may be emotionally tempestuous... Try to let go of your own anger or annoyance. Don't take the Dramatic person's emotional reactions personally and don't be frightened by the drama.
6. Avoid jealousy... Dramatic individuals like to charm other people. Try feeling flattered and turned on by the warm attentions of others to your mate and have a good time at the party. (pp. 139–140)

There are drama queens in all sectors though they are likely to be found in the more human resource orientated world. They can do very well in

PR, marketing and training, particularly, if they are talented. But they certainly remain hard working for their ever-suffering reports.

9.5 Obsessive-compulsive (diligent, conscientious)

This disorder is more common in men and around 1 per cent of the population exhibit the symptoms. They are often known for their zealous perfectionism, attention to detail, rigidity and formality. They are also often the workaholics; those who really 'live' the work ethic. They are competent, organized, thorough and loyal. They enjoy, even in their holidays and leisure time, intense, detailed, goal-orientated activities.

These managers show a preoccupation with orderliness, perfectionism and mental and interpersonal control, at the expense of flexibility, openness and efficiency. They make for the most anal of bureaucrats. They are always preoccupied with details, rules, lists, order, organization or schedules to the extent that the major point of the business activity is lost and forgotten. All show perfectionism that interferes with task completion (e.g. unable to complete a project because his or her own overly strict standards are not met). And of course they demand it in others, however unproductive it makes them. These managers are often workaholics often excluding leisure activities and friendships. They are seriously driven workaholics. They have a well-deserved reputation for being overconscientious, scrupulous and inflexible about matters of morality, ethics or values.

Amazingly, they are unable to discard worn-out or worthless objects even when they have no sentimental value. They hoard rubbish at home and in the workplace. They are reluctant to delegate tasks or to work with others unless they submit to exactly his or her way of doing things. They do not let go and pay the price. They are misers towards both self and others; money is viewed as something to be hoarded for future catastrophes. Because they never fully spend their budget, they never get it increased. In short, they show rigidity and stubbornness... very unpleasant to work for.

Conscientious, obsessive-compulsives rise through the ranks through hard work. But at certain levels they start to derail because they have problems making quick decisions, setting priorities and delegating. They tend to want to check the details again and again. They function best as right-hand-man to leaders with strong conceptual skills and visions. They are very self-disciplined and put work first. They are often not very emotionally literate and can be fanatical and fundamentalist about moral, political and religious issues. They can find it difficult to relax and throw things away. Their relationships are marked by conventionality and coolness. They are faithful, responsible but unromantic and unemotional. They can be seen as mean, overcautious.

The obsessive-compulsive manager *must* have everything done *perfectly*. They get wrapped up in details and lose sense of directions and priorities. They can be tyrannical bosses super-attentive to time, orderliness and cleanliness. They are driven by 'oughts' and 'shoulds' and expect others to do likewise. They make rules for themselves and others but don't see themselves as rigid, perfectionistic and controlling. They are the overbearing, fault-finders of the business world. They are driven to achieve respect and approval and control their and others', dangerous impulses, desires and feelings.

Oldham and Morris (1991) describe the following psychiatric criteria:

(1) Perfectionism that interferes with task completion, for instance, inability to complete a project because own overly strict standards are not met.

(2) Preoccupation with details, rules, lists, order, organization or schedules to the extent that the major point of the activity is lost.

(3) Unreasonable insistence that others submit to exactly his or her way of doing things, or unreasonable reluctance to allow others to do things because of the conviction that they will not do them correctly.

(4) Excessive devotion to work and productivity to the exclusion of leisure activities and friendships (not accounted for by obvious economic necessity).

(5) Indecisiveness: decision making is either avoided, postponed or protracted, for instance, the person cannot get assignments

done on time because of ruminating about priorities (do not include if indecisiveness is due to excessive need for advice or reassurance from others).

(6) Overconscientiousness, scrupulousness and inflexibility about matters of morality, ethics or values (not accounted for by cultural or religious identification)

(7) Restricted expression of affection

(8) Lack of generosity in giving time, money or gifts when no personal gain is likely to result.

(9) Inability to discard worn-out or worthless objects even when they have no sentimental value. (pp. 71–72)

Hogan and Hogan (2001) called these types Diligent because they are concerned with doing a good job, being a good citizen and pleasing authority. They note that the Diligent type is hard working, careful, planful, meticulous and have very high standards of performance for themselves and other people. They live by these rules and expect others to do so too, and they become irritable and erratic when others do not follow their rules. What is most distinctive is their conservatism, their detail orientation, their risk aversion, but they are also thought of as reliable, dependable and predictable. They are often desirable organizational citizens who can always be relied upon to maintain standards, do their work competently and professionally, and treat their colleagues with respect.

Hogan and Hogan note that they are good role models who uphold the highest standards of professionalism in performance and comportment. They are popular with their bosses because they are so completely reliable but not necessarily with those who report to them. However, they are fussy, particularly, nit-picking, micro-managers who deprive their subordinates of any choice or control over their work. Their sin is micro-management. This alienates their staff who quite soon refuse to take any initiative and simply wait to be told what to do and how to do it. Diligent, conscientious, obsessive-compulsives also cause stress for themselves; their obsessive concern for quality and high performance makes it difficult for them to delegate. It also makes it difficult for them to prioritize their tasks. They also have problems with vision and the big picture. Consequently, they have a kind of ambivalent status as managers and can function in some environments at certain levels.

Diligent, obsessive-compulsives tend to become stressed by heavy workloads. They respond to increased workloads by working longer and harder (not smarter), and they fall further and further behind and thus find this intolerable. They often become a bottle neck to productivity – because everything must pass through them, be checked and revised by them, be approved by them and they won't let anything go that isn't completed according to their standards. They perhaps too closely supervise their staff. It can help making suggestions regarding prioritizing work, and by reflecting on the big picture.

De Haan and Kasozi (2014) provide a description of the difficult obsessive-compulsive manager whom they call the responsible workaholic:

> The Responsible Workaholic becomes the Troublesome Princeling when she loses the confidence and support of those she relies on in the visionary tapestries that she is weaving. In this circumstance her tremendous energy and experience are seen as being devoted to control and double-checking, rather than to activities that are a real benefit in her organization. She becomes fussy and gets caught up in irrelevant details. She becomes slow and reluctant to share the fruits of her work. She may become controlling and inflexible. The Troublesome Princeling's unhelpful overdrive is mostly triggered when there are unusual risks or when her creative ideas are not taken on board and actively supported by others internally and externally. She will then find herself increasingly making more and more suggestions and creating more and more elaborate proposals that others pay less and less attention to. Consequently she is experienced as a maverick, brilliant but self-obsessed, and lacking in realism, pragmatism and detachment. At her most challenged she finds it impossible to delegate or even to identify priorities, and she gets obsessed with unrealistic standards. Her behaviour is seen as controlling, inflexible and unhelpful and her princely position is only tolerated because of her prior accomplishments or because she keeps putting in enormous time and effort. (p. 147)

In everyday language Oldham and Morris (1991) describe nine characteristics of these types:

(1) **Hard work**: The Conscientious person is dedicated to work, works very hard, and is capable of intense, single-minded effort.

(2) **The right thing**: To be Conscientious is to be a person of conscience. These are men and women of strong moral principles and values. Opinions and beliefs on any subject are rarely held lightly. Conscientious individuals want to do the right thing.

(3) **The right way**: Everything must be done 'right', and the Conscientious person has a clear understanding of what that means, from the correct way to balance the cheque book, to best strategy to achieve the boss's objectives, to how to fit every single dirty dish into the dishwasher.

(4) **Perfectionism**: The Conscientious person likes and projects to be complete to the final detail, without even minor flaws.

(5) **Love of detail**: Conscientious men and women take seriously all the steps of any project. No detail is too small for Conscientious consideration.

(6) **Order**: Conscientious people like the appearance of orderliness and tidiness. They are good organisers, cataloguers, and list makers, and they appreciate schedules and routines.

(7) **Pragmatism**: Conscientious types approach the world and other people from a practical, no-nonsense point of view. They roll up their sleeves and get to work without much emotional expenditure.

(8) **Prudence**: Thrifty, careful, and cautious in all areas of their lives, Conscientious individuals do not give in to reckless abandon or wild excess.

(9) **Accumulation**: A 'pack rat', the Conscientious person saves and collects things (storing them in orderly bundles), reluctant to discard anything that has, formerly had, or someday may have, value for him or her. (p. 57)

They also offer tips for dealing with these types:

1. Be humorously tolerant. Let the Conscientious person have his or her habits...
2. Stay flexible...
3. Don't wait for the Conscientious person to change. Bring your strengths to the relationship and use them...
4. Don't expect compliments or easy expressions of affection; these are not a barometer of how a Conscientious person feels about you...
5. Avoid arguments and power struggles at all costs. Conscientious people must win – it's their nature. Conscientious men and women are consummate arguers and may nit-pick and split hairs until you walk out or give in...
6. Appreciate and enjoy the security and stability that the Conscientious person brings to the relationship. Be reassured that he or she takes care of your life so well. (pp. 67–68)

The diligent, conscientious type can do very well in business. Certain jobs demand obsessive-compulsive-checking, such as health and safety and quality control. But, like all the other disorders, it is too much of this trait that leads to serious problems both for the individual and his or her staff.

9.6 Conclusion

As noted many times before, the paradox of the derailed leader is that they have often had a very successful early career. Their abilities and personalities seem to have helped them climb the greasy pole of corporate success only to dramatically 'fall from grace'. Furthermore, it has been observed that certain personal characteristics seem to benefit people well in different work sectors like disinhibited theatricality in the creative industries and careful checking in the world of engineering.

This chapter has been about four executive types whose personality disorders become demons in the sense that their strengths become their weaknesses. Under stress and pressure, their dark-side disorders lead to significant problems for all around them. Furthermore, if the stress is chronic rather than intermittent and acute, it can lead to sudden and dramatic derailment.

Chapter 10

The sick executive

10.1 Introduction

People continue working whilst physically ill. Most have struggled to work with a bad cold. Many have continued at work whilst suffering pain possibly self-inflicted as in a hangover or with a migraine. Some people suffer from chronic conditions like lower back pain which means they are in chronic pain. Some others may experience tinnitus which can affect their communication and judgement.

Some executives become addicts and those addictions cloud their judgements. Others succumb to a wide range of stress-related illnesses, which can take their toll in many ways. In this chapter we question how physical illness may impair a leader's judgement and behaviour.

Although it seems perfectly obvious to most people, *health* as such remains difficult to clearly define. In 1948, the WHO defined it as 'a complete state of physical, mental and social well-being and not merely the absence of disease or infirmity'. This definition proved very helpful for three reasons. First, it saw health in *positive* terms, not negative terms – that is, health is not being sick with various signs and symptoms of illness. Next, it took what we now call a *biopsychosocial perspective* recognizing the integration of various dimensions of health. Third, it included the first mention of *social well-being* which has been the focus of much subsequent research.

Some people want to broaden the concept even more in order to look at the political and sociological factors like poverty and injustice that relate to health status. For most people, there is a *wellness – illness continuum* from serious acute and chronic illnesses at one extreme and high levels of flourishing mental and physical health at the other.

In the past, however, it was common to divide mind and body seeing physical and mental well-being as distinct. We now know that there are both *psychosomatic* illnesses and *somapsychic* illnesses, where mental problems cause physical problems and vice versa. It has been argued that thinking about health has moved from the dualistic view (mind and body are separate) to a mechanistic biomedical approach which is reductionistic because it reduces health status and behaviour exclusively to physical functioning. However, the psychosocial models of health and illness prevailed into the now-accepted *biopsychosocial* model with these three factors becoming inter-related and interdependent.

The biomedical approach assumes that ill health and disease is directly (and exclusively) caused by diseases and their specific pathological processes. The biopsychosocial approach suggests we best understand chronic condition by also understanding the patient and the physical and social context of the health care system.

Historically, physicians have always taken a patient's psyche (personality, beliefs and values) and their social circumstances and context into consideration when treating them. Osler, a great nineteenth-century expert in internal medicine, noted: 'The good physician treats the disease but the great physician treats the patient who has the disease'. Whilst the biopsychosocial approach to health and illness has always been articulated in one form or another, the stunning success of pharmacotherapy over the past 20–30 years led to a resurgence of the biomedical model.

The biopsychosocial approach to health understands the nature/nurture interaction. It accepts conscious and unconscious influences on health and wellness. Most of all, it understands reciprocal determinism which accepts that social factors may influence psychological factors which change the physiological factors.

10.2 The biopsychosocial approach to health

This now well-established model argues for the *interplay* of three aspects of a person's life: biological, psychological and social factors. *Biological* factors refer to body functioning. *Psychological* factors refer to the ideas, (cognition), feelings (emotions) and drives (motivations) that influence a person's lifestyle. *Social* factors like the family, community, culture and nation that one grows up in which are also seen to be also pivotal to health.

We believe that extreme hubristic behaviour is a syndrome, constituting a cluster of features ('symptoms') evoked by a specific trigger (power), and usually remitting when power fades. 'Hubris syndrome' is seen as an acquired condition, and therefore different from most personality disorders which are traditionally seen as persistent throughout adulthood. The key concept is that hubris syndrome is a disorder of the possession of power, particularly power which has been associated with overwhelming success, held for a period of years and with minimal constraint on the leader. The ability to make swift decisions, sometimes based on little evidence, is of particular importance – arguably necessary – in a leader. Similarly, a thin-skinned person will not be able to stand the process of public scrutiny, attacks by opponents and back-stabbings from within, without some form of self-exultation and grand belief about their own mission and importance. Powerful leaders are a highly selected sample and many criteria of any syndrome based on hubris are those behaviours by which they are probably selected – they make up the pores of the filter through which such individuals must pass to achieve high office ...

Dictators are particularly prone to hubris because there are few, if any, constraints on their behaviour. Here, this complex area is not covered but one of us has considered the matter elsewhere. Hitler's biographer, Ian Kershaw entitled his first volume '1889–1936 Hubris' and the second '1936–1945 Nemesis'. Stalin's hubris was not as marked or as progressive as Hitler's. As for Mussolini and Mao both had hubris but probably each also had bipolar disorder. Khrushchev was diagnosed as having hypomania and there is some evidence that Saddam Hussein had bipolar disease. Being elected to high office for a democratic leader is a significant event. Subsequent election victories appear to increase the likelihood of hubristic behaviour becoming hubris syndrome. Facing a crisis situation such as a looming or actual war or facing potential financial disaster may further increase hubris. But only the more developed cases of hubris deserve classification as a syndrome exposed as an occupational hazard in those made vulnerable by circumstance.

10.3 In sickness and in power

A surprising number of politicians at various times and in various countries have been ill. David Owen (2009), both a trained medical doctor and a high-ranking British politician, has written a book subtitled 'Illness in heads of government during the last 100 years'. He was interested in how various illnesses affect decision making and also the dangers of trying to keep these illnesses secret. In doing so, he makes little distinction between physical, psychological and psychiatric illnesses. Furthermore, he showed that often at critical times in their political lives and those of their country, they were essentially unfit to hold power.

His particular interest is in hubris, which is very similar to subclinical narcissism which he sees as a major factor in political leader derailments. In their paper, Owen and Davidson (2009) noted:

A review of biographical sources of mental illness in US Presidents between 1776 and 1974 showed that 18 (49%) Presidents met criteria suggesting psychiatric disorder: depression (24%), anxiety (8%), bipolar disorder (8%) and alcohol abuse/dependence (8%) were the most common. In 10 instances (27%) a disorder was evident during presidential office, which in most cases probably impaired job performance. The overall (49%) rate of psychiatric disorder was in tune with US population rates of mental illness, but the rate of depression was greater than expected in males, which has been reported as 13% in the US population. (p. 4)

Table 10.1 is adapted from Owen's work. What is surprising is three things. First, how many politicians appeared to have a number of serious illnesses. Second, how often these illnesses were little known or reported during the politicians' time of power. Third, the possibly significant effects of those illnesses on the politicians' judgement.

It is quite possible that senior business executives also experience periods of acute and possibly chronic illnesses. This inevitably impacts on their interactions with the board and the decisions they make. Often these illnesses are covered up as much as they are in politicians. It seems, however, that there are no books on business executives as on politicians by Owen.

10.4 Stress and illness at work

It is 'tough at the top'. Many executives suffer from acute and chronic anxiety and worry, which can easily lead to stress-related illnesses such as migraines, ulcers and irritable bowel syndrome. Many of these illnesses require medication and sometimes time off work, which can significantly impact on executive decision making.

So what is stress? The word 'stress' is derived from the Latin word *stringere*, which means 'to draw tight'. First, many definitions exist: some believe stress can and should be *subjectively* defined (i.e. what I say about how I feel); others feel one needs an *objective* definition (perhaps physical measures of saliva, blood or heart beat). Second, some researchers believe a *global* definition is appropriate (there is one general thing called stress); others emphasize that stress is *multidimensional* (it is made up of very different features). Third, should you define it by the outside stimulus factors that *cause* it or rather how *people respond* to it? That is, if somebody does not experience something as stressful, can we really call it a stressor?

There are various models or theories that try to describe and understand stress. The simplest perhaps is the demand-control theory that looks at the various psychological and physical demands put on the person to behave in a particular way and the control or decision latitude they have in delivery then. High-demand, low-control situations are worst. Another way of describing this is challenge and support.

Table 10.1 Illnesses in famous politicians

Leader Name	Title (years)	Related Illnesses to Hubris	Impairment Evident to Others or Sought Treatment
George W. Bush	President of the USA (2001–2009)	• History of alcohol-related problems • Overactive thyroid gland	Yes
Jacques Chriac	President of France (1995–2007)	• Stroke	Yes
Tony Blair	British prime minister (1997–2007)	• None	Yes
Ariel Sharon	President of Israel (2001–2006)	• Stroke • Cerebral vascular incident • Small hole in heart that led to complications • Bleeding into the brain – led to medically induced coma	Yes
Saddam Hussein	President of Iraq (1979–2003)	• Bipolar disorder	Yes

(Continued)

Leader Name	Title (years)	Related Illnesses to Hubris	Impairment Evident to Others or Sought Treatment
Boris Yeltsin	President of Russia (1991–1999)	• Lower back pain • Cardiac ischaemia • Reliance on painkillers and alcohol • Heart attacks • Sleep apnoea • Hypothyroidism	Yes
George H. W. Bush (Sr.)	President of the USA (1989–1993)	• Atrial fibrillation (diagnosed after difficulties when jogging) • Thyrotoxicosis	Yes
Margaret Thatcher	British prime minister (1979–1990)	• None	Yes
Ronald Reagan	President of the USA (1981–1989)	• One of two politicians diagnosed with Alzheimer's after leaving office • Limited attention span	Yes

(Continued)

Leader Name	Title (years)	Related Illnesses to Hubris	Impairment Evident to Others or Sought Treatment
Leonid Brezhnev	General Secretary of the Central Committee of the Communist Party (1964–1982)	• High blood pressure • Heart attacks • Arteriosclerosis of the brain from Alvarez disease • Only able to concentrate for around 3 hours a day	Yes
Jimmy Carter	President of the USA (1977–1981)	• Haemorrhoids	
Josip Broz Tito	President of Yugoslavia (1953–1980)	• High blood pressure • Heart attacks • Cardiomobile – meant he only had 1 or 2 hours of concentration a day	Yes
Harold Wilson	British prime minister (1974–1976)	• One of two politicians diagnosed with Alzheimer's after leaving office	Yes

(Continued)

Leader Name	Title (years)	Related Illnesses to Hubris	Impairment Evident to Others or Sought Treatment
Edward Heath	British prime minister (1970–1974)	• Hypothyroidism (sometimes referred to as myxoedema)	Yes
		• Atrial fibrillation of the heart ('rip-roaring heart failure')	
Richard Nixon	President of the USA (1969–1974)	• Alcoholic abuse	Yes
		• Paranoia	
Georges Pompidou	President of France & Co-Prince of Andorra (1969–1974)	• Waldenström syndrome	Yes
		• Influenza	
		• Haemorrhoids	
Willy Brandt	Chancellor of the Federal Republic of Germany (1969–1974)	• Depressive symptoms that interfered with politics	Yes
Lyndon Johnson	President of the USA (1963–1969)	• Heart attacks	Yes
		• Depression	
		• Acute cholecysistis (caused post-operation depression)	
		• Hypersexuality	
		• Bipolar – 1	

(Continued)

Leader Name	Title (years)	Related Illnesses to Hubris	Impairment Evident to Others or Sought Treatment
Charles de Gaulle	President of the French Republic (1959–1969)	• Depression • Malignant Malaria • Prostatic adenoma	Yes
Lyndon B. Johnson	President of the USA (1963–1969)	• Bipolar 1 disorder	Yes
John F. Kennedy	President of the USA (1961–1963)	• Addison's disease • Amphetamine abuse	Yes
Harold MacMillan	British prime minister (1957–1963)	• Urinary retention • Prostate cancer • Hypochondria	Yes
Dwight Eisenhower	President of the USA (1953–1961)	• Type 'A' personality • Hypertension • Crohn's Disease	Yes
Anthony Eden	British prime minister (1955–1957)	• Amphetamine abuse	Yes
Winston Churchill	British prime minister (1940–1945; 1951–1955)	• Major Depressive Disorder: cyclothymic features • Alcohol and drug abuse • Brain apoplexy	Yes

(Continued)

Leader Name	Title (years)	Related Illnesses to Hubris	Impairment Evident to Others or Sought Treatment
Joseph Stalin	General Secretary of the Central Committee of the Communist Party (1922–1952)	• High blood pressure • Brain haemorrhaging	Yes
Franklin D. Roosevelt	President of the USA (1933–1945)	• Paranoia • Minor haemorrhages	Yes
Adolf Hitler	Führer of Germany (1934–1945)	• Parkinson's disease • Hepatitis • Heart attacks • Neurotic Psychopath – bordering schizophrenia • Drug abuse (cocaine; bull testosterone, but not as a replacement of his monorchism) • Paranoia	Yes
Benito Mussolini	Head of the Italian Government and Duce of Facism (1925–1945)	• Bipolar Disorder	Yes
Neville Chamberlain	British prime minister (1937–1940)	• None	Yes
Stanely Baldwin	British prime minister (1935–1937)	• Deafness (thought to be cause of resignation)	No

(Continued)

Leader Name	Title (years)	Related Illnesses to Hubris	Impairment Evident to Others or Sought Treatment
James Ramsey MacDonald	British prime minister (1929–1935)	• Glaucoma • Mild dementia	Yes
Calvin Coolidge	President of the U.S. (1923–1929)	• Major Depressive Disorder	Yes
Bonar Law	British prime minister (1922–1923)	• Laryngeal cancer	Yes
Warren Harding	President of the U.S. (1921–1923)	• Heart trouble Depression	Yes
David Lloyd George	British prime minister (1916–1922)	• None	Yes
Woodrow Wilson	President of the USA (1913–1921)	• Anxiety Disorder • Major Depressive Disorder • Personality change due to stroke	Yes
Paul Deschanel	President of France (1920)	• Elepnor's Syndrome • Drug abuse • Frontotemporal Dementia	Yes
Herbert Asquith	British prime minister (1908–1916)	• Alcohol abuse • Hypertension	Yes
Henry Campbell-Bannerman	British prime minister (1905–1908)	• Heart attacks	Yes
Theodore Roosevelt	President of the USA (1901–1909)	• Bipolar Disorder	Yes

In most management jobs, leaders are both supported and challenged. They are supported by peers, subordinates and superiors, who also challenge them to work harder and 'smarter'. Thus, it is possible to think of the average manager in terms of support and challenge thus:

- **Much support, little challenge**: Managers in this role are in the fortunate position of good technical and social support, but the fact they are under-challenged probably means that they under-perform. They may actually be stressed by boredom and monotony.
- **Much support, much challenge**: This combination tends to get the most out of managers as they are challenged by superiors, subordinates, shareholders and customers to 'work smarter' but are given the appropriate support to succeed.
- **Little support, much challenge**: This unfortunate, but very common, situation is a major cause of stress for any manager because he or she is challenged to work consistently hard but only offered minimal emotional, informational (feedback) and physical (equipment) support.
- **Little support, little challenge**: Managers in some bureaucracies lead a quiet and unstressed life because they are neither challenged nor supported, which usually means neither they nor their organization benefits. They belong to the 'psychologically quit but physically stay' employee.

Most of the models and theories about stress consider how three factors lead to stress. They are essentially things about the *make-up of the individual*, particularly their personality, ability and biography. Second, there are features about the *environment* (job, family, organization), usually but not exclusively considered in terms of the work environment. Third, there is how the individual and the environment perceive, define but more importantly try to *cope* with stress, strains and pressures. The argument is that there are individual, environmental and coping factors that considered together determine whether, when and why individuals and group experience stress.

Two people with similar experience and qualifications and in the same job or family situation can experience very different levels of stress – one gets ill and goes absent whilst others soldier on. Why? First, there are the anxious worriers (sometimes called neurotics). People with 'negative affectivity', namely those with a mix of anxiety, irritability, neuroticism and self-deprecation, tend to be less productive, less job satisfied and more prone to absenteeism. Neurotics tend to dwell on their mistakes, disappointments and shortcomings and focus more on the negative aspects of the world in general. They seem more prone to experiencing stress and less able to cope with it.

Another possible cause is fatalists. Individuals develop a general expectancy regarding their ability to control their lives. People who believe that the events that occur in their lives are the result of their own behaviour and/or ability; personality and effort are said to have the expectancy of internal control, whereas those who believe events in their lives to be a function of luck, chance, fate, God(s), powerful others or powers beyond their control, comprehension or manipulation are said to have an expectancy of external control. People with internal locus of control tend to see threatening events at work as less stressful and they cope with it better than managers with external locus of control.

Third, there is the competitive, frantic person. The Type A (supposed heart attach prone) pattern is characterized by excessive and competitive drive and an enhanced sense of time urgency. This behaviour pattern is multidimensional, having many components such as an intense sustained desire to achieve, an eagerness to complete, persistent drive for recognition, a continuous involvement in deadline activities, a habitual propensity to accelerate mental and physical functions and consistent alertness. They bring about their own stress.

How does a person with stress attempt to cope? One distinction that has been made was between *problem*-focused coping (aimed at problem-solving or doing something to alter the source of stress) and *emotion*-focused coping (aimed at reducing or managing the emotional distress that is associated with, or cued by, a particular set of circumstances). Emotion-focused responses involve denial, others involve positive reinterpretation of events and still others involve the seeking out of social support. Similarly, problem-focused coping can potentially involve several distinct activities, such as planning, taking direct action, seeking assistance, screening out particular activities and sometimes stopping acting for an extended period. It is argued that, for various reasons, individuals tend to adopt and habitually use a few of the coping patterns, which may or may not be successful. However, it does appear that people can be taught or trained to relinquish less successful coping strategies and adopt others.

One personal factor that seems to play an important role in determining resistance to stress is the familiar dimension of optimism/pessimism. Optimists are hopeful in their outlook on life, interpret a wide range of situations in a positive light and tend to expect favourable outcomes and results. Pessimists, by contrast, interpret many situations negatively and expect unfavourable outcomes and results. Optimists are much more stress-resistant than pessimists.

Optimists and pessimists adopt sharply contrasting tactics for coping with stress. Optimists concentrate on problem-focused coping – making and enacting specific plans for dealing with sources of stress. In addition, they seek social support – the advice and help of friends and others – and refrain from engaging in other activities until current problems are solved and stress is reduced. Pessimists tend to adopt rather different strategies, such as giving up in their efforts to reach goals with which stress is interfering and denying that the stressful events have even occurred. Furthermore, they have different attributional styles: the optimist attributes success internally and failure externally and vice versa. Indeed, that is how optimism and pessimism are both measured and maintained.

Another individual difference factor that seems to distinguish stress-resistant people from those who are more susceptible to its harmful effects is hardiness or resilience. This term refers to a cluster of characteristics rather than just one. Hardy people appear to differ from others in three respects. They show higher *level of: commitment* – deeper involvement in their jobs and other life activities; *control* – the belief that they can, in fact, influence important events in their lives and the outcomes they experience; and challenge – they *perceive change as a challenge* and an opportunity to grow rather than as a threat to their security.

Together, these characteristics tend to arm hardy persons with high resistance to stress. People classified as high in hardiness report better health than those with low hardiness, even when they encounter major stressful life changes.

We can recognize stress by its consequences. The list is long but can usually be categorized under three headings (See Table 10.2):

Table 10.2 Three symptoms of burnout

Physiological symptoms	A noticeable decline in physical appearance; Chronic fatigue and tiredness; Frequent infections, especially respiratory infections; Health complaints, such as headaches, backaches, stomach and skin problems; Signs of depression, change in weight or eating habits.
Emotional symptoms	Boredom or apathy: lack of affect and hopelessness; Cynicism and resentfulness; Depressed appearance, sad expressions, slumped posture; Expressions of anxiety, frustration, tearfulness.
Behavioural symptoms	Absenteeism, accidents; Increase in alcohol or caffeine consumptions; increase smoking; Obsessive exercising; Irrational quick to fly off the handle; Reduced productivity: inability to concentrate or complete a task.

Individuals often try to cope with their stress by lifestyle changes, by attempting relaxation or meditation techniques or by signing up for therapy. There are also organizational symptoms of stress like high absenteeism and labour turnover, a deterioration in labour relations and a reduction of quality control even theft and arson. Some attempt to reduce a worker's stress by job redesign, organizational restructuring and introducing stress management programme.

10.5 Burnout

Burnout is the outcome of physical, psychological and emotional exhaustion. Boredom, the opposite of a heavy workload, may cause it. At work, poor communication among supervisors, peers, subordinates and clients is a common cause. Too much responsibility with too little support is also found to contribute to it. Having to acquire new and specialized skills too frequently to do quite different, important but meaningless tasks is yet another cause.

Classic causes and consequences of burnout are the following well-established facets of alienation: first, *meaninglessness* – the idea that there seems no purpose, inherent worth or meaning in day-to-day work; second, *estrangement* from the goals of the organization – assigning personally low value to those things the organization values highly; third, *powerlessness* – the expectancy that, whatever one does, it will not relate to success or happiness.

First, victims of burnout complain about physical exhaustion. They have low energy and feel tired much of the time. They report many symptoms of physical strain, such as frequent headaches, nausea, poor sleep and changes in eating habits. *Second*, they experience emotional exhaustion. Depression, feelings of helplessness and feelings of being trapped in one's job are all part of the syndrome. *Third*, people suffering from burnout often demonstrate a pattern of mental or attitudinal exhaustion, often known as depersonalization. They become cynical about others, tend to treat them as objects rather than as people and hold extremely negative attitudes towards their organization. In addition, they tend to derogate themselves, their jobs, their managers and even life in general. *Finally*, they often report feelings of low personal accomplishment.

People suffering from burnout conclude that they have not been able to accomplish much in the past and assume that they probably will not succeed in the future. Burnout is this syndrome of emotional, physical and mental exhaustion, coupled with feelings of low self-esteem or low self-efficacy, resulting from prolonged exposure to intense stress. Not much fun really.

10.6 Workaholism

Oates (1971) claimed to have invented the neologism 'workaholic' meaning the addiction to work and the compulsion or the uncontrollable need to work incessantly. But unlike other forms of addiction that are held in contempt, workaholism is frequently lauded, praised, expected and even demanded. Signs of this 'syndrome' include boasting about the house of work, invidious comparisons between self and others on the amount of work achieved, inability to refuse requests for work and general competitiveness. He offered six pieces of advice to the workaholics:

> Admit that you are a workaholic, powerless to do anything about it without help beyond yourself. Make a fearless inventory of all the busy-work you do which is not essential or part of your job and throw it overboard. Make a plan to spend part of each weekend in meditation. Remember something that you enjoyed doing when a teenager, and do it again. If you read at all, find something you do not have to read as part of your job. Meet some new people you have not met before, and renew contact with some old acquaintances with whom you have lost touch.

Other advice includes re-evaluating the whole economy, pattern, productivity and purpose of holidays. The dangers of workaholism are seen to be not only the physical and mental illness of the workaholic himself or herself, but also of the spouse who might become hyperactive or alcoholic and the children of workaholics.

Machlowitz (1980) has defined workaholics as people whose desire to work long and hard is intrinsic and whose work habits almost always exceed the prescriptions of the job they do and the expectations of the people with whom, or for whom, they work. All true workaholics are intense, energetic, competitive and driven but who also have *strong self-doubts*. They prefer labour to leisure and can – and do – work anytime and anywhere. They tend to make the most of their time and blur the distinctions between business and pleasure.

All workaholics have these traits and may be subdivided into four distinct types (See Table 10.3):

Table 10.3 Different types of workaholic

The *dedicated* workaholic	These are quintessentially the single-minded, one-dimensional workaholics frequently described by lay people and journalists. They shun leisure and are often humourless and brusque.
The *integrated* workaholic	This type does integrate outside features into the work. Thus, although work is 'everything' it does sometimes include extracurricular interests.
The *diffuse* workaholic	This type has numerous interests, connections and pursuits which are far more scattered than those of the integrated workaholic. Furthermore, they may change jobs fairly frequently in pursuit of their ends.
The *intense* workaholic	This type approaches leisure (frequently competitive sport) with the same passion, pace and intensity as work. They become as preoccupied by leisure as work.

To some extent, it is thought that workaholism is an *obsessive-compulsive neurosis* characterized by sharp, narrowed, focused attention, endless activity, ritualistic behaviours and a 'strong desire to be in control'. It is perhaps linked to perfectionism, pathological ambition, even the obsessive-compulsive personality disorder.

However, the aetiology of this 'syndrome' is seen to lie in childhood where workaholism is fairly easily recognized. Machlowitz (1980) argues that some children are driven from within, but others are pushed by parents, for example, by reinforcement. That is, parents threaten to withdraw love if ever-increasing expectations are not fulfilled.

Furthermore, parents may encourage workaholism by providing a model for their children. But, because the parents are so busy, they may be poor parents in that they are inattentive.

Machlowitz (1980) offered a number of reasons why workaholics shun vacations and time-off: they have never had a good experience of holidays either because they have expected too much or chose the wrong type; as their jobs are their passion, they do not feel that they need to get away from it all; traditional forms of recreation seem like a waste of time and incomprehensible to them; the preparation for and anxiety that precedes taking a holiday are more trouble than they are worth; and, finally, workaholics are afraid that they would lose complete control of their jobs if they left for a holiday.

Research in the topic of workaholism and related topics like burnout and engagement has been steady for the past thirty years, attempting to describe and delineate the syndrome of high work involvement and drive to work but low work enjoyment. It is a study of the *joylessness of work* but almost exclusively with white-, as opposed to blue-collar workers. Workaholism is often thought of as working both excessively and compulsively. The current interest is in the very opposite of workaholism, namely work engagement characterized by vigour, energy and resilience; dedication, enthusiasm and pride; and absorption and engrossment at work.

There have been some impressive attempts to build a model of the antecedents, consequences and dimensions of workaholism such as that of Ng et al. (2007). The model specifies three types of antecedents (dispositions, socio-cultural experiences and behavioural reinforcements), dimensions of workaholism (affect, cognitive and behavioural), consequences (satisfaction, mental health, career success) and overall long- and short-term performance. Much of the research has been concerned with definitions and distinctions using different methodologies like distinguishing between the work enthusiast, the workaholic, the enthusiastic workaholic, the unengaged worker, the relaxed worker and the disenchanted worker.

10.7 Addictions

Table 10.1 shows how many politicians suffered from addictions. Newspaper reports also often document how many executives are accused of one form of addiction or another. Most people think of addictions primarily in terms of drugs. There is a long list of substances that people can and do become addicted to. These include alcohol, stimulants (like cocaine), opiates, hallucinogens, marijuana and tobacco, and barbiturates. The term originally meant physiological overdependence on a drug which altered the biochemistry of an individual such that increasing doses were required to have the desired effect.

Addiction involves the exposure to something and then seeking to repeat the experience very often. Over time the addiction becomes established. There is regular and increasing consumption with the takers knowing their habit is expensive, unhealthy and possibly illegal but seemingly unable to 'kick the habit'. It is a complex process that involves biological, psychological and social factors.

Some addiction researchers are interested in why some particular drugs or activities have such a propensity to become addictive. Others are fascinated by why some individuals seem more susceptible than others. Some scientists are fascinated by the environmental and social condition and feature that makes addictions more or less likely. Others look at attempts at recovery and relapse from addiction.

These days all types of behaviours are described as addictive. A recent film on 'sex addiction' has opened up the debate again. What is addictive and what not? How can these seemingly irrational and deeply unhealthy behaviours be explained? Can you simply put the suffix 'aholism', of course derived from alcoholism, after any word like 'work' and expect to have described and delineated a real, meaningful problem or is that little more than lazy journalistic typing and categorizing?

An addiction is a reward-driven activity over which an individual has 'impaired control'. It is an activity to which a person gives an unhealthy priority because of their disordered motivational system. Addictions are associated with cravings and withdrawal symptoms. Many researchers focus on that substance (alcohol, chocolate, drugs) or behaviour that seems to give pleasure, relief or excitement. They are interested in the extent to which people do things to get those stimuli and the positive and negative balances they make to do so.

Yet it seems clear that definitions of addictions vary considerably across time and culture. Thus, undesirable, pathological and pathetic addiction in one culture at one time may, to an outsider or indeed a historian looking back, seem perfectly adaptive. It could be argued that, in some job sectors at certain times, it is effectively a job *requirement* to become addicted to work. Employers want to see an employee totally dedicated to their work, ignoring their family, their health and indeed government laws on working hours. The totally work-obsessed worker is seen to be a hero in the organization and those who don't show that commitment half-hearted, slovenly, even work shy. Clearly, this is using the concept of addiction in a very specific and non-orthodox way.

However, the concept of addiction has been applied much more widely. Thus, there are gambling, sex and work addicts. There are now many 'aholic' terms like 'chocaholic' or 'workaholic', which all try to employ an addiction like alcoholism.

With regard to drugs, the psychiatric literature distinguishes between substance dependence and abuse. Both have technical meanings. Dependence has very specific characteristics like *tolerance* (people take more and more for limited affect), *withdrawal symptoms* (on not taking the drug), *obsessions* with trying to get hold of the drug; a *deterioration* in all social, occupational and recreational activities; and *continued use* with full knowledge of all the danger that is being done.

Abuse means using the drug whilst fulfilling various school, home and work obligations; using in dangerous situations (driving at work); using for illegal behaviour; using despite persistent negative side effects.

Over the years, different theories, models or approaches have arisen to describe all sorts of addictions. This partly reflects the complexity of the issue and the number of factors involved. Most of these approaches are supplementary rather than contradictory, but they clearly put their emphasis on different factors.

The original idea was that people had some particular profile or flaw or vulnerability that made them prone to specific or all addictions. However, the concept has not been successful. Yet, psychologists and psychiatrists have continued to explore the issue. Some psychiatrists see addiction as a consequence of mental illness like depression or anti-social personality disorder. The idea is that risk-takers or the mentally ill are vulnerable to become reliant on drug taking as a crutch. They are more likely to experiment and ignore or downplay any potentially adverse consequences.

Therapists also point out how addicts and drug-dependent people use drugs to compensate or cope. Drugs are used to numb feelings, reduce painful emotional states or reduce internal conflict. It may help loneliness or make up for a lack of gratifying relationships with others. For young people, drugs may help with the anxiety associated with intimacy. They feel they can only say and do things when under the influence of the drugs and therefore, in time, they become dependent on specific drugs for effective social functioning.

10.8 Conclusion

Nearly every adult has a medical history which includes some chronic or acute illness from back pain to cancer. The causes of these illnesses are manifold but some can be provoked by stress. There is no reason to expect that business leaders are exempt from these problems: indeed the often unhealthy lifestyle which they choose or are forced to lead may well make them more susceptible to illnesses. The question is the consequences of those illnesses and treatment for those. It is quite possible that the executives who seek to hide their illnesses (i.e. alcoholism, depression) or take strong medication can have their judgements on all sorts of issues impeded. In this sense, their illnesses are a major cause of their derailment.

Chapter 11

Prevention and management of the dark side

11.1 Introduction

People who have worked with, and for, a derailing dark-side manager often puzzle about how they were selected or promoted in the first place; what events or issues made them apparently derail; and how long it took the organization to do anything about it.

Many have pointed out the great costs of derailment to the organization: people leaving, bad business decisions, share prices dropping, even the total collapse of the whole company. The practical question is simple: how to best prevent people from derailing and, equally important, how to manage those who are showing early signs of derailment?

The answer lies in better selection, training and coaching as well as putting into place systems that monitor for early signs of derailment.

Charan and Colvin (1999) argue that CEOs fail primarily due to their unwillingness to remove ineffective managers, a problem in the leadership domain. However, a deeper analysis suggests that the real cause is that failed CEOs cannot admit that they have made bad staffing decisions, a problem in the intrapersonal domain. Equally important is the dark-side tendencies in the CEOs themselves.

One important point needs to be made, particularly about selection. When people complete a standard dark-side measure it is often surprising how many 'risk issues' show up. That is, they indicate that under stress and pressure an executive mighty show a host of potentially derailing behaviours.

Very few, if any, people have no 'dark-side' in the sense that under stress and pressure less attractive features of their personality or coping style never emerge. To find the perfectly adapted, operative, paragon of justice and integrity in the workplace is virtually impossible. Biographic and other analyses have demonstrated just how much 'dark side' some very famous and effective leaders have (see Chapter 8). Some very successful and effective leaders have had a very dark side: but one of which they were aware and able to control.

But is it possible to reduce and even eliminate bullying, corruption and Machiavellianism at work? The answer with selection and other strategies is that appropriate interventions can significantly lower the probability of derailment. No system is going to detect all potential derailers, but they can increase the likelihood that serious selection errors do not frequently occur.

There is also the issue of living with, but continuing to employ, a derailing executive. Just as those who have bipolar disorder often say the 'ups' are worth the 'downs' in the sense that the energy and elation of the manic phases compensates for the pain and gloom of the depressive phase, so it is occasionally acceptable to keep employed someone with very strong dark-side tendencies. Thus, the obsessiveness of a designer, the creativity of a marketing person or the coldness of a researcher may be acceptable if they deliver in other ways.

It has frequently been observed that a derailed leader's early career success was often responsible for their later failure because they failed to learn. At various times in a work career, people have to learn to let go of old, odd, dysfunctional assumptions and beliefs and behaviours. Furthermore, they need to acquire new skills and ideas. This often means exposing oneself to learning situations that can be threatening and which may involve failure.

Some organizations do a good job in preparing people for senior positions. Through a series of planned experiences and courses, they hope to transition them to take on the responsibilities of higher management. All potential leaders need to upgrade and extend their social and technical skills and move from tactical to strategic thinking. Both incompetent and derailed leaders often have too narrow a range of experience and an overemphasis and reliance on either technical or social skills.

Senior leadership is often about dealing calmly and rationally with ambiguous, threatening and uncertain situations. The inflexible and non-adaptable executive seems often to change their mindset and grow to meet changing situations.

There are a range of transitions that most people go through. These include promotion to senior and then general management, losing a supportive boss or coherent team, going through a difficult merger or simply experiencing disruptive organizational change. Some are offered coaching, mentoring and other ways to help over this period. They might be given a mature and functional team. Most importantly, they are given feedback on their strengths, limitations and blind spots.

Early researchers in the area proposed some simple ideas. Brubaker and Coble (1997) argued that all senior leaders have to ask themselves what they are currently doing to avoid derailment. They need to listen to others' assessments of their own leadership and seek open and honest feedback regarding themselves. They noted how important it was to take care to create a culture in which staff members feel comfortable entertaining conflicting ideas. They also suggested that it can be useful to think about which steps managers took as they ascended the career ladder, so that they can capitalize on their ability to make good choices. This can be a process that will tell them what they need to do in the present. Positive images from the past can be inspiring in the present. Successful managers need to build a strong support base with fellow employees and build trust throughout the organization. Staff will perceive managers as being sincere when they listen actively and when they follow through with concrete steps to assure others they have been heard. They argue that all managers should brainstorm with trusted colleagues to find solutions to hypothetical situations that call for difficult decisions. This exercise will help one to realize that there are many factors to consider and that there is more than one solution for a specific situation.

However, they quite rightly pointed out that it is important to realize that both the individual and the organization can make mistakes that can lead to derailment. Organizational derailment could be as a result of many factors: moving people so quickly that they are unable to successfully complete a job; moving people vertically from one low-challenging job to another could result in them not learning from new experiences; appointing too many self-orientated managers to the fast track, where their aggressiveness, arrogance and autonomous styles begin as strengths but end as liabilities; additionally, some managers might be giving too much attention during feedback sessions to what the workers did rather than to how they did it – at times the most important issue at stake.

11.2 Three issues: Selection, development and transitioning

Although bad management and derailed leadership are widespread, they are to some extent preventable. Hogan et al. (2009) have argued that derailment can be minimized through closer attention to the problem in selection, development and job transitions.

11.2.1 Selection

Hogan et al. (2009b) note that derailed executives resemble successful executives in that both groups are bright, ambitious, and technically and socially skilled. As has been mentioned many times, many have had impressive track records, and identified as 'talented'. Furthermore, all successful leaders have a dark side and often many career setbacks. In this sense they are not that easy to differentiate between those likely to succeed and fail.

Given that we know the major causes of derailment, an obvious solution is to use a dark-side measure, such as the Hogan Development Survey to assess dark sides. Indeed, there is evidence that people are more aware of the necessity of 'selecting out' and the dangers of the dark side. Thus, many have argued that assessing dark-side characteristics could help identify derailment potential (Khoo & Burch, 2008).

Hogan et al. (2009b) note another problem that there are often not enough good managers to go around. The base rate for managerial incompetence is about 50% and the pool maybe shrinking. Furthermore, an organization has to deal with the people they have at the moment. It takes a long time to 'change the guard' and the selection option is only a long-term solution.

The advantage of using a select-out or coaching instrument such as the HDS is that it has multiple uses. An example is presented in Figure 11.1. A potential candidate completes the questionnaire online. A report is then sent to the person sponsoring the test. The report highlights the risk areas, and it is written to give the person advice as how to interpret it as well as concentrate on the very specific issues.

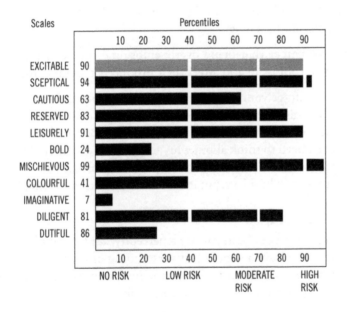

Figure 11.1 An HDS Profile

11.2.1.1 Developmental recommendations
The following developmental recommendations concern the dimensions where your score was in the *Moderate* or *High* risk zone.

11.2.1.1.1 Excitable

First, remember your strengths – when you are at your best, you are an active, energetic and interesting person who can infuse intensity and purpose in an organization. If you can learn to control your tendency to be annoyed or discouraged and modify the way you express your emotions, you will be even more helpful to others.

Second, listen closely to feedback from people you trust; this will be particularly helpful in allowing you to persevere when you become discouraged about a person or a project and begin to think about breaking off your participation.

Third, recognize that you tend to get overly enthusiastic about people or projects. Reflect on this tendency and learn to control your initial excessive burst of enthusiasm. That way, you will reduce the likelihood of being discouraged later.

Fourth, remember that being overly emotional can send unintended messages to your team and affect their productivity and performance.

Finally, encourage yourself to stick with your plans and strategies and 'ride out' the difficult periods when you might get discouraged. Change your expectations from 'I knew this wouldn't work' to 'Things aren't going well, I need to think about why, and what to do next to keep them moving forward'. The more often you persist in solving your problems, the more you will build a reputation of being steady and reliable.

11.2.1.1.2 Sceptical

When you are at your best, you are a perceptive and insightful judge of people and you have a superior understanding of organizational politics. You are a good resource for identifying potential hidden agendas and for analysing and solving social and political problems.

You will tend to distrust your coach; you should suspend judgement and give your coach a chance to try to help you. The same is true for others who care about you – you need to make an extra effort to appreciate what they are telling you and why.

Be careful how you communicate with others. When you believe you are expressing honest opinions, others may see you as being argumentative. Be open to others' points of view.

You should try to be less critical and judgemental. Tell a trusted friend that you are trying to become more tolerant. Ask him or her to tell you when you are being excessively critical, defensive or sensitive – and listen to his or her feedback.

11.2.1.1.3 Leisurely

You are independent, socially skilled and able to say 'no' diplomatically. You make few demands of others, expect to be left alone to do your work in your own way.

You see more incompetence in the world than others do. Although you may think others are naïve, you could profit from their optimism and trust.

Understand that you may become irritable when others try to coach you. Allow yourself to be more easily influenced by friends or family, and be more willing to do the little extra things they ask you to do.

Limit the promises you make to others, but be sure to fulfil the promises and commitments you do make.

11.2.1.1.4 Mischievous

Other people may think that you follow your own agenda and don't consider how your decisions impact them. As a result, they may be as reluctant to make commitments to you as you seem to be in return. Thus, you need to be careful to follow through on all your good faith commitments.

If you find circumstances have altered the conditions under which you made a commitment, then negotiate the changes with the people to whom you have made the promise – rather than simply going on about your business.

You tend to have a higher tolerance for risk than most people. Be aware that not everyone is as adventurous as you seem to be.

You may have disappointed others by not following through. You need to acknowledge your errors and make amends – rather than trying to explain the situation away.

At your best, you are charming, spontaneous and fun. You adapt quickly to changing circumstances, you handle ambiguity well, you add positive energy to social interactions, and people like being with you.

11.2.1.1.5 Diligent

You have high standards for performance and are planned and organized. In addition, you provide structure and order for your staff.

Tackle issues with outside-the-box thinking. Try not to solve every problem in the same way.

Practice delegating to your staff. This provides them with valuable developmental experiences and opportunities to learn.

Your high standards result in high quality work. However, be careful not to criticize others continually who do not share your values for impeccable work.

The advantage of using such a test is that it can be used in both coaching and selection. However, there are other measures which are being developed to detect potential derailment. One such recent test is the B-Scan. The B-Scan 360 is a measure of corporate psychopathy. It is a new instrument that uses ratings of others to measure psychopathic features in workplace settings with a four factor model (Mathieu et al., 2013). There are other ways to measure the disorders. Thus, De Fruyt and others have shown how it is possible to derive dark-side measures from bright-side measures looking for either extreme scores or else combinations of facets (Wille & De Fruyt, 2014).

Certainly these measures can alert selectors to issues they may choose to investigate further in selection. No test scores alone should be used to make a select-out decision. However, they do often signal issues and areas that need further investigation.

11.2.2 Development

This is mainly done through four methods: self-awareness training, skill development, coaching/mentoring and stretch assignments.

11.2.2.1 Self-awareness through feedback

The key to development is self-awareness, but this alone is not sufficient. Potentially derailing managers must also improve their social and business skills, particularly emotional self-regulation and social interaction.

Hogan et al. (2009b) argue that all managers need to develop self-awareness in two areas: (1) how others perceive them and (2) their dark-side tendencies. The use of a 360-degree feedback process, comparing ratings provided by superiors, peers and subordinates with self-ratings is now widespread. It is often the feedback from peers and subordinates that is most useful as they have most 'data' on the individual. They experience their management style and values on a daily basis. If there is a big and consistent disparity (gap) between what leaders/managers say about themselves (i.e. rate the work related behaviour) and the comments/ratings of all the staff and colleagues, this should flash a serious warning signal.

Regular, specific and accurate feedback hopefully enhances self-awareness and promotes desirable behaviour change. Hogan et al. (2009b) have, however, noted that feedback is most effective in improving performance under particular conditions (a) for the lowest rated managers, (b) when the feedback is intended to be used for development (as opposed to administrative decisions), (c) when coaches help managers review their feedback and set specific improvement goals and (d) when managers share their development plans with co-workers and ask for suggestions.

Alimo-Metcalf (1998) reviewed the literature on the importance of 360-degree feedback on the development of transformational leadership. She noted:

Remarkably persistent themes have emerged from research using 360-degree feedback. These can be listed as follows below:

- Managers, in general tend to rate themselves higher in management competence and leadership effectiveness than do their colleagues and also rate them (i.e. their boss, peers and staff).
- Managers' self-ratings are less highly related to the ratings others make of them than peers', bosses' and staffs' ratings are with one another.

- Managers' self-ratings are less accurate than others' ratings when compared to 'objective criterion measures'.
- Taken together, the ratings that the managers' 'others' provide for the manager, predict team performance.
- Staff are more satisfied with their managers and their job when their perceptions of their manager matched the manager's self-perceptions. More 'successful' managers (as rated by their staff and their boss) are less likely to inflate self-ratings of leadership.
- Managers who have 'inflated' self-ratings:

    (i) over-estimate their influence
    (ii) are likely to misjudge and misdiagnose their own need for improvement.

Staffs' perceptions of a manager's effectiveness relate significantly to bosses' ratings of performance and promotion, but managers' self-ratings of leadership are not related to these measures.

The stronger the relationship between a manager's self-perceptions with that of their staff, the more likely they are to be perceived by their staff as transformational. (p. 36)

Her argument is that multi-rater feedback is useful because it increases self-awareness and focuses on discrepancies. The data suggest feedback does help performance improvement but only on the behaviours/skills that managers/leaders decide to work on. She also considers the tricky and sensitive issue of sex differences in both ratings and leadership

The issue for all 360-degree measures lies in the behaviours rated. Clearly, the more dark-side ratings are used, the better. At the moment few 360-degree questionnaires are designed to assess dark-side and derailing issues.

11.2.2.2 Intrapersonal skills

Self-awareness is not enough. Being aware of one's dark side and derailers is insufficient. Potential derailers need skills training.

Hogan et al. (2009b) suggest that all methods for helping managers develop intrapersonal skills have six features in common: first, competent assessments; second, helping managers identify their implicit theories and personal goals; third, focusing on the faulty assumptions, emotional hot-buttons and self-defeating schema; fourth, understanding how the self-defeating schemas are no longer adaptive; fifth, reprogramming the faulty schemas and replacing the associated counterproductive behaviours with more constructive behavioural alternatives; sixth, addressing the difficulty of changing habitual behaviour.

Many of the skills required are 'soft skills'. Managers need the benefits of negotiation skills as well as performance management skills training. Some also need something of a business education so that they become more able to search out and interpret business data.

There are many issues concerning skills training, the most obvious of which is what type of training is most efficient and effective in delivering skills. That is a big topic and not appropriate here. Suffice it to say that a careful audit needs to be made of which crucial skills are necessary and secondly which types of training are likely to be most successful.

11.2.2.3 Coaching/mentoring

Coaching and mentoring has become very popular as a way of helping executives. Some refer to mentors as experienced people within the organization who effectively coach, whilst coaches are external experts and professors who are hired for specific assignments.

One of the most cost-effective and beneficial things any good interpersonal manager, leader or supervisor can do is offer mentoring. The word comes from Homer's *Odyssey* where Mentor was a tutor to Odysseus's son Telemachus. Mentor was a 'wise and trusted advisor'.

The idea is that (young) new people in an organization need help, advice and nurturing. Mentoring is about education, support and encouragement. The mentor and mentee meet regularly to discuss business issues so that the latter learns to perform at the maximum of their potential as quickly as possible. Some organizations facilitate and support (even demand) mentoring. They make employee development a priority and offer formal rewards to those who engage in mentoring.

The mentoring process, then, is where an experienced, more senior supervisor/leader is committed to providing developmental assistance, guidance and support to a less experienced mentee. Mentors can (and should) provide mentees with coaching, challenging assignments, exposure, protection and sponsorship.

Many organizations like to follow specific rules. Thus, for instance, it is suggested that mentors should: first establish the goals, and rules to play by; they need to model all desirable behaviours; they need to be as impartial and non-judgemental as possible. Their task is to build awareness and confidence, extend analytic skills and deepen, strengthen and expand networks within and outside the organization. It is *not* their job to become a personal therapist and try to sort out the mentee's psychological problems and personal relationships. It is not their primary task to get the mentee promoted. They are not there to be directive, prescriptive or proscriptive, or, for that matter, give business advice.

There are benefits to mentor as well as mentee. They have 'step children' in the organization. They stay in touch with another generation and they learn from them. They grow their influence base from below. There are costs and benefits to mentoring. Mentees develop feelings of accomplishment, a sense of competence in addition to new perspectives and knowledge. Mentors can also acquire new (often technological) skills, support and an ally in their mentee. Mentors often talk of feelings of quasi-immortality watching their mentees grow and succeed.

There are costs if the relationship turns sour. Mentors have talked of exploitation and backstabbing. Others perceive the time and effort not worth it. Some mentors have also been accused of nepotism by jealous non-mentored people. However, there is evidence to suggest if the programme is voluntary on both sides, the two are well matched, the mentor is trained and there is management support for the whole process, then they can be a great success.

One question is how mentor and mentee are paired. What is the criterion? Who makes the decision: a learning and development specialist, the mentor, the mentee, the mentees boss? Should there be some sort of speed dating exercise to have a good 'sniff around' one another? How does one ensure the process is standardized across the organization? Should it be voluntary or compulsory? These are no easy or straightforward questions.

Many of the same issues apply to coaching. The sparse literature on the evidence for the efficacy of coaching suggests that four factors predict the efficacy of coaching in terms of reaching desired outcomes. First, readiness for coaching which is a mixture of willing and able to learn, to change, to embrace challenge. The coach needs to activate readiness, remove barriers and resistance or move on. Furthermore, he or she needs to respond to the client's preferences. Second, there is the relationship between the coach and protégé. The coach should explore and exploit the therapeutic alliance which is about collaboration, consensus and support. It is about building and maintaining a positive, open, productive and hopefully transformative alliance.

The third ingredient is about expectation of improvement, finding new paths to goals and 'agency thinking'. Coaches need to speak the message that successful change or progress is possible. They actuate hope by credibility building at the beginning of the relationship. The final ingredient is the application of a theory and therapy. Theories organize observation. Some coaches share them, others don't. But clearly the good coach needs to know what works for whom. But coaches need to know about the business world and the dilemma of conflict of interests between the client and the organization.

The client–coach mission and relationship is a bit like the patient–therapist one. However, typically patients have more serious problems and poorer adjustment than business clients. Also, therapists work at a deeper emotional level than a coach. Therapists see more of the patient and contact is nearly always face-to-face. Coaches focus on the workplace, therapists on all aspects of functioning.

Coaching only works if the client is able, ready and willing. It works well if the bond is good and if the coach instils hope for change. Moreover, coaches can be alerted to the necessity of dark-side interventions in the sense that they need to be able to detect common derailers and confront issues before things get too difficult.

11.2.2.4 Stretch assignments

Some organizations believe that the most effective developmental strategies are experiential. Thus, they provide each new manager with a set of stretch assignments whose aim is to test and develop individuals. The assignments are not a test in the sense that there is some success versus failure outcome score. The idea is to expose a person to a range of particular challenges so that they see to what extent they have the skills and resilience to meet them.

If the assignments are well planned and monitored they could easily provide an excellent opportunity to detect early signs of derailment.

11.2.3 Transition management

McCall and Lombardo (1983, p. 11) noted that the causes of derailment are 'all connected to the fact that situations change as one ascends the organizational hierarchy'. Others have also observed that most derailment occurs after a transition to a more senior job usually one or two below board level. Promotion brings more responsibility, scrutiny, ambiguity and office politics. Leaders can be put under a great deal of acute and chronic stress.

It appears that executives need three to six months to adjust to a new job. It is often lonely at the top. Executive teams frequently have problems. For most, the task is simultaneously to get along with, but also get ahead of, colleagues to get the top job: the CEO. So there are issues around hidden agendas and competitiveness.

What are the typical problems of executive teams and how to deal with them? The first is *bloated membership*. Everybody wants to 'sit on the board' and be 'on the top team'. It has been said that the only thing worse than not being on the board is being on the board. Any CEO needs to be clear about who is on the board *and why* and resist the cancerous growth of those who feel, want or believe they deserve to be at the heart of power.

The second is the *naked ambition* of the many team members. There is no easy solution to dealing with the pathologically, ambitious. But, at least, bringing succession planning out into the open helps control some blind ambition. The teams need to specify a timetable, personal criteria for the top job and the process by which the boss is appointed.

The third is *conspiracy of silence*. Surprising perhaps, big boys often cope with issues by never mentioning them. Teams often try to deal with emotional issues by ignoring them. There needs to be a rule about what can and cannot be discussed, when and why. It is often the personal pathology of the CEO that dictates what is taboo and what is not.

A fourth issue is *resisting centrifugal forces*. Board members can, quite literally, head off in different directions. Their values and priorities can soon lead to the executive team losing its cohesiveness and focus. This is most frequently the problem where individuals have difficulty delegating. The CEO must become aware of the existence and power of these forces upon the members and, therefore, of the necessity to ensure uniformity of approach. Members are pulled in different directions at the same time and need help with the focus and alignment.

A fifth problem is not unique to top teams but can be very destructive and it refers to the *ambiguity in roles*. Executive team members are answerable to many different constituencies. More importantly it is not always clear how decisions are made. Executives need to specify very clearly *how* the group is to make decisions and, of necessity, to stick to them.

The sixth problem is the personal but not *hidden agendas of individuals*. The boardroom is an ideal place, some believe, to have fun to promote personal causes. The solution is quite simple: have a clear agenda and stick to it. Boards need to be told on a regular basis what they are there for.

Hogan et al. (2009b) argue that transition management takes place in two phases: preparation for a new role and integration into that new role. Preparation involves creating a plan based on a realistic job preview, assessing risk factors and building a relationship with the new boss, peers and reports. They note that at this point special attention should be paid to strengths that could become liabilities and seemingly previously ignored weaknesses that could become liabilities.

The most important part of a successful transition is dealing with a new boss and board. The best practices include setting expectations and regularly clarifying them, developing mechanisms for monitoring progress and understanding the political landscape.

11.3 Reducing derailment potential

A number of recommendations have been made around this topic (See Tables 11.1 to 11.4). In a to-the-point article on the topic, Zhang et al. (2013) ask three relevant questions which they attempt to answer:

Table 11.1 How to Reduce Your Derailment Potential

Take a 360-degree assessment instrument to increase your awareness of potential problems that can lead to derailment	Select an instrument that assesses your effective and ineffective leadership behaviours to check your blind spots.
Solicit feedback on a routine basis	At regular intervals, try to get feedback from those immediately around you (peers, manager, colleagues, etc.) to identify areas you can be more effective.
Take responsibility for your own development	Understand what the demands and expectations are for your role, compare your strengths and weaknesses to these and create a development plan.
Learn what skills and abilities are needed in positions you aspire to through observations, interviews, and available organizational information	New skills and behaviours are needed as you progress. Seeking support, setting a development plan and filling any gaps in knowledge and skills are key.

Table 11.2 How to Reduce Others' Derailment Potential

Determine what motivates our direct reports and pay attention to it	Coupling messages of improvement with opportunity is likely to excite employees and make them less likely to feel hurt by criticism.
Be clear about the demands and expectations of the job, including behavioural components	Make sure employees know what is important, why it is important, and the consequences of not paying attention to that needed behaviour.
Hire individuals who can contribute to your group in diverse ways so that you have a balanced, complementary group	Everyone has strengths and weaknesses, and building a diverse group can create learning opportunities between group members.
Delegate and empower your group	Learning by doing can be far more effective than talking about the new behaviours. Talk to the staff member about the specific development goal in mind and why they've been given it.
Deal with problem employees in a direct, timely manner	The longer you delay a difficult conversation, the more opportunity there is for a problem to get out of hand. Address problems in a positive way, preferably with improvement areas and opportunity.

Table 11.3 How to Reduce Your Organization's Derailment Potential

Offer zigzag (or lateral plus vertical movement) career paths over vertical movement alone	Exposing managers to different areas of the organization can broaden their perspective as well as help them build critical relationships
Provide support and coaching for managers during transition	Managers need to not only be prepared for new roles, but they need to also be supported once they are in them.

(Continued)

Provide information about the behaviours and expectations required in the job	At the higher levels, behavioural job expectations become more important. Employees need to know what these are and need to be able to assess their proficiency in them. A realistic job preview can better prepare them for success in the role.
Offer assessments of potential problems as well as strengths	By providing employees with this insight, you can help them form a more balanced view of their leadership behaviours.
Offer training on how to provide effective feedback from different sources across career stages	If employees know how to deliver effective feedback and are encouraged to do so, then derailment behaviours are more likely to be identified sooner and addressed more effectively.

11.4 Self-help

A number of books are essentially self-help books in that they give advice to people on how they should 'wrestle with their demons' once they know their dark-side profile. Thus, Dotlich and Cairo (2003) offer the following advice for each of the disorders (Table 11.4).

Table 11.4 How to deal with each disorder

Arrogance	First, determine if you really fit the arrogant profile. Second, find truth-tellers in your organization and get them to give honest feedback. Third, use set backs that you may experience to cross back over the line before big failure hits.
Melodrama	First, 'dial down the volume'. Second, get someone to videotape you in action. Third, identify the circumstances that cause you to cross the line. Fourth, make time to reflect and really listen.
Volatility	First, empower a 'trusted advisor' to give you a volatility alert. Second, learn to take a step back, as well as where necessary forward. Third, ask what is and is not happening and how I can influence the action.

(Continued)

Excessive Caution	First, prioritize and put you time and effort into the key matters. Second, do something different and break routine. Third, focus on past success to reduce the fear of failure. Fourth, confront your fears by imagining worst case scenarios.
Habitual Distrust	First, analyses the 'why' behind the distrust of so many. Second, reconfigure a key relationship and work on your suspicions. Third, practice giving positive feedback to others. Fourth, recognize how distrust is hurting your career.
Aloofness	First, map out your network to determine allies (get savvy). Second, rehearse your messages so that people here clearly what you want to say. Third, pay attention to your (lack) of impact and try harder to 'get through'.
Mischievousness	First, take ownership of what you are really doing. Second, determine which rules are (really) important to follow. Third, role play being on the receiving end of your mischief. Fourth, confide in a coach and listen carefully to them.
Eccentricity	First, determine the price you are prepared to play for your 'non conformity'. Second, surround yourself with people who can execute your ideas. Third, recognize the gap between your intention and the impact you want.
Passive Resistance	First, note the gap between how you are feeling and what you are saying/doing. Second, put yourself in the place of people that you work with. Third, work on potential areas of conflict. Fourth, look to other successful leaders for models.
Perfectionism	First, examine the costs of your approach and style: being stressed out and missing opportunities. Second, prioritize the key jobs and learn to live with imperfection. Third, give up the perfectionistic behaviour and your obsessiveness.
Eagerness to Please	First, identify what you really believe. Second, pick a fight: a small scale conflict. Third, defend someone who is worth defending.

11.5 Conclusion

Prevention is better than cure. It is also cheaper but it is also more problematic. The (very) high cost of management derailment and the renewed interest in the area have provoked an interest in the selection and development of managers from a dark-side perspective.

Until comparatively recently, the standard selection procedure was to specify particular competencies relevant to a job and then seek sufficient behavioural evidence that a candidate had them. There is now a realization that this has two problems. First, it is assumed that the more of a competency the person has, the better: the concept of a linearity. However, thanks to an understanding of the spectrum hypothesis and the work on strengths, it has been realized that within great strengths there maybe weaknesses. Second, thanks to the development of various measures, there is now a concern with how and when to select out those having potential derailers. In this sense selection has become derailer sensitive.

The second issue is how to deal with those that have been selected and to try and prevent them derailing particularly when transitioning jobs. These include attempts to increase self-awareness, develop new skills, have help from a coach or mentor or take part in 'stretch assignments' that teach skills, self-awareness and resilience.

Bibliography

Aaslad, M.S., Skogstad, A., Notelaers, G., Nielsen, M.B. & Einarsen, S. (2009). The prevalence of destructive leadership behaviour. *British Journal of Management, 21,* 438–452.

Adorno, T., Frenkel-Brunswick, D., Levinson, D. & Sanford, N. (1948). *The Authoritarian Personality.* New York: Harper.

Aguilera, R.V. & Vadera, A.K. (2008). The dark side of authority: Antecedents, mechanisms, and outcomes of organisational corruption. *Journal of Business Ethics, 77,* 431–449.

Alimo-Metcalfe, B. (1998). 360 Degree Feedback and Leadership Development. *International Journal of Selection and Assessment, 6,* 35–44.

American Psychiatric Association (2000). *Diagnostic and Statistical Manual of Mental Disorders* (4th revised edition). Washington: APA.

——. (2014). *Diagnostic and Statistical Manual of Mental Disorders* (5th edition). Washington: APA.

Anand, V., Ashforth, B. & Joshi, M. (2004). Business as usual. *Academy of Management Executive, 18,* 1–33.

Andreasen, C.S., Griffiths, M.D. & Gjertsen, S.R. (2013). The relationships between behavioural addictions and the five-factor model of personality. *Journal of Behavioral Addictions, 2,* 90–99.

Aquino, K., Reed, H., Thau, S. & Freeman, D. (2007). A grotesque and dark beauty. *Journal of Experimental Social Psychology, 43,* 385–392.

Ardelt, M. (2000). Still stable after all these years. *Social Psychology Quarterly, 63,* 392–405.

Argandoña, A. (2001). Corruption: The corporate perspective. *Business Ethics: A European Review, 10,* 163–175.

Arnulf, J.K. & Gottschalk, P. (2013). Heroic leaders as white-collar criminals: An empirical study. *Journal of Investigative Psychology and Offender Profiling, 10,* 96–113.

Arthaud-Day, M.L., Certo, S.T., Dalton, C.M. & Dalton, D.R. (2006). A changing of the guard: Executive and director turnover following corporate financial restatements. *Academy of Management Journal, 49(6),* 1119–1136.

Ashforth, B. & Anand, V. (2003). The normalisation of corruption in organisations. *Research in Organisational Behaviour, 25*, 1-52.

Babiak, P. (1995). When psychologists go to work: A case of an industrial psychopath. *Applied Psychology: An International Review, 44*, 171-188.

Babiak, P., & Hare, R. (2006). *Snakes in Suits*. New York: Regan Books.

Babiak, P., & Hare, R.D. (2012). The *B-Scan* 360 Manual.

Baird, J.E., & Zelin, R.C. (2009). An examination of the impact of obedience pressure on perceptions of fraudulent acts and the likelihood of committing occupational fraud. *Journal of Forensic Studies in Accounting and Business, Winter, 1*, 1-14.

Balthazar, O., Cooke, R. & Potter, R. (2006). Dysfunctional culture, dysfunctional organisation. *Journal of Management Psychology, 21*, 709-732.

Bandura, A., Barbaranelli, C, Caprara, G. & Pastorelli, C. (1996). Mechanisms of moral disengagement in the exercise of moral agency. *Journal of Personality and Social Psychology, 80*, 125-135.

Barber, R. (2001). Hackers profiled-who are they and what are their motivations? *Computer Fraud and Security, 2*, 14-17.

Baucus, M.S. & Near, J.P. (1991). Can illegal corporate behaviour be predicted? An event history analysis. *Academy of Management Journal, 34*, 9-36.

Baumeister, R., Campbell, J., Krueger, J. & Volis, K. (2003). Does high self-esteem cause better performance, interpersonal success, happiness and healthier lifestyles. *Psychological Science in the Public Interest, 4*, 1-44.

Beck, J.C. (2010). Dangerous severe personality disorder: The controversy continues. *Behavioural Sciences and the Law, 28*, 177-288.

Becker, J. & O'Hare, D. (2007). Machiavellians' motives in organisational citizenship behaviour. *Journal of Applied Communication Research, 35*, 246-267.

Beenen, G. & Pinto, J. 2009. Resisting an epidemic of organizational-level corruption: An interview with Sherron Watkins. *Academy of Management Learning & Education, 8*, 275-289.

Benning, S., Patrick, C., Bloniger, D., Hicks, B. & Iacono, W. (2005). Estimating facets of psychopathy from normal personality traits. *Assessment, 12*, 3-18.

Benson, M.L. & Simpson, S.S. (2009). *White-Collar Crime: An Opportunity Perspective. Criminology and Justice Series*, Routledge: New York.

Berglas, S. (2009). Six tips on hiring a business coach. *Forbes Magazine*, retrieved from: http://www.forbes.com/2009/12/04/hiring-business-coach-entrepreneurs-management-berglas.html.

Bergstorm, K. (2011). "Don't feed the troll": Shutting down a debate about community expectations on Reddit.com. *First Monday, 16*.

Bhattacharya, U. & Marshall, C.D. (2012). Do they do it for money? *Journal of Corporate Finance, 18*, 92–104.

Binns, A. (2012). Don't feed the trolls! Managing troublemakers in magazines' online communities. *Journalism Practice, 6(4)*, 547–562.

Bishop, J. (2014a). The effect of de-individuation of the internet troller on criminal procedure implementation: An interview with a hater. *International Journal of Cyber Criminology, 7*, 28–48.

Bishop, J. (2014b). Representations of 'trolls' in mass media communication: A review of media-texts and moral panics relating to 'internet trolling'. *International Journal of Web Based Communities, 10*, 7–24.

Bjørkelo, B. (2013). Workplace bullying after whistleblowing: Future research and implications. *Journal of Managerial Psychology, 28*, 306–323.

Black, P.J., Woodworth, M. & Porter, S. (2013). The big bad wolf? The relationship between the dark triad and the interpersonal assessment of vulnerability. *Personality and Individual Differences*. doi: 10.1016/j.paid.2013.10.026.

Blonigen, D., Carlson, S., Krueger, R. & Patrick, C. (2003). A twin study of self-reported psychopathic personality traits. *Personality and Individual Differences, 35*, 179–197.

Board, B.J. & Fritzon, K. (2005). Disordered personalities at work. *Psychology, Crime & Law, 11*, 17–32.

Boddy, C. (2010). Corporate psychopaths and productivity. *Management Services*, Spring, 26–29.

——. (2011). *Corporate Psychopaths: Organisational Destroyers*. Basingstoke: Palgrave McMillan.

Bollaert, H. & Petit, V. (2010). Beyond the dark side of executive psychology: Current research and new directions. *European Management Journal, 28(5)*, 362–376.

Bookman, Z. (2008). Convergences and omissions in reporting corporate and white collar crime. *DePaul Business & Commercial Law Journal, 6*, 347–392.

Boone, C. & de Brabander, B. (1997). Self-reports and CEO locus of control research: A note. *Organisational Studies, 18(6)*, 949–971.

Bracken, D. & Timmreck, C. (2001). Success and sustainability, in Bracken, D., Timmreck, C. & Church, A. (2001) *The Handbook of Multi-Source Feedback*. San Francisco: Jossey Bass, pp. 478–494.

Brehemer, B. (1980). In one word: Not from experience. *Acta Psychologica*. Elsevier, 45, 223–241.

Brightman. (2009). Workplace bullying after whistleblowing: Future research and implications. *Journal of Managerial Psychology, 28*, 306–323.

Brubaker, D. & Coble, L. (1997). *Staying on Track: An Educational Leader's Guide to Preventing Derailment and Ensuring Personal and Organizational Success.* Thousand Oaks: Corwin Press.

Buckels, E.E., Trapnell, P.D. & Paulhus, D.L. (2014). Trolls just want to have fun. *Personality and individual Differences, 67,* 97–102.

Bushman, B. & Baumeister, R. (1998). Threatened egoism, narcissism, self-esteem and direct and displaced aggressions. *Journal of Personality and Social Psychology, 75,* 219–229.

Byrd, A.L., Kahn, R.E. & Pardini, D.A. (2013). A validation of the inventory of callous-unemotional traits in a community sample of young adult males. *Journal of Psychopathology and Behavioural Assessments, 35,* 20–34.

Campbell, W. (2001). Is narcissism really so bad? *Psychological Inquiry, 12,* 214–216.

Campbell, W., Bush. C., Brunell, A. & Sheldon, J. (2005). Understanding the social costs of narcissism. *Personality and Social Psychology Bulletin, 31,* 1358–1368.

Campbell, J-L. & Göritz, A.S. (2013). Culture Corrupts! A qualitative study of organisational culture in corrupt organisations. *Journal of Business Ethics, 120,* 291–311. doi: 10.1007/s10551-013-1665-7.

Caprara, G. & Capanna, C. (2006). Moral disengagement in the exercise of civic-ness, in L. Zsolnai (ed.), *Interdisdicplinary Yearbook of Business Ethics.* New York: Lang, pp. 87–98.

Capretta, C., Clark, L.P. & Dai, G. (2008). Executive derailment: Three cases in point and how to prevent it. *Global Business and Organisational Excellence, 27(3),* 48–56.

Carson, M.A., Shanock, L.R., Heggestad, E.D., Andrew, A.M., Pugh, S.D. & Walter, M. (2012). The relationship between dysfunctional interpersonal tendencies, derailment potential behaviour, and turnover. *Journal of Business and Psychology, 27(3),* 291–304.

Casciaro, T. & Lobo, M.S. (2005). Competent jerks, lovable fools, and the formation of social networks. *Harvard Business Review, 83(6),* 92–99.

Caspi, A., Moffitt, T., Silva, P., Krueger, A. et al. (1994). Are some people crime prone? *Criminology, 32,* 163–195.

Charan, R. & Colvin, G. (1999). Why CEOs fail. *Fortune,* 21 June.

Chatterjee, A. & Hambrick, D.C. (2007). It's all about me: Narcissistic chief executive officers and their effects on company strategy and performance. *Administrative Science Quarterly, 52,* 351–385.

Chatterkee, A. & Hambrick, D.C. (2011). Executive personality, capability cues, and risk taking: How narcissistic CEOs react to their successes and their stumbles. *Administrative Science Quarterly, 56(2)*, 202–237.

Choo, F. & Tan, K. (2007). An 'American Dream' theory of corporative executive fraud. *Accounting Forum, 31*, 203–215.

Christiansen, N., Quirk, S., Robie, C. & Oswald, F. (2014). Light already defines the darkness. *Industrial and Organisational, 7*, 138–142.

Christie, E. & Geis, F. (1970). *Studies in Machiavellinaism*. London: Academic Press.

Chui, R. (2014). A multi-faceted approach to anonymity online: Examining the relationships between anonymity and anti-social behaviour. *Journal of Visual Worlds Research, 7(2)*, 1–13.

Cisek, S., Sedikides, C., Hart, C., Godwin, H., Benson, V. & Liversedge, S. (2014). Narcissism and consumer behaviour. *Frontiers in Psychology, 5*, 232.

Claxton, G., Owen, D. & Sadler-Smith, E. (2013). Hubris in leadership: A peril of unbridled intuition? *Leadership*, doi: 10.1177/1742715013511482.

Cleckley, H. (1941). *The Mask of Sanity*. St. Louis: C. V. Mosby.

Clements, C. & Washbush, J. (1999). The two faces of leadership: Considering the dark side of leader-follower dimensions. *Journal of Workplace Learning, 11*, 170–175.

Comité Européen Des Assurances. (2004). *Terrorist Acts Against Computer Installations and the Role of the Internet in the Context of International Terrorism*. Retrieved from: http://www.insuranceeurope.eu/uploads/Modules/Publi cations/1225358536_annexel90.pdf

Conway, M. (2003). Hackers as terrorists? Why it doesn't compute. *Computer Fraud and Security, 12*, 10–13.

Cooke, R.A. & Lafferty, J. (1989). *Organizational Culture Inventory*. Plymouth: Human Synergistics.

Cooke, R.A. & Rousseau, D.M. (1988). Behavioral norms and expectations: A quantitative approach to the assessment of organizational culture. *Group and Organization Studies, 13*, 245–273.

Coolidge, F.L., Moor, C.J., Yamazaki, T.G., Stewart, S.E. & Segal, D.L. (2001). On the relationship between Karen Horney's tripartite neurotic type theory and personality disorder features. *Personality and Individual Differences, 30*, 1387–1400.

Corry, N., Merritt, R., Mrug, S. & Pamp, B. (2008). The factor structure of the narcissistic personality inventory. *Journal of Personality Assessment, 90*, 593–600.

Cowen, A.P. & Marcel, J.J. (2011). Damaged goods: Board decisions to dismiss reputationally compromised directors. *Academy of Management Journal, 54(3)*, 509–527.

Craig, R. & Amernic, J. (2011). Detecting Linguistic traces of destructive narcissism at-a-distance in a CEO's letter to shareholders. *Journal of Business Ethics, 101*, 563–575.

Croall, H. (2007). 'White collar crime, consumers and victimization', in G. Geis & H. Pontell (eds), *International Handbook of White Collar Crime*. New York: Springer.

Crocker, J. & Wolfe, C. (2001). Contingencies of self worth. *Psychologist Review, 108*, 593–623.

Crysel, L.C., Crosier, B.S. & Webster, G.D. (2013). The dark triad and risk behaviour. *Personality and Individual Differences, 54*, 35–40.

Daboub, A.J., Rasheed, A.M.A., Priem, R.M. & Gray, D.A. (1995). Top Management Team Characteristics and Corporate Illegal Activity. *The Academic of Management Review, 20*, 138–170.

Dahlberg, L. (2001). Computer-mediated communication and the public sphere: A critical analysis. *Journal of Computer Mediated-Communication, 7*, 1–26. doi:0.1111/j.1083-6101.2001.tb00137.x

Dailey, P. (2011). Why leaders fail? *European Business Review*, July 2011.

Dattner, B. & Hogan, R. Can you handle failure? *Harvard Business Review*, April 2011, 117–121.

De Haan, E. & Kasozi, A. (2014). *The Leadership Shadow: How to Recognise and Avoid Derailment, Hubris and Overdrive*. London: Kogan Page.

Deal, T. & Kennedy, A. (1982). *Corporate Culture*. Reading: Addison-Wesley.

Delobbe, N., Haccoun, R.R. & Vandenberghe, C. (2002). *Measuring Core Dimensions of Organisational Culture: A Review of Research and Development of a New Instrument*. Unpublished manuscript. Belgium: Universite catholique de Louvain.

den Nieuwenboer, N.A. & Kaptein, M. (2008). Spiraling down into corruption: A dynamic analysis of the social identity processes that cause corruption in organisations to grow. *Journal of Business Ethics, 83*, 133–146

Denton, J. (2000). Management Derailment. Unpublished manuscript. University of Stellenbosch.

Denton, J.M. & van Lill, J.B. (2006). Management Derailment. *XIMB Journal of Management, 3(2)*, 231–250.

Desimone, J. (2014). Will exploring the darkness prove enlightening. *Industrial and Organisational Psychology, 7*, 126–130.

Dilchert, S., Ones, D. & Krueger, R. (2014). Maladapative personality constructs, measures and work behaviors. *Industrial and Organisational Psychology, 7*, 98–155.

Dixon, N. (1981). *On the Psychology of Military Incompetence*. London: Jonathan Cape.

Donath, J. (1999). Identity and deception in the virtual community, in M.A. Smith & P. Kollock (eds), Communities in Cyberspace. New York: Routledge, pp. 29–59.

Dotlich, D. & Cairo, P. (2003). *Why CEOs Fail*. New York: Jossey Bass.

Douglas, H., Bore, M. & Munro, D. (2012). Distinguishing the dark triad: evidence from the five-factor model and the hogan development survey. *Psychology, 3(2)*, 237–242.

Duchon, D. & Burns, M. (2008). Organisational narcissism. *Organisational Dynamics, 37*, 354–364.

Dunkelberg, J. & Robin, D.P. (1998). The anatomy of fraudulent behaviour. *Business Horizons, 41(6)*, 77–82.

Dweck, C.S. (2012). *Mindset: How You Can Fulfill Your Potential*. Constable & Robinson.

Dyce, A. (1997). The Big Five factors of personality and their relationship to the personality disorders. *Journal of Clinical Psychology, 53*, 587–593.

Emler, N. (2005). *The Costs and Causes of Low Self-Esteem*. Unpublished paper: LSE.

Ernst, E. (1995). How to become a charlatan. *The Skeptic, 9*, 6–7.

Esbec, E. & Echeburua, E. (2011). New criteria for personality disorders in DSM-V. *Actas Esp. Psiquiatr, 39*, 1–11.

Eysenck, H. (1964). *Crime and Personality*. London: Routledge & Kegan Paul.
——. (1977). *Crime and Personality*. London: Routledge & Kegan Paul.

Eysenck, H. & Eysenck, S. (1973). The Personality of Female Prisoners. *British Journal of Psychiatry, 122*.

Eysenck, H. & Gudjonsson, G. (1989). *The Causes and Cures of Criminality*. New York: Plenum.

Falk, C. (2005). Ethics and hacking: The general and the specific. *Norwich University Journal of Information Assurance, 1*, 1–10.

Farrington, D. (2003). Key results from the first forty years of the Cambridge Study in Delinquent Development, in T.P. Thornberry and M.D. Krohn (eds), *Taking Stock of Delinquency: An Overview of Findings from Contemporary Longitudinal Studies*. New York: Springer, pp. 137–183.

Feldman, P. (1993). *The Psychology of Crime*. Cambridge: Cambridge University Press.

Finkelstein, S. (2003). *Why Smart Executives Fail*. New York: Portfolio.

Finney, H. & Lesieur, H. (1982). A contingency theory of organisational crime. *Research in the Sociology of Organisations, 1*, 255–299.

Fossati, A., Pincus, A.L., Borroni, S., Munteanu, A.F. & Maffei, C. (2014). Are pathological narcissism and psychopathy different constructs or different names for the same thing? A study based on Italian nonclinical adult participants. *Journal of Personality Disorders, 28*, 394–418.

Furnham, A. (1998). *The Psychology of Managerial Incompetence*. London: Whurr.

——. (2000). *The Hopeless, Hapless and Helpless Manager*. London: Whurr.

——. (2003). *Mad, Sad and Bad Management*. Cirencester: Management Books.

——. (2014). What you can and can't change: Lay perspectives on Seligman's Guide. Unpublished paper.

Furnham, A. Chapman, A., Wilson, E. & Persuad, R. (2013). Treatment hurts: Lay theories of graded exposure in the treatment of four anxiety disorders. *European Journal of Psychotherapy and Counseling, 15*, 253–273.

Furnham, A. & Crump, J. (2005). Personality traits, types and disorders. *European Journal of Personality, 19*, 167–184.

Furnham, A., Crump, J. & Ritchie, W. (2013). What it takes: Ability, demographic, bright and dark side trait correlates of years to promotion. *Personality and Individual Differences, 55*, 952–956.

Furnham, A., Hughes, D.J. & Marshall, E. (2013). Creativity, OCD, Narcissism, and the Big Five. *Thinking Skills and Creativity, 10*, 91–98.

Furnham, A., Hyde, G. & Trickey, G. (2013). The values of work success. *Personality and Individual Differences, 55*, 485–489.

——. (2014a). Do your dark side traits fit? Dysfunctional personalities in different work sectors. *Applied Psychology: An International Review, 63*, 589–606.

——. (2014b). The dark side of career preference: Dark side traits, motives, and values. *Journal of Applied Social Psychology, 44*, 106–114.

Furnham, A., Richards, S.C. & Paulhus, D.L. (2013). The dark triad of personality: A 10 year review. *Social and Personality Psychology Compass, 7(3)*, 199–216.

Furnham, A. & Thompson, J. (1991). Personality and self-reported delinquency. *Personality and Individual Differences, 12*, 585–593.

Furnham, A. & Trickey, G. (2011). Sex differences in dark side traits. *Personality and Individual Differences, 50*, 517–522.

Furnham, A., Trickey, G. & Hyde, G. (2012). Bright aspects to dark side traits: Dark side traits associated with work success. *Personality and Individual Differences, 52*, 908–913.

Gaddis, B.H. & Foster, J.L. (2013). Meta-analysis of dark side personality characteristics and critical work behaviours among leaders across the globe: Findings and implications for leadership development and executive coaching. *Applied Psychology: An International Review*. doi: 10.1111/apps.12017.

Gao, Y. & Rain, A. (2010). Successful and unsuccessful psychopaths: A neurobiological model. *Behavioural Sciences and Law, 28*, 194–210.

Gebauer, J.E., Sedikides, C., Verplanken, B. & Maio, G.R. (2012). Communal Narcissism. *Journal of Personality and Social Psychology, 103(5)*, 854–878.

Gerstner, W.C., König, A., Enders, A. & Hambrick, D.C. (2013). CEO Narcissism, audience engagement, and organisational adoption of technological discontinuities. *Administrative Science Quarterly, 58(2)*, 257–291.

Gino, F., Gu, J. & Zhong, C.-B. (2009). Contagion or restitution? When bad apples can motivate ethical behaviour. *Journal of Experimental Social Psychology, 45(6)*, 1299–1302.

Glover, N., Miller, J.D., Lynam, D.R., Crego, C. & Widiger, T.A. (2012). The five-factor narcissism inventory: A five-factor measure of narcissistic personality traits. *Journal of Personality Assessment, 94(5)*, 500–512.

Goldman, A. (2008). Company on the couch: Unveiling toxic behaviour in dysfunctional organisations. *Journal of Management Inquiry, 17(3)*, 226–238.

——. (2011). Demagogue to dialogue: An alternative to toxic leadership in corporate downsizing. *Organisational Dynamics, 40*, 235–241.

Gonzalez-Mulé, E., DeGeest, D.S., Kiersch, C.E. & Mount, M.K. (2013). Gender differences in personality predictors of counterproductive behaviour. *Journal of Managerial Psychology, 28(4)*, 333–353.

Gottfredson, M. & Hirschi, T. (1990). *A General Theory of Crime*. Stanford: Stanford University Press.

Gottschalk, G. (2010). Entrepreneurship in organised crime. *International Journal of Entrepreneurship and Small Business, 9(3)*, 295–307.

Gottschalk, P. (2012). Conceptual framework for police deviance applied to police crime court cases. *International Journal of Law and Management, 54(3)*, 222–233.

Gottschalk, P. (2014). *Financial Crime and Knowledge Workers – An Empirical Study of Defense Lawyers and White-Collar Criminals*. New York: Palgrave Macmillan.

Graham, J. (1996). Machiavellian project manager. *International Journal of Project Management, 14*, 67–74.

Greenberg, G. (2010). *Insidious Workplace Behaviour*. London: Routledge.

Grijalva, E., Harms, P.D., Newman, D.A., Gaddis, B.H. & Fraley, R.C. (2013). Narcissism and leadership: A meta-analytic review of linear and nonlinear relationships. *Personnel Psychology*, 1–47.

Gudjonsson, G., Einarsson, E., Bragason, O. & Sigurdsson, J. (2006). Personality Predictors of Self-Reported Offending in Icelandic Students. *Psychology, Crime and Law, 12*, 383–393.

Guenole, N. (2014). Maladaptive personality at work. *Industrial and Organisational Psychology, 7*, 85–89.

Hambrick D. & Mason P. (1984). Upper echelons theory: The organization as a reflection of its top managers. *Academy of Management Review, 9*, 193–343.

Hare, R. (1999). *Without Conscience*. New York: Guilford Press.

Harms, P.D., Spain, S.M. & Hannah, S.T. (2011). Leader development and the dark side of personality. *The Leadership Quarterly, 22*, 459–509.

Hayward, M., Forster, W., Saravathy, S. & Frederickson, B. (2010). Beyond hubris: How highly confident entrepreneurs rebound to venture again. *Journal of Business Venturing, 25*, 569–578.

Heaven, P., Newbury, K. & Wilson, V. (2004). The Eysenck psychoticism dimension and delinquent behaviours among non-criminals. *Personality and Individual Differences, 36*, 1817–1825.

Heinze, P., Allen, R., Magai, C. & Ritzler, B. (2010). Let's get down to business: A validation study of the psychopathic personality inventory among a sample of MBA students. *Journal of Personality Disorders, 24(4)*, 487–498.

Helman, C. (1990). *Culture, Health and Illness*. London: Wright.

Herring, S.C., Job-Sluder, K., Sheckler, R. & Barab, S. (2002). Searching for safety online: Managing 'trolling' in a feminist forum. *The Information Society, 18(5)*, 371–383.

Higgs, M. (2009). The good, the bad, and the ugly: Leadership and narcissism. *Journal of Change Management, 9(2)*, 165–178.

Hill, P.L. & Roberts, B.W. (2012). Narcissism, well-being, and observer-rated personality across the lifespan. *Social Psychological and Personality Science, 3(2)*, 216–223.

Hogan, R. (2007a). *Personality and the Fate of Organisations*. Hillsdale, NJ:. Erlbaum.

Hogan, R. (2007b). Personal Communication. London.

Hogan, R., Barrett, P. & Hogan, J. (2009a). *Hogan Business Reasoning Inventory Manual*. Tulsa Hogan Assessments.

Hogan, R. & Hogan, J. (1997). *Hogan Development Survey Manual*. Tulsa: Hogan Assessments.

——. (1999). *Hogan Development Survey Manual*. Tulsa: Hogan Assessments.

——. (2001). Assessing leadership: A view from the dark side. *International Journal of Selection and Assessment, 9*, 40–51.

Hogan, R., Hogan, J. & Kaiser, R. (2009b). Management derailment, in S. Zedeck (ed.), *American Psychological Association Handbook of Industrial and Organizational Psychology*. New York: American Psychological Association.

Hogan, J., Hogan, R. & Kaiser, R. (2011). Management Derailment, in S. Zedeck (ed.), *American Psychological Association Handbook of Industrial and Organisational Psychology*. Washington, DC: American Psychological Association.

Hogan, R. & Kaiser, R. (2008). Learning the lesson in executive selection. *Leadership in Action, 27*, 22–24.

Holtzman, N.S. & Strube, M.J. (2012). People with dark personalities tend to create a physically attractive veneer. *Social Psychological and Personality Science, 4(4)*, 461–467

Horney, K. (1950). *Neurosis and Human Growth: The Struggle Toward Self-Realization*. N. Y.: W.W. Norton & Company Inc.

Jansen, E. & James, V. (1995). *NetLingo: The Internet Dictionary*. Oxarnd Netlingo Inc.

Jausovec, N. & Jausovec, K. (2012). Sex differences in mental rotation and cortical activation patterns: Can training change them? *Intelligence, 40*, 151–162.

Joanson, P.K., Lyons, M. & Bethell, E. (2013). The making of Darth Vader: Parent-child care and the dark triad. *Personality and Individual Differences*. doi: 10.1016/j.paid.2013.10.006.

Johns, G. (1999). A multi-level theory of self-serving behaviour in and by organisations. *Research in Organisational Behaviour, 21*, 1–38.

Joiner, R., Gavin, J. & Duffield, J. (2005). Gender, Internet identification and Internet anxiety: Correlates of Internet use. *CyberPsychology & Behavior, 8*, 371–378.

Jonason, P.K. (2014). Personality and politics. *Personality and Individual Differences, 71*, 181–184.

Jonason, P.K., Koenig, B. & Tost, J. (2010). Living a *fast* life: The dark triad and life history theory. *Human Nature, 21*, 428–442.

Jonason, P.K., Li, N.P. & Teicher, E.A. (2010). Who is James Bond?: The dark triad as an agentic social style. *Individual Differences Research, 8(2)*, 111–120.

Jonason, P.K. & McCain, J. (2012). Using the HEXACO model to test the validity of the dirty dozen measure of the dark triad. *Personality and Individual Differences, 53*, 935–938.

Jonason, P.K. & Webster, G.D. (2010). The dirty dozen: A concise measure of the dark triad. *Psychological Assessment, 22(2)*, 420–432.

Jonason, P.K., Webster, G.D., Schmitt, D.P., Li, N.P. & Crysel, L. (2012). The antihero in popular culture: Life history theory and the dark triad personality traits. *Review of General Psychology, 16(2)*, 192–199.

Jones, D.N. & Figueredo, A.J. (2012). The core of darkness: Uncovering the heart of the dark triad. *European Journal of Personality, 27(6)*, 521–531.

Jones, D.N. & Paulhus, D.L. (2011a). Differentiating the dark triad within the interpersonal circumplex, in L.M. Horowitz & S. Strack (ed.), *Handbook of Interpersonal Psychology: Theory, Research, Assessment, and Therapeutic Interventions*. New York: Wiley & Sons, pp. 249–269.

Jones, D.N. & Paulhus, D.L. (2011b). The role of impulsivity in the dark triad of personality. *Personality and Individual Differences*, 51, 679–682.

Joseph Rowntree Foundation (1996). Social Policy Research Document 93, Joseph Rowntree Foundation.

Judge, T.A., Piccolo, R.F. & Kosalka, T. (2009). The bright and dark sides of leader traits: A review and theoretical extension of the leader trait paradigm. *The Leadership Quarterly, 20*, 855–875.

Juvonen, J. & Gross, E.F. (2008). Extending the school grounds? Bullying experiences in cyberspace. *Journal of School Health, 78*, 496–505.

Kaisr, R.B., LeBreton, J.M. & Hogan, J. (2013). The dark side of personality and extreme leader behaviour. *Applied Psychology: An International Review*, doi: 10.1111/apps.12024.

Kaiser, R., LeBreton, J. & Hogan, J. (2015). The dark side of personality and extreme leader behaviour. *Applied Psychology, 64*, 56–92.

Kaiser, R. & Overfield, D. (2011). Strengths, strengths overused and lopsided leadership. *Consulting Psychology Journal, 63*, 89–09.

Kaplan, R. & Kaiser, R. (2006). *The Versatile Leader*. San Francisco: Pfeiffer.

Kaplan, R. & Kaiser, R. (2009). Stop overdoing your strengths. *Harvard Business Review, 87(2)*, 100–103.

Kessler, S.R., Bandelli, A.C., Spector, P.E., Borman, W.C., Nelson, C.E. & Penny, L.M. (2010). Re-examining Machiavelli: A three-dimensional model of Machiavellianism in the workplace. *Journal of Applied Social Psychology, 40(8)*, 1868–1896.

Kets de Vries, M.F.R. (2006a). *The Leader on the Couch: A Clinical Approach to Changing People and Organizations*. Chichester: John Wiley & Sons Ltd.

——. (2006b). The Spirit of Despotism. *Human Relations, 59*, 195–220.

——. (2012). Star Performers: Paradoxes wrapped up in Enigmas. *Organisational Dynamics, 41*, 143–182.

——. (2013). Are you a mentor, a helper or a rescuer? *Organisational Dynamics, 42(4)*, 239–247.

———. (2014). The psycho-path to disaster coping with SOB executives. *Organisational Dynamics, 43*, 17–26.

Khoo, H.S. & Burch, G.S.J. (2008). The 'dark side' of leadership personality and transformational leadership: An exploratory study. *Personality and Individual Differences, 44*, 86–97.

Kibling, T. & Lewis, T. (2000). *Employment Law*. London: Legal Action Group.

Kshetri, N. (2005). Pattern of global cyber war and crime: A conceptual framework. *Journal of International Management, 11*, 541–562.

Kuszewski, A. (2011). You can increase your intelligence. *Scientific American, March 7*, 1–8.

Langan-Fox, J., Cooper, C. & Klimoski, R. (2007). *Research Companion to the Dysfunctional Workplace*. Cheltenham: Edward Elgar.

Larsson, H., Andershed, H. & Lichtenstein, P. (2006). A genetic factor explains most of the variation in the psychopathic personality. *Journal of Abnormal Psychology, 115*, 221–223.

Larsson, S., Svensson, M. & de Kaminski, M. (2013). Online piracy, anonymity and social change: Innovation through deviance. *Convergence: The International Journal of Research into New Media Technologies, 19*, 95–114.

Lee, K. & Ashton, M.C. (2014). The dark triad, the big five, and the HEXACO model. *Personality and Individual Differences*. doi: 10.1016/j.paid.2014.01.048.

Lee, K., Ashton, M.C., Wiltshire, J., Bourdage, J.S., Visser, B.A. & Gallucci, A. (2013). Sex, power, and money: Prediction from the dark triad and honesty-humility. *European Journal of Personality, 27*, 169–184.

L'Etang, H. (1980). Alcohol and leadership. *Alcohol and Alcoholism, 15(4)*, 167–171

Levenson, M.R., Kiehl, K.A. & Fitzpatrick, C.M. (1995). Assessing psychopathic attributes in a noninstitutionalised population. *Journal of Personality and Social Psychology, 68*, 151–158.

Ligon, G.S., Harris, D.J. & Hunter, S.T. (2012). Quantifying leader lives: What historiometric approaches can tell us. *The Leadership Quarterly, 23*, 1104–1133.

Ligon, G.S., Hunter, S.T. & Mumford, M.D. (2008). Development of outstanding leadership: A life narrative approach. *The Leadership Quarterly, 19*, 312–334.

Lilienfeld, S.O., Lynn, S.J., Ruscio, J. & Beyerstein, B.L. (2010). *Fifty Great Myths of Popular Psychology: Shattering Widespread Misconceptions About Human Behavior*. Chichester: Wiley-Blackwell.

Lilienfeld, S.O., Walkdman, I.D., Landfield, K., Watts, A.L., Rubenzer, S. & Faschingbauer, T.R. (2012). Fearless dominance and the U.S. presidency: Implications of psychopathic personality traits for successful and unsuccessful political leadership. *Journal of Personality and Social Psychology, 103(3)*, 489–505.

Lindebaum, D. (2013). Pathologizing the healthy but ineffective: Some ethical reflections on using neuroscience in leadership research. *Journal of Management Inquiry, 22(3)*, 295–305.

Listwan, S.J., Piquero, L.N & Van Voorhis, P. (2010). Recidivism among a white-collar sample: Does personality matter, *Australian and New Zealand Journal of Criminology, 43(1)*, 156–174.

Liu, D., Liao, H. & Loi, R. (2012). The dark side of leadership: A three-level investigation of the cascading effect of abuse supervision on employee creativity. *Academy of Management Journal, 55(5)*, 1187–1212.

Lombardo, M. & Eichinger, R. (1999). *Preventing Derailment*. Greensboro. Centre for Creative Leadership.

——. (2006). The leadership machine. (3rd edition). The Leadership Machine. Minnesota: Lominger Ltd.

Lombardo, M.M., Ruderman, M.N. & McCauley, C.D. (1988). Explanations of success and derailment in upper-level management positions. *Journal of Business and Psychology, 2(3)*, 199–216.

Lynam, D.R., Gaughan, E.T., Miller, J.D., Miller, D.J., Mullins-Sweatt, S-M. & Widiger, T.A. (2011). Assessing the basic traits associated with psychopathy: Development and validation of the elemental psychopath assessment. *Psychological Assessment, 23*, 108–124.

Machlowitz, M. (1980). *Workaholics*. New York: Mentor.

Mahmut, M.K. & Menictas, C. (2011). Validating the factor structure of the self-report psychopathy scale in a community sample. *Psychological Assessment, 23(3)*, 670–678.

Mars, G. (1982). *Cheats at Work*. London: Unwin.

——.(1984). *Cheats at Work*. London: Unwin.

——. (2006). Changes in Occupational Deviance. *Crime, Law and Social Change, 4455 (4)*, 283–296.

Mathieu, C., Hare, R.D., Jones, D.N., Babiak, P. & Neumann, C.S. (2013). Factor structure of the B-Scan 360: A measure of corporate psychopathy. *Psychological Assessment, 25*, 288–293.

Mathieu, C., Neumann, C.S., Hare, R.D. & Babiak, P. (2014). A dark side of leadership: Corporate psychopathy and its influence on employee well-being and job satisfaction. *Personality and Individual Differences, 59*, 83–88.

Mazar, N., Amir, O. & Ariely, D. (2008). The dishonesty of honest people: A theory of self-concept maintenance. *Journal of Marketing Research, 155*, 633–644.

McCall, M. (1998). *High Flyers*. Cambridge: HBS Press.

McCall, M. & Lombardo, M. (1983). *Off the Track: Why and How Successful Executives Get Derailed*. Report 21. Greensboro: Centre for Creative Leadership.

McCartney, W.W. & Campbell, C.R. (2006). Leadership, management, and derailment: A model of individual success and failure. *Leadership and Organisation Development Journal, 27(3)*, 190–202.

McCosker, A. (2014). Trolling as provocation: YouTube's agnostic publics. *Convergence: The International Journal of Research into New Media Technologies, 20*, 201–217.

Mealey, L. (1995). The sociobiology of sociopathy: An integrated evolutionary model. *Behavioral & Brain Sciences*, 18: 523–599.

Miller, L. (2008). *From Difficult to Disturbed*. New York: AMACOM.

Miller, J.D. & Lynam, D. (2001). Structural models of personality and their relation to antisocial behavior: A meta-analytic review. *Criminology*, 39: 765–798.

Miller, J.D., Gentile, B. & Campbell, W.K. (2013). A test of the construct validity of the five-factor narcissism inventory. *Journal of Personality Assessment, 95(4)*, 377–387.

Miller, J.D., Gentile, B. Wilson, L. & Campbell, W.K. (2012). Grandiose and vulnerable narcissism and the DSM-5 pathological personality trait model. *Journal of Personality Assessment, 95(3)*, 284–290.

Moore, C. (2008). Moral disengagement in processes of organisational corruption. *Journal of Business Ethics, 80*, 129–139.

Moore, P.J., Heuvelman, A. & Verleur, R. (2010). Flaming on YouTube. *Computers in Human Behaviour, 6*, 1563–1546.

Morrison, A., White, R. & Van Velsor, E. (1992). *Breaking the Glass Ceiling*. Boston: Addison – Wesley.

Moscoso, S. & Salgado, J.F. (2004). 'Dark Side' personality styles as predictors of task, contextual, and job performance. *International Journal of Selection and Assessment, 12(4)*, 356–362.

Musteen, M., Barker III, V.L. & Baeten, V.L. (2010). The influence of CEO tenure and attitude toward change on organisational approaches to innovation. *The Journal of Applied Behavioural Science, 46(3)*, 360–387.

Nevicka, B., Ten Velden, F.S., de Hoogh, A.H.B. & van Vianen, A.E.M. (2011). Reality at odds with perceptions: Narcissistic leaders and group performance. *Psychological Science, 22(10)*, 1259–1264.

Newton, N.A. & Khanna, C. (2008). Workplace failure: Mastering the last taboo. *Consulting Psychology Journal: Practice and Research, 60(3)*, 227–245.

Ng, T., Sorensen, K. & Feldman, D. (2007). Dimensions, antecedents and consequences of workaholism. *Journal of Organisatonal Behaviour, 28*, 111–136.

Ng, H.S., Tam, K-M. & Shu, T-M. (2011). The money attitude of covert and overt narcissists. *Personality and Individual Differences, 51(2)*, 160–165.

Oates, W. (1971). *Confessions of a Workaholic: The Facts about Work Addiction.* New York: World Publishing Company.

O'Boyle, E.H., Jr., Forsyth, D.R., Banks, G.C. & McDaniel, M.A. (2012). A meta-analysis of the dark triad and work behaviour: A social exchange perspective. *Journal of Applied Psychology, 97(3)*, 557–579.

Oldham, J. & Morris, L. (1991). *Personality Self-Portrait.* New York: Bartam Books.

——. (2000). *The New Personality Self-Portrait.* New York: Barton Books.

Oldham, J.M. & Skodol, A.E. (1991). Personality disorders in the public sector. *Hospital and Community Psychiatry, 42(5)*, 481–487.

Otway, L. & Vignoles, V. (2006). Narcissism and childhood recollections. *Personality and Social Psychology Bulletin, 32*, 104–116.

Ou, A., Tsui, A., Kinicki, A., Waldman, D., Xioa, Z. & Song, L. (2014). Humble Chief Officers' connections to top management team integration and middle managers. *Administrative Science Quarterly, 59*, 34–72.

Ouimet, G. (2010). Dynamics of narcissistic leadership in organisations: Towards an integrated research model. *Journal of Managerial Psychology, 25(7)*, 713–72.

Owen, D. (2006). Hubris and nemesis in heads of government. *Journal of the Royal Society of Medicine, 99(11)*, 548–551.

——. (2009). *In Sickness and in Power.* London: Methuen.

Owen, D. & Davidson, J (2009). Hubris Syndrome. *Brain, 132*, 1396–1406.

Pailing, A., Boon, J. & Egan, V. (2013). Personality, the dark triad, and violence. *Personality and Individual Differences.* doi: 10.1016/j.paid.2013.11.018.

Palazzo, G., Krings, F. & Hoffrage, U. (2012). Ethical blindness. *Journal of Business Ethics, 109*, 323–338.

Paris, J. (2012). Modernity and Narcissitic personality disorder. *Personality Disorders: Theory, Research, and Treatment,* doi: 10.1037/a0028580

Paulhus, D.L. (2013). The dark tetrad of personality: Relevance to nefarious groups. Power Point Presentation: University of British Columbia.

Paulhus, D.L. & Williams, K.M. (2002). The dark triad of personality: Narcissism, Machiavellianism, and psychopathy. *Journal of Research in Personality, 36*, 556–563.

Paunonen, S., Lonqvist, J.-E., Verkasalo, M., Levkas, S. & Nisswen, V. (2006). Narcissism and emergent leadership in military cadets. *Leadership Quarterly, 17*, 475–488.

Pech, R.J. & Slade, B.W. (2007). Organisational sociopaths@ rarely challenged, often promoted. Why? *Society and Business Review, 2(3)*, 254–269.

Pelletier, K.L. (2010). Leader toxicity: An empirical investigation of toxic behaviour and rhetoric. *Leadership, 6(4)*, 373–389.

Pendleton, D. & Furnham, A. (2012). *Leadership: Everything You Want to Know.* Basingstoke Palgrave McMillan.

Peter, L. (1985). *Why Things Go Wrong.* London: Unwin.

Peters, D.C. (2010). Personality disorders and biosocial trait theories: The argument for radical legal reform. *Behavioural Sciences and the Law, 28*, 289–302.

Peterson, S.J., Walumbwa, F.O., Byron, K. & Myrowitz, J. (2009). *Journal of Management, 35(2)*, 348–368.

Petrides, K.V., Vernon, P.A., Schermer, J.A. & Veselka, L. (2011). *Twin Research and Human Genetics, 14*, 35–41.

Philips, W. (2011). LOLing at tragedy: Facebook trolls, memorial pages, and resistance to grief online. *First, 6 (12)*, Retrieved from: http://firstmonday .org/ojs/index.php/fm/article/view

Phillips, J.G. & Butt, S. (2006). Personality and self-reported use of mobile phones for games. *CyberPsychology & Behavior, 9*, 753–758.

Pickett, K. & Pickett, J. (2002). *Financial Crime Investigation and Control.* NY: Wiley & Sons.

Pinto, J., Leana, C.R. & Pil, F.K. (2008). Corrupt organisations or organisations of corrupt individuals? Two types of organisation-level corruption. *Academy of Management Review, 33(3)*, 685–709.

Piquero, A., Paternoster, R., Mazerolle, P., Brame, R. & Dean, C. (1999). Onset Age and Offence Specialisation. *Journal of Research in Crime and Delinquency, 36 (3)*, 275–299.

Porath, C. & Pearson, C. (2010). The cost of bad behavior. *Organizational Dynamics, 39*, 64–71.

Porter, S., Bhanwer, A., Woodworth, M. & Black, P.J. (2013). Soldiers of misfortune: An examination of the dark triad and the experience of schadenfreude. *Personality and Individual Differences.* doi: 10.1016/j.paid.2013.11.0.

Qast, L.N., Wohkittel, J.M., Center, B.A., Chung, C.T. & Vue, B. (2010). Managerial Behavior Associated with Managerial Derailment in the US and Several Asian Countries.

Raine, A. (1993). *The Psychopathology of Crime: Criminal Behavior as a Clinical Disorder.* San Diego: Academic Press.

Raskin, R. & Hall, C. (1981). The Narcissistic Personality Inventory. *Journal of Personality Assessment, 45*, 159–162.

Rauthmann, J.F. & Kolar, G.P. (2012). How "dark" are the dark triads? Examining the perceived darkness of narcissism, Machiavellianism, and psychopathy. *Journal of Personality and Individual Differences, 53*, 884–889.

——. (2013). Positioning the dark triad in the interpersonal circumplex: The friendly-dominant narcissist, hostile-submissive Machiavellian, and hostile-dominant psychopath? *Personality and Individual Differences, 54*, 622–627.

Rauthmann, J.F., Kappes, M. & Lanzinger, J. (2014). Shrouded in the veil of darkness: Machiavellians but not narcissists and psychopaths profit from darker weather in courtship. *Personality and Individual Differences*. doi: 10.1016/j.paid.2014.01.020.

Resick, C.J., Whitman, D.S., Weingarden, S.M. & Hiller, N.J. (2009). The bright-side and the dark-side of CEO personality: Examining core self-evaluations, narcissism, transformational leadership, and strategic influence. *Journal of Applied Psychology, 94(6)*, 1365–1381.

Rogers, M. (2001). A Social Learning Theory and Moral Disengagement Analysis of Criminal Computer Behavior: An ExploratoryStudy." Unpublished Doctoral Dissertation.

Ronson, J. (2011). *The Psychopath Test*. London: Picador.

Rosenthal, S. (2007). *Narcissism and Leadership. A Review and Research Agenda*. Working Paper: Center for Public Leadership, Harvard University.

Rosenthal, S.A. & Pittinsky, T.L. (2006). Narcissistic leadership. *The Leadership Quarterly, 17*, 617–633.

Ross, S. (2013). Talent derailment: A multi-dimensional perspective for understanding talent. *Industrial and Commercial Training, 41*, 12–17.

Russell, G. (2011). Psychiatry and politicians: The 'hubris syndrome'. *The Psychiatrist, 35*, 140–145.

Samenow, S. (1984). *Inside the Criminal Mind*. New York: Times books.

Schein, E.H. (1990). Organizational culture. *American Psychologist, 45*, 109–119.

Scherer, K.T., Baysinger, M., Zolynsky, D. & LeBreton, J.M. (2013). Predicting counterproductive work behaviours with sub-clinical psychopathy: Beyond the five factor model of personality. *Personality and Individual Differences, 55*, 300–305.

Schwartz, M. (2008). The trolls among us. *The New York Times*. Retrieved from: http://www.nytimes.com/2008/08/03/magazine/03trolls-t.html?pagewanted=all&_r=0

Seleim, A. & Bontis, N. (2009). The relationship between culture and corruption: A cross-national study. *Journal of Intellectual Capital, 10(1)*, 165–184.

Seligman, M. (2007). *What You Can Change...and What You Can't*. London: Nicholas Brearley.

Shachaf, O. & Hara, N. (2010). Beyond vandalism: Wikipedia trolls. *Journal of Information Science, 36*, 357-370.

Shipper, F. & Dillar, J.E., Jr. (2000). A study of impending derailment and recovery of middle managers across career stages. *Human Resource Management, 39(4)*, 331-345.

Smith, S.F. & Lilienfeld, S.O. (2013). Psychopathy in the workplace: The knowns and unknowns. *Aggression and Violent Behaviour, 18(2)*, 204-218.

Spain, S.M., Harms, P. & Lebreton, J.M. (2013). The dark side of personality at work. *Journal of Organisational Behaviour, 35*, S41-S60.

Stellar, J.E. & Willer, R. (2014). The corruption of value: Negative moral associations diminish the value of money. *Social Psychological and Personality Sciences, 5*, 60-66.

Stevens, G.W., Deuling, J.K. & Armenakis, A.A. (2012). Successful psychopaths: Are they unethical decision-makers and why? *Journal of Business Ethics, 105*, 139-149.

Sturgeon, J. (2005). Are you a bad boss? Unique Opportunities: The Physician's Response.

Sulea, C., Fine, S., Fischmann, G., Sava, F.A. & Dumitru, C. (2013). Abusive supervision and counterproductive work behaviours. *Journal of Personnel Psychology, 12(4)*, 196-200.

Sumner, C., Byers, A., Boochever, R. & Park, G.J. (2012). Predicating dark triad personality traits from Twitter usage and a linguistic analysis of Tweets. *Machine Learning and Applications (ICMLA), 2012 11th International Conference, 2*, 386-393.

Sutherland, E.(1940). The White-collar criminal. *American Sociological Review 5*, 1-12.

Takala, T. (2010). Dark leadership, charisma and trust. *Psychology, 1*, 59-63.

Toney, F. & Brown, S. (1997). The incompetent CRO. *The Journal of Leadership Studies, 4(3)*, 84-98.

Tosi, H.L., Werner, S., Katz, J.P. & Gomez-Mejia, L.R. (2000). How much does performance matter? A meta-analysis of CEO pay studies. *Journal of Management, 26(2)*, 301-339.

Tourish, D. & Vatcha, N. (2005). Charismatic leadership and corporate cultism at Enron: The elimination of dissent, the promotion of conformity and organisational collapse. *Leadership, 1(4)*, 455-480.

Tracy, J. & Robins, R. (2007). "Death of a (Narcissistic) Salesman". An integrative model of fragile self esteem. *Psychological Enquiry, 14(1)*, 57-62.

Treadway, D., Shaughnessy, B., Breland, J., Yang, J. & Reeves, M. (2013). Political skill and the job performance of bullies. *Journal of Management Psychology, 28*, 273–289.

Troy, C., Smith, K.G. & Domino, M.A. (2011). CEO demographics and accounting fraud: Who is more likely to rationalize illegal acts? *Strategic Organisation, 9(4)*, 259–282.

Trzesniewski, K., Donellan, M., Moffit, R., Robins, R., Poulton, R. & Caspi, A. (2008). *Low Self-Esteem During Adolescence Predicts Poor Health, Criminal Behaviour, and Limited Prospects During Adulthood.* Paper under review.

van Velsor, E. & Leslie, J.B. (1995). Why executives derail: Perspectives across time and cultures. *Academy of Management Executive, 9(4)*, 62–72.

Veselka, L., Giammarco, E.A. & Vernon, P.A. (2014). The dark triad and the seven deadly sins. *Personality and Individual Differences.* doi: 10.1016/j. paid.2014.01.055.

Veselka, L., Schermer, J.A. & Vernon, P.A. (2011). Beyond the big five: The dark triad and supernumerary personality inventory. *Twin Research and Human Genetics, 14(2)*, 158–168.

——. (2012). The dark triad and an expanded framework of personality. *Personality and Individual Differences, 53*, 417–425.

Victor, B. & Cullen, J. (1988). The Organisational Bases of Ethical Work Climates. *Administrative Science Quarterly, 33*, 101–126.

Vidding, E., Blair, R.J.R., Moffitt, T.E. & Plomin, R. (2005). Strong genetic link for psychopathic syndrome in children. *Journal of Child Psychology and Psychiatry, 46*, 592–597.

Vince, R. & Mazen, A. (2014). Violent Innocence: A contradiction at the heart of leadership. *Organization Studies, 35*, 189–207.

Vohs, K.D., Redden, J.P. & Rahinel, R. (2013). Physical order produces healthy choices, generosity, and conventionality, whereas disorder produces creativity. *Psychological Science, 24(9)*, 1860–1867.

Walton, M. (2007). Leadership toxicity – an inevitable affliction of organisations? *Organisations & People, 14*, 19–27.

Waters, J. (1978). Catch 22.5: Corporate morality as an organisational phenomenon. *Organisational Dynamics, 6*, 3–18.

Watts, A.L., Lilienfield, S.O., Smith, S.F., Miller, J.D., Campbell, W.K., Walkman, I.D., Rubenzer, S.J. & Faschingbauer, T.J. (2013). The double-edged sword of grandiose narcissism: Implications for successful and unsuccessful leadership among U.S. presidents. *Psychological Science*, doi: 10.1177/0956797613491970.

Weber, E.U., Blais, A-R. & Betz, N.E. (2002). A domain-specific risk-attitude scale: Measuring risk perceptions and risk behaviours. *Journal of Behavioural Decision Making, 15*, 263–290.

Webster, G.D. & Jonason, P.K. (2013). Putting the 'IRT' in 'Dirty': Item response theory analyses of the dark triad dirty dozen – an efficient measure of narcissism, psychopathy, and Machiavellianism. *Personality and Individual Differences, 54*, 302–306.

Weisburd, D. & Waring, E. (2001). *White-Collar Crime and Criminal Careers*. New York: Cambridge University Press.

Westphal, J.D., Park, S.H., McDonald, M. & Hayward, M.L.A. (2012). Helping other CEOs avoid bad press: Social exchange and impression management support among CEOs in communications with journalists. *Administrative Science Quarterly, 57(2)*, 217–268.

Widiger, T.A. (2011). Integrating normal and abnormal personality structure: A proposal for DSM - V. *Journal of Personality Disorders, 25(3)*, 338–363.

Widiger, T.A. & Clark, L.A. (2000). Toward DSM-V and the classification of psychopathology. *Annual Review of Clinical Psychology, 5*, 197–222.

Widiger, T.A. & Costa, P.T., Jr. (2013). *Personality Disorders and The Five-Factor Model of Personality*. Washington: American Psychological Association.

Widiger, T.A., Livesley, W.J. & Clark, L.A. (2009). An integrative dimensional classification of personality disorder. *Psychological Assessment, 21(3)*, 243–255.

Wille, B. & DeFruyt, F. (2014). Fifty Shades of personality. *Industrial and Organisational Psychology, 7*, 121–124.

Wille, B., de Fruyt, F. & de Clercq, B. (2013). Expanding and reconceptualising aberrant personality at work. *Personnel Psychology, 66*, 173–223.

Williams, F.I., Campbell, C., McCartney, W. & Gooding, C. (2013). Leader derailment: The impact of self-defeating behaviours. *Leadership & Organisation Development Journal, 34*, 85–97.

Williams, K.M., Nathanson, C. & Paulhus, D.L. (2010). Identifying and profiling scholastic cheaters: Their personality, cognitive ability, and motivation. *Journal of Experimental Psychology: Applied, 16*, 297–307.

Winterstein, Beate P., Silvia, Paul J., Kwapil, Thomas R., Kaufman, James C., Reiter-Palmon, Roni and Wigert, Benjamin (2011). "Brief assessment of schizotypy: Developing short forms of the Wisconsin Schizotypy Scales". *Psychology Faculty Publications*. Paper 59. http://digitalcommons.unomaha.edu/psychfacpub/59

Wright, K. & Furnham, A. (2014). What is narcissistic personality disorder? Lay theories of narcissism. *Psychology, 5*, 1120–1130.

Wulach, J. (1988). The Criminal Personality as a DSM-III-R Antisocial, Narcissistic, Bordreline and Histrionic Personality Disorder. *International Journal of Offender Therapy and Comparative Criminology, 32,* 185–199.

Zettler, I. & Solga, M. (2013). Not enough of a 'dark' trait? Linking Machiavellianism to job performance. *European Journal of Personality, 27(6),* 545–554.

Zhang, Y., Leslie, J.B. & Hannum, K.M. (2013). Trouble ahead: Derailment is alive and well. *Thunderbird International Business Review, 55,* 95–102.

Zibarras, L.D., Port, R.L. & Woods, S.A. (2008). Innovation and the 'dark side' of personality: Dysfuntional traits and their relation to self-reported innovative characteristics. *Journal of Creative Behaviour, 42(3),* 201–215.

Zimbardo, P.G. (2004). A situationalist perspective on the psychology of evil: Understanding how good people are transformed into perpetrators, in A.G. Miller (ed.), *The Social Psychology of Good and Evil.* New York: Guilford Press, pp. 21–50.

Zona, F., Minoja, M. & Coda, V. (2013). Antecedents of corporate scandals: CEO's personal traits, stakeholder's cohesion, managerial fraud, and imbalanced corporate strategy. *Journal of Business Ethics, 113,* 265–283.

Zweig, J.M., Dank, M., Yahner, J. & Lachman, P. (2013). The rate of cyber dating abuse among teens and how it relates to other forms of teen dating violence. *Journal of Youth and Adolescence, 42,* 1063–1077.

Appendix

Leadership risk assessment report

This is an edited and shortened report from an organization which specializes in dark-side leadership assessment. We have their permission to use this. It gives an excellent example of a report that could be used in selection or coaching.

Leverage (Brinkmeyer), K.R., Parsons, N.E., CDR Assessment Group, Inc. (1998). CDR Leadership Risk Assessment Report. Tulsa, OK

Introduction

Why leaders may ultimately derail

Leaders derail for a wide range of reasons. Consider for a moment a leader that you are aware of whom you believe is not performing well and is heading towards (or seems apt to) derailment. Without a doubt, there are distinct characteristics demonstrated by this individual that conflict with expectations for effective leadership behaviours and competencies.

Often, behaviours directly related to those identified in this Risk Assessment Report do not result in termination. However, without awareness of their impact and focused effort to change them, these risk factors or potential leadership derailment behaviours erode the positive perception of a leader's performance over time.

Over the short term, a leader's damaging behaviours identified by this report may affect the team or subordinates more so than they affect the leader. Depending on the organizational climate and practiced values, these leadership behaviours identified as risk factors may go virtually ignored or undetected by senior executives. Over time and gone unchecked, negative leadership behaviours described in this report can create real havoc, fear, tension, discomfort and significant costs to the organization. Again, the purpose of this Leadership Risk Assessment Report is to equip you with clear and comprehensive information to help you manage any risk factors you may have that could derail your success, damage your relationships with others or that could obstruct organizational results.

Universal leadership derailers

Leadership success and derailment largely depend upon two factors: (1) the perceptions of others about your performance which includes your relationships with them; and (2) your contributions or results produced for the good of the organization. Overwhelmingly, the first of these is the most critical in terms of leadership derailment. A leader may have produced outstanding results; yet if he/she has damaged relationships along the way, or has operated with a lack of integrity, derailment may be inevitable. Universally, or across organizations, leadership derailers can be defined as:

Leadership Derailers	Examples
Erosion or betrayal of trust	Lack of integrity, loss of credibility, over-focus on personal agenda, failure to meet commitments
Failure to deliver and be accountable	Slow to act, studies issues and solutions too long, waits for instruction, short on results
Failure to adapt	Resists change, difficulty with multiple priorities, lacks flexibility
Lack of courage and decisiveness	Risk aversive, freezes under uncertainty, fails to assert views; avoids making decisions
Creating or endorsing a dysfunctional work environment	Failure to support, inappropriate emotionality or lack of 'emotional intelligence', hostile work environment

(Continued)

Leadership Derailers	Examples
Failure to develop people and organization	Fails to coach, mentor others, or provide developmental resources; and, unconcerned with bench strength, organizational growth planning issues
Lacks forward-looking and inspirational approach	Lacks a vision, can't rally troops to produce; does not build enthusiasm towards stretch goals
Lack of objectivity and broadmindedness	Narrow views, undervalues diversity, strives to preserve personal wishes and bias, not perceived as fair, does not consider sufficient views or sufficient data in decision making

Risk factors for derailment

Defining Risk Factors and High Scores

This report defines eleven leadership risk factors that can inhibit leadership effectiveness and can lead to derailment. A 'high risk' is identified by scores at or above the 90th percentile. Scores below the 90th percentile, though useful for development, are not considered 'high risks'.

Of these eleven risk factors, some are generally more damaging to leadership effectiveness than others. Also, certain combinations of high scores or elevations may be more or less detrimental than others. *It is not uncommon to have a couple of high scores or elevations in scores.* Furthermore, the impact of leadership behaviours resulting from these risk factors will vary based upon specific organizational values, strategic objectives, performance contributions and social effectiveness.

Risk factor scale definitions and behavioural examples:

Each of the risk factors described below features: (1) a definition, (2) linkage to universal leadership derailers and (3) example of behaviours.

False Advocate – This scale represents behaviours that are passively detrimental-they are not always obvious to those who are being acted out against-but serve to undermine agendas, go against the status quo, or put up barriers to success. Leaders with high scores appear outwardly supportive and on-board while sabotaging effectiveness through defiance, resentment, procrastination and resistance. False advocates regularly betray the trust of others though it may take time for their behaviour to be revealed because of the covert nature of their activities. *Examples: Blaming others for failure to perform; saying one thing and doing another; and, not living up to commitments.*

Worrier – This scale represents an unwillingness to make decisions due to fear of failure or criticism. Worriers impede progress, over-study, over-review and slow down performance. Worriers are not decisive, seem to lack courage and fail to adapt promptly to changing demands. *Examples: Stonewalling decisions; having associates perform unnecessary non-value added tasks just to appease personal comfort level; and, being slow to act and risk aversive.*

Cynic – This scale describes those who are skeptical, mistrustful, pessimistic, always looking for problems, constantly questioning decisions and ideas, and who resist innovation. Cynics lack a forward thinking and inspirational approach; may lack objectivity in decision making and are poor at adapting to changing business needs. *Examples: Resisting innovation with statements like: 'We have always done it this way ... or, it'll never work ... '; communicating doubt and pessimism about the business future or projects; and, not showing trust in others to perform independently.*

Rule Breaker – This scale depicts those who ignore rules, test the limits, do what feels good, jeopardize company resources, and who do not think through the consequences of their behaviour or decisions. In leadership roles, Rule Breakers can lose credibility and betray trust by violating rules and may be prone to fostering a dysfunctional work environment because of their impulsive and often destructive behaviour. *Examples: Failure to comply with safety rules; spending more funds than expenditure authority may permit; and, skinny-dipping at a company sponsored function.*

Perfectionist – This scale describes the leaders that micro-manage, cling to details, have a high need to control, set unreasonably high standards, have difficulty setting priorities, and struggle with relating to the big strategic picture. Perfectionists betray trust due to their compulsive need to control, may lack objectivity and broadmindedness and may struggle with adapting to change. *Examples: Keeping control by monitoring process details unnecessarily; requiring too many updates from associates on work progress; and, nitpicking errors instead of welcoming new concepts, ideas or solutions.*

Egotist – This scale reveals the leader who: is self-centred, has a sense of entitlement, takes credit for others' accomplishments, is viewed as a hard-nosed competitor, has a sense of superiority and expects to be looked up to. Egotists betray trust by stealing credit, create dysfunctional work environments because of their self-obsession; and lack objectivity in decision making. *Examples: Putting personal agenda ahead of the needs team; refusing to admit mistakes or pay attention to feedback; and, behaving like a dictator or as a pompous member of royalty.*

Pleaser – This scale describes those who depend on others for feedback and approval, are eager to please the boss, avoid making decisions alone, are unwilling to challenge the status quo, refuse to rock the boat and may help others while letting their own accountabilities flounder. Pleasers in leadership roles may fail to deliver results, may lack courage and may create a dysfunctional work environment by failure to support or go to bat for others. *Examples: Acting as an order taker who needs to be told what to do; failure to defend their team's position; and focusing more on the relationship with the boss than with associates or peers.*

Hyper-Moody – This scale typifies those with unpredictable emotional swings, moodiness, volatility, potentially explosive outbursts and vacillation of focus or interest in projects and people. Hyper-Moody leaders may hurt their credibility by their inconsistent moods and actions. They may erode or betray trust due to their emotional swings; create a poor or dysfunctional work environment and may lack a forward thinking and inspirational approach. *Examples: Showing a roller-coaster of emotions when pressed with changing priorities; yelling one minute then charming someone the next; and, creating a tenuous environment where associates have no idea what temperament to expect next.*

Detached – This scale pertains to a tendency to: withdraw, fade away, fail to communicate, avoid confrontation, be aloof, tune others out and be reticent about interfacing with people. Detached leaders may fail to deliver by not asserting views thus giving the appearance of a lack of courage or indifference; may fail to develop others; and may create a dysfunctional work environment due to a lack of communication or by the appearance of a lack of concern for others. *Examples: Not speaking up at meetings (with a tendency to fade into the wallpaper); maintaining minimal or distant relationships with associates; and, reluctance to become involved in group dynamics.*

Upstager – This scale describes leaders with an excessive need to be around others, to be dramatic and histrionic, to dominate meetings and air time, to constantly sell a personal vision and viewpoint, and to demonstrate an inability to go with the tide. Upstagers may not do well developing others because of their need for constant attention and may not make decisions objectively due to their relentless passionate views. *Examples: Missing social cues, pushing too hard on the wrong people and not letting others take centre stage.*

Eccentric – This scale depicts those who are quite unusual in their thinking and behaving, creative, perhaps whimsical or even weird or peculiar in some ways. Eccentrics may have difficulty adapting to cultural standards and may erode trust and credibility due to their odd ways. *Examples: Dressing or behaving in non-conforming ways; alienating customers by their bizarre or off-the-wall remarks; and, making statements from 'left field'. (Actual comments from high scorers, 'I can feel my molecules moving' and 'We are looking for a house where there are trees and birds and where we can hear the earth breathe'.)*

RISK FACTORS – *Scale by Scale Review for Duke Sample*

False Advocate   **58%**

0–49% – Not a Risk Factor   50–90% –
                                             Development Need   High Risk

Forthright about agendas and timelines   Procrastination, quiet resistance
False agreement,

                                             fail

to follow through,

defiance

Behaviours associated with scores in this range include:

- Independence and being content to work without team assistance
- Comfortable setting own timelines and agenda
- Willing to work without structure or guidance
- Hesitance about sharing information and successes; preferring to use knowledge to push personal success.
- Difficulty sustaining relationships due to extreme independence.
- Putting off tasks that are deemed personally irrelevant.
- May be at odds with the philosophy of a team approach or agenda.

Worrier   **44%**

    0–49% – Not a Risk Factor

50–90% –
Development Need   High Risk

  Makes snap decisions, comfortable with
Refrains from action,

Indecisive, slow to act

uncertainty appears
non-confident

Leaders who receive scores in this range tend to be easy-going, comfortable making decisions in ambiguous problem areas and unafraid of making mistakes.

Cynic

71%

0–49% – Not a Risk Factor

50–90% –
Development Need   High Risk

Trusting, optimistic, gives space for
Distrustful, pessimistic,

Questions motives, reluctant

experimenting

supporter

requires undue

justification

Behaviours associated with scores in this range include:

- Astute observer of subtle cues concerning fairness and equity issues
- Skilled at finding the 'flaw' in a plan or idea
- Able to play hardball in negotiations; won't believe everything that others' say
- Pessimistic view about 'compelling' future goals and aspirations
- Lack of focus on team spirit and morale
- Tendency to over question and seek unrealistic justification
- Implementation may take time in order to first clear scepticism

Rule Breaker

90%

0–49% – Not a Risk Factor

50–90% –
Development Need   High Risk

Abides by rules, thinks through consequences   Mischievous, tests the limits
Impulsive, lacking

in self-discipline,

ignores rules

High risk behaviours associated with scores in this range include:

- Tendency to be impulsive and may not learn from failures and mistakes.
- Personal motivation drives behaviour, even if it means violating established rules.
- Tendency to disregard rules, tradition and potentially organizational values.
- May not think through consequences of own behaviour
- Lack of self-discipline can lead to professional indiscretions.

Perfectionist

14%

0–49% – Not a Risk Factor

50–90% –
Development Need

High Risk

Flexible, willing to improvise

Meticulous, planful Needs order &

predictability, strict

standards for behaviour

Leaders who receive scores in this range tend to be flexible, willing to improvise on how work is completed and unlikely to micro-manage their staff.

Egotist   **95%**

0–49% – Not a Risk Factor

50–90% –
Development Need   High Risk

Modest, interested in others' point of view   Disregards negative feedback, puts
Arrogant, sense of

entitlement,   own interest ahead of team's

authoritarian

High risk behaviours associated with scores in this range include:

- May be insensitive to customer or associates' issues or concerns.
- Habitual management tactics may include intimidation, force or competition.
- Tendency to see him/herself as the brightest and smartest.
- May be dogmatic or stubborn.
- Sense of entitlement about rewards and projects
- May view information sharing as a waste of time.
- Tend to view team decision making as tedious and unnecessary.
- May not consider all factors or views when making decisions
- Associates are pawns in the high scorer's game.

Pleaser   **20%**

0–49% – Not a Risk Factor   50–90% –
                                                          Development Need   High Risk

Willing to confront superiors, goes to bat   Overly collaborative, requires
Unwilling to rock the

for troops   participation from others
boat, focuses on

pleasing superiors,

depends on others

Leaders who receive scores in this range tend to be willing to go to bat for their staff, are generally willing to state their views and won't feel compelled to confer with the team on every decision.

Hyper-Moody   87%

0–49% – Not a Risk Factor   50–90% –
Development Need   High Risk

Tends to express emotions in a mature
Volatile, brooding,

& consistent manner
emotional rollercoaster

Some moodiness, intense at

times – especially under pressure

Behaviours associated with scores in this range include:

- Strong sense of urgency
- Passionate about views and personal causes
- Bursts of energy that lead to high levels of accomplishment
- Being prone to alternate between enthusiasm and disappointment about people and projects
- Lacking poise in times of high stress or ambiguity
- Having 'hot buttons' that may cause emotional displays or pushy behaviour
- Blurting out and trying to catch words
- Appearing sporadic on vision and goal attainment.

Detached   **32%**

0–49% – Not a Risk Factor   50–90% –
                                              Development Need   High Risk

Participates and expresses views, shows   Misses social or political cues,
may Aloof. distant, avoids

interest in associates, is visible, willing to   appear unresponsive or inaccessible,
conflict, isolates

participate in conflict resolution   prefers being alone to participating
lacks diplomacy

Leaders with scores in this range tend to be socially connected, are willing to assert views, will speak up during controversial or stressful times and are available to staff for feedback and to discuss their career development.

Upstager   83%

0–49% – Not a Risk Factor   50–90% –
                                            Development Need   High Risk

Effective to excellent listening skills, will   May exaggerate views, talk more
than Melodramatic,

present views without dominating air time   listen, tend to push own views too
histrionic,

shows respect for others views   often
attention seeking

Behaviours associated with scores in this range include:

- Spends sufficient time with customers and team members
- Perceived as energetic and as keeping things lively
- Strong sales inclination and willing to express views
- Tending to overstate or exaggerate causes leaving customers' and associates weary and likely to dismiss or disregard the message
- May not pick up on the impact personal style has on others
- Zeal to sell personal vision to the team may intimidate others
- Tendency to talk when listening could lead to learning

Eccentric   **11%**

0–49% – Not a Risk Factor   50–90% –
                                                 Development Need   High Risk

Practical, logical and down to earth. Realistic   May see things differently, have some
Odd, lack of

and conforms to social norms   unusual habits, and may not always
focus, social

                                                 be attentive or focused

blunderer

Leaders with scores in this range tend to be practical decision makers, are adept at maintaining focus and planning, will focus on results and are skilful at meeting social and cultural expectations.

Report summary

Summary of your potential leadership risks
There are two primary areas of risk for you.

First, you relish spontaneity and risk-taking and therefore you have a tendency to act impulsively and without thinking through the potential outcomes of your actions. Although your related tendencies to be free spirited and to foster a non-bureaucratic work environment can be amusing, it is important to remember that rules and procedures are necessary in order to maintain a safe and fair work environment that has minimal liability.

Second, you are very self-confident and assertive and you tend to see yourself as a uniquely talented contributor; perhaps well above others. These qualities can work for you in high-profile situations where it is important that you make a powerful impression. On the other hand, you also tend to have a sense of entitlement for accolades and respect and this sense of superiority can be offensive or alienate associates and team members. Further, because you are so self-confident, you may manage by intimidation and fail to inspire the troops towards achieving common goals.

It is also important to be aware of your elevations in scores for the False Advocate, Cynic, Hyper-Moody and Upstager scales.

As a leader, others may find that you appear supportive but don't follow through in action and, because you seem annoyed by interruptions, your troops may avoid coming to you even when the need arises. Be careful not to put off tasks you deem personally irrelevant or that do not promote your preferred self-image.

Be careful not to doubt others' intentions so readily and don't misuse your eagle-eye abilities by questioning or disputing every issue that comes up.

You feelings tend to be apparent to others because you fervently express your emotions or because you tend towards mood swings or brooding. Remember that, although perfectly natural to you, others may not be as comfortable with your 'spirit' and expressiveness. It is important to keep a handle on how your mood swings affect the team's morale and effectiveness.

Selling your vision of how things should be is a strong tendency for you, and it can work in situations where you need to garner resources or market to your client base. However, the intensity with which you express your ideas may be off-putting to some and communications can break down as a result. Soften your touch and practice active listening so that others don't see you as too forceful with your personal views or agenda.

Developmental ideas and suggestions

- Collect performance feedback (regularly) on your leadership behaviours from associates.
- Work with a skilled leadership coach or trained mentor one-to-one to develop strategies for offsetting and neutralizing risks.

- Share this Leadership Derailer Report information with team members and ask for their support with not allowing these risks to inhibit the team's performance or output. Keep in mind that they observe these behaviours on a more regular basis and will most likely appreciate your candidness, willingness to ask for help and will respect your desire to improve.
- Be forthright about your intentions and views.
- Remember that your professional reputation depends to some degree on your ability to meet timelines that are imposed by others and by the level of support you afford others.
- Be careful not to procrastinate on tasks you deem personally irrelevant.
- Lighten up! Being negative exacerbates the stress of heavy workloads.
- Partner with others who are more trusting and upbeat than you.
- Don't be an obstacle to innovation; allow and endorse others' creative expression before looking for flaws.
- Try to alleviate extreme emotional reactions by actively tempering initial enthusiasm and through contingency planning so that there are fewer unexpected developments.
- Identify your 'hot buttons', those issues which when mentioned cause you to bristle or brood.
- Practice letting others' comments 'roll off' and try not to over-react when things don't go your way.
- Respect your team's need to be left alone; don't fix things that aren't broken.
- Practice listening so that you might learn how others perceive things.
- Ease up on your need to convince others of your point of view; pick your battles wisely.

Career planning

In order to minimize your risk factors, keep the following career recommendations in mind:

The best work roles for you are those where you can trust your associates and where you feel comfortable with their expectations and recommendations. Also, make sure you are in an environment where your contributions are valued. This is not always easy to achieve and it may be an ongoing struggle as you try to further your career.

Environments that allow you to solve problems in a high profile way-free of bureaucracy and regulation-and that are progressive in policies and reward programs will be most satisfying for you.

Index